HOW TO BUILD A
CATHEDRAL

HOW TO BUILD A
CATHEDRAL

*Constructing the story of
a medieval masterpiece*

Malcolm Hislop

BLOOMSBURY
LONDON · BERLIN · NEW YORK · SYDNEY

First published in Great Britain in 2012 by
Bloomsbury Publishing Plc
50 Bedford Square
London WC1B 3DP
UK

Copyright © 2012 Ivy Press Limited

ISBN 978-1-4081-7177-6

All rights reserved. No part of this publication may be
reproduced, stored in a retrieval system or transmitted
in any form or by any means, electronic, mechanical,
photocopying, recording or otherwise, without the
prior consent of the publisher.

A CIP catalogue record for this book
is available from the British Library

Colour origination by Ivy Press Reprographics

Printed in China

This book was conceived, designed and produced by
Ivy Press
210 High Street, Lewes,
East Sussex BN7 2NS
UK
www.ivy-group.co.uk

Creative Director: PETER BRIDGEWATER
Publisher: JASON HOOK
Editorial Director: CAROLINE EARLE
Art Director: MICHAEL WHITEHEAD
Design: JC LANAWAY
Project Editor: JAMIE PUMFREY
Illustrator: ADAM HOOK

Contents

Introduction	6
Devising the Plan	10
Building the Walls	36
Taking the Strain	60
Raising the Roof	78
Reaching to Heaven	104
The Cathedral in Color	128
Seeking the Light	146
Shaping the Stone	168
Furnishing the House of God	190
Timeline	214
Cathedral Locations	218
Glossary	220
Resources	221
Index	222
Acknowledgments	224

Introduction

Designed and built without reinforced concrete, steel frames, power tools, or computers, yet raised on vast scales to extremely high standards of craftsmanship, the cathedrals of medieval Europe are both structural and aesthetic masterpieces and have every right to be ranked among the world's most inspiring architectural achievements. These buildings engage and impress in different ways, but they all elicit a common desire to know more about how they were made and the kind of people that worked on them. It is in sympathy with this desire that the emphasis of this book falls: upon the practical processes and upon the people that contributed to the erection of a medieval cathedral.

The focus of this book is on the Gothic, an approach to architecture that began to take hold toward the middle of the twelfth century and which maintained its dominance for nearly 400 years. It differed markedly from the Romanesque style that had preceded it and marked a new dynamic centered within the up-and-coming states of northern Europe rather than in the south, where the influence of Roman architecture was strongest. The single most significant element that shaped the Gothic style was the pointed arch, a feature that probably had its origins in Islamic architecture. It was the pointed arch on which the vertical character of the Gothic cathedral was based, creating not only a new aesthetic but also allowing the development of a quite distinct structural system. For the Gothic was more than a style, it was also a system of engineering.

GOTHIC STYLE
Pointed arches, flying buttresses, and high vaults were characteristic of the Gothic style of cathedral building.

The Gothic great church made its first appearance in a developed form in the Île de France at the abbey of St. Denis near Paris, ca. 1140, although this was probably a coalescence of existing elements in a systematic fashion instead of a completely new invention. While France may be viewed as the birthplace of the Gothic, remaining at the heart of Gothic culture throughout the Middle Ages, England also made an important early contribution to the development of the structural system, because it was here that the use of the pointed arch in vault construction was introduced, an advancement that had a profound effect on the approach to cathedral design and on the character of the cathedral. England developed its own version of the Gothic, although it was far from insular, being open to influence from France and beyond. France, however, was the motor that powered the spread of the style to other parts of Europe, including Germany and Spain, where the early Gothic cathedrals of the thirteenth century are French in style and which were in a number of cases masterminded by French architects.

It was only later that these two parts of the world developed their own versions of the Gothic. Italy's architectural identity was considerably stronger, a robust stone-building tradition having been derived from antiquity. Consequently, the impact of the Gothic in this region was more muted than elsewhere, and the pronounced verticality that characterizes the style in northern Europe does not materialize even in Milan Cathedral, arguably the greatest of the Italian Gothic cathedrals. Despite being one of the tallest cathedrals in Europe, the general proportions that were employed there are such that it appears comparatively squat.

Proportions were the bedrock of design in the Middle Ages, and this meant an understanding of geometry, because the proportions used by the cathedral builders were based on geometrical relationships. This might suggest a highly theoretical approach to design, but, in fact, the architect's knowledge was in some measure formulaic—his geometry, for instance, was of a very practical nature—and to a great extent empirical. Rules were worked out through experience, a system that could prove very costly to some church authorities, as is demonstrated by the numerous building collapses that occurred during the medieval period.

KING AND MASTER MASON
Building a cathedral required funds from a wealthy patron, then the responsibility for bringing the project to fruition became the preserve of the highly skilled master mason, who combined the roles of architect, structural engineer, and master builder.

Vaults and towers gave the greatest cause for concern, because both were areas made vulnerable by the cathedral builder's desire for verticality and height. The introduction of pointed rib vaulting to the central aisles of great churches provided a more effective and economical method of vaulting a large area and, at the same time suited the vertical character of the Gothic. Stone vaults proliferated, however, the outward pressure exerted on the walls by the inclined angle of the pointed rib produced a problem. In the twelfth century, the master builder overcompensated for this by raising massively constructed buttresses. It was only gradually that the principle of thrust and counterthrust became better understood, so that buttresses attained more reasonable proportions, together with a purpose that was decorative as well as structural.

Indeed, this ability of the medieval cathedral builder to absorb the structural framework of a church into the overall decorative plan is a measure of the craft-based nature of the fine arts. Stoneworkers, for example, ranged from those who laid the stones in position, be it high-quality ashlar work or rubble walling, to those who cut the stones, through to those endowed with the highest level of skill, who produced the sculpture. However, woodworkers, glaziers, metalworkers of various kinds, painters, and tilers all included artists within their ranks, and all made a significant contribution to the decoration of a cathedral.

INTRODUCTION

SCULPTURAL EMBELLISHMENT
As cathedral engineering became more sophisticated, so did the aesthetic—elegantly sculpted decoration was integral to the design of a Gothic great church.

While this is primarily a book about cathedrals, the term is used in a broad sense to encompass all great church architecture, on the grounds that the strict definition of a cathedral as a church containing the throne of a bishop is too prescriptive in its meaning for a book of this type. It would, for example, exclude Westminster Abbey, which is one of the greatest and most innovative of all English churches, for although it had a brief period as a cathedral (1540–50), it is arguable as to whether this really counts, because it came after the medieval period with which we are concerned had ended. However, to discuss the development of English cathedral architecture without a mention of Westminster Abbey, which was greatly influential, would be to create a considerable lacuna. Similarly, the omission of the abbey of St. Denis from a book on cathedrals concentrating on the Gothic period might have the effect of lessening a thorough understanding of the subject.

Nor would it be easy to know where to draw the line in the case of those cathedrals that were not built as such but only had the status bestowed upon them at a later date. To take one example, Gloucester Cathedral was an abbey church throughout the medieval period, only becoming a cathedral at the Reformation yet Gloucester plays a very important part in architectural history, because it was the first great church to adopt the Perpendicular style. St. Albans Cathedral, which was also an abbey church in the Middle Ages, did not become a cathedral until the nineteenth century. In England, prior to the Reformation, a number of cathedrals, including Canterbury and Durham, were also monasteries. What distinguishes these buildings from the great churches of other monastic houses is simply that they contained the seat of a bishop.

The truth is that cathedral architecture did not exist in isolation, and there is little to distinguish it from the design and construction techniques that were used in other churches of the period. The main differentiating factor is one of scale. Large-scale churches in the Middle Ages were generally high-quality buildings, but it is also the case that some smaller buildings were also extremely influential, due to the status of their builders. The royal chapels of the Ste.-Chapelle in Paris and of St. Stephen in Westminster Palace, for example, were both buildings that had an important impact on cathedral architecture, and, for that reason, should be considered as great church architecture and of direct relevance to the subject in hand. It is also true that the large body of highly trained personnel, on whom the cathedral builders drew, were generally peripatetic workers, traveling from one site to another as the opportunities arose. They made no distinction between abbey, cathedral, and parish church in seeking out employment and practicing their skills. Whatever the building, the working practices were similar; the building worker could adapt himself to the circumstances.

The book is arranged in eight chapters. Each of the first five describe a stage in the construction sequence, the intention being to describe how the project progressed from its inception. Starting with the design stage, we move, in turn, to the raising of the walls, the buttresses, the vaults and roofs, and, finally, the towers and spires. The three succeeding chapters describe the approaches to the design and construction of the windows, sculpture, and, lastly, the cathedral furnishings, including tile pavements, screens, choir stalls, decorative ironwork, and stained glass. The overall aim is to provide a sense of how the construction of a cathedral advanced and the methods, materials, and personnel that were involved.

Pages of narrative text are accompanied by drawings and interspersed with double-page feature illustrative spreads on particular aspects of design and construction. In addition, the book features a series of reconstruction drawings that leads us through the building of a cathedral, demonstrating how a project might have progressed. The example used here is Salisbury Cathedral, a structure that was completed in a single building campaign lasting forty-eight years between 1218 and 1266. This example may be unusual in its compact plan, but it demonstrates what could be achieved on a virgin site if funding remained steady throughout the project. There is also a sixteen-page color section that includes a number of medieval illustrations of building sites, which convey contemporary perspectives of the phenomenon, together with examples of some of the colorful trappings with which many cathedrals were once endowed but that are now much less evident than they once were.

Further information toward the end of the volume includes a timeline illustrating some of the significant events in the great age of cathedral building, maps showing the locations of many of the buildings mentioned in the text, a glossary that gives explanations for some of the more technical vocabulary, and a resource page providing suggestions on where to find out more about the subject. It is certainly a subject worth pursuing, and it is hoped that this introduction to the world of the medieval cathedral builders will whet the appetite for more.

SALISBURY CATHEDRAL
This cathedral-building project took forty-eight years to complete—relatively swift by medieval standards. The commissioned illustrations in this book follow the cathedral's progression from ground plan to spire.

evising
the Plan

DEVISING THE PLAN

Introduction

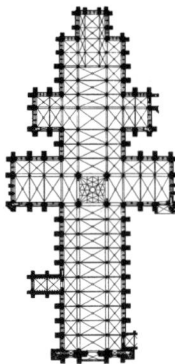

THE CREATION OF A CATHEDRAL was a partnership between the patron, usually (although not always) a high-ranking ecclesiastic, and his master builder. The initial conception came from the former, and there is no doubt that some churchmen, such as Suger, Abbot of St. Denis, near Paris, and Bernard, Abbot of Clairvaux, in Burgundy, had strongly held opinions on the architectural quality of a great church, based on their religious convictions. Such a figurehead was immensely important in providing the impetus, in raising the funds, and in providing the unflinching leadership that projects of such magnitude required.

While the patron was key in getting the enterprise off the ground and maintaining its trajectory in order to bring things to a successful technical conclusion, it was necessary to secure the services of an effective architect. There were probably some instances of clergymen acting in a design capacity, but, generally, this role was filled by a master mason, a man with a craft-based training who combined the functions of architect, structural engineer, and builder.

In the Middle Ages, it was important to be confident in one's choice of architect; instances of structural failure were far too common, and the daring scale of some Gothic buildings must have only made the commonly held concern about long-term stability more acute. The consequences of choosing unwisely could be disastrous. It was the master mason, Hugh de Goldclif, who was deemed responsible for the collapse of the new work on the west front of St. Alban's Abbey in Hertfordshire, ca. 1200, caused by a failure to cover the partially built walls to prevent water penetration. At around the same date, the fall of the central tower of Beverley Minster in Yorkshire, following the erection of a spire on top of it, was blamed on the incompetence of the masons who failed to provide sufficient support to counter the extra weight.

With so much at risk, it is hardly surprising to learn that the task of finding the right man was not something that was taken lightly. When the eastern arm of Canterbury Cathedral was severely damaged by fire in 1174, several craftsmen, both English and French, were called in to advise on its repair. It was only after they had each given their opinions that a Frenchman, William of Sens, was appointed "on account of his lively genius and good reputation." Reputation, indeed, was crucial in an age in which an architect's knowledge was largely empirical, and there were few yardsticks other than his existing works by which to measure a master's competence.

Introduction

William of Sens, "a man active and ready, and as a craftsman most skillful in both wood and stone … addressed himself to the procuring of stone from beyond the sea. He constructed ingenious machines for loading and unloading the ships, and for lifting masonry and stones. He delivered molds for shaping the stones to the sculptors who were assembled and diligently prepared other things of the same kind." He was, in other words, responsible for all the technical and logistical aspects of the construction work.

This practical dimension was the most important factor when considering the design and construction of a great church. While the master masons of the medieval period may have adhered to certain rules of design and construction because these had evolved from accumulated experience, they were not always the same rules. Instead of a universal theoretical understanding of structures, they developed a series of regional practices that usually worked, although they might not adhere to any universally accepted set of rules.

The point is underlined by the discussions that centered around the new cathedral of Milan, begun in 1386, where several consultant architects, both French and German, were called in to advise on the structural character of the church. One of the most striking aspects of the episode is the profound measure of disagreement that existed between experienced master builders from different parts of Europe.

Such consultations are a sign that the master mason was not left to his own devices and that patrons were active in ensuring the structural integrity of a building in so far as it was in their power. An architect had to be prepared to be able to justify his design. While the degree of control that patrons might be able to exercise over the technical aspects of a plan might be limited, they were much better positioned to influence the aesthetics of a design, and there is little doubt that this was a matter for consultation, discussion, and compromise.

Something of the process is hinted at in surviving medieval architectural drawings, which appear to have been intended for the purpose of demonstrating the effect of the intended structure for the benefit of the patron. Collections survive from several medieval cathedrals, including Strasbourg, Reims, Ulm, Vienna, and Cologne. The fact that several plans were sometimes prepared suggests that the patrons took an active interest in the formulation of the design. The influence of the two parties varied according to their respective strengths, but there is little doubt about the collaborative nature of the exercise.

DEVISING THE PLAN

Designing a Great Church

Medieval great churches were, above all things, functional buildings that were designed for worship, and it was this primary purpose that determined the outlines of the ground plan. Because the rituals of Christian worship did not differ in their essentials from one great church to another, a good deal of uniformity can be discerned within the general layout and lines of circulation.

The religious focus of the cathedral was the sanctuary, or presbytery, which was always situated close to the east end of the church. The sanctuary housed the high altar, which stood on a slightly elevated platform approached by steps. It also accommodated the clergy that officiated at the celebration of Mass.

The offices, or religious services, were sung, so an important adjunct to the sanctuary was the choir, which lay immediately to the west. It was here that the stalls of the choristers were situated, facing one another across a central aisle. It is worth noting at this point that the term "choir" is also widely used in a broader sense to denote the whole of the eastern arm of a great church. For clarity, the qualified terms "liturgical choir" or "ritual choir" are sometimes used in referring specifically to where the choristers sit during Mass.

Sanctuary and choir formed a unit separated from the rest of the church in which the main acts of worship could be carried out undisturbed. In addition, however, a cathedral housed numerous other chapels where services were celebrated. The most significant of these was the Lady chapel, where the special devotion felt for the Virgin Mary in the Middle Ages could be celebrated. In England, where the cult of the Virgin was particularly strong, many Lady chapels were built projecting prominently from the east end of the church. Many other smaller chapels were required, each containing an altar and each with its own dedication, in order to cater for the daily celebration of Mass by the large numbers of priests attached to a great church.

Another universal component of a cathedral was the nave, which occupied the western arm of the church and which comprised a large open space of considerable length, usually flanked by arcades giving onto the side aisles. Although naves were used for religious purposes, principally by lay worshippers, and contained altars at which Mass could be celebrated, their great size suggests that a large part of their purpose was to provide both an imposing ceremonial setting for infrequent ritual events and an architectural impact that engendered a sense of reverence and awe.

Notre-Dame de Paris Choir

The choir and sanctuary formed the ritual hub and dramatic climax of the cathedral, the religious significance of the area being emphasized architecturally by the rise in floor level from the nave to the choir and from the choir to the sanctuary. In Viollet le Duc's reconstruction of Notre-Dame de Paris shown here, the enclosed nature of the area is apparent. The choir is separated from the nave by the rood screen—a decorative partition with a representation of the Crucifixion. The north and south sides of the choir are screened from the aisles by the high backs of the choristers' stalls, and the apsidal (semicircular) east end by a screen.

These essential elements, together with centuries of evolved tradition, acted as limitations upon the design. In addition, the character of the site imposed physical constraints. Many cathedrals built in the Gothic era occupy more ancient loci than the existing superstructure might imply and often succeed one or more churches of earlier date. Sometimes, elements of these earlier churches might be incorporated into the new building, as at Chartres, where the cathedral was substantially destroyed by fire in 1194. Here, the eleventh-century crypt and the twelfth-century west front, which were the only elements to survive the fire, were both retained in the rebuilding that followed. For structural reasons, the presence of the crypt had to be taken into account in the design of the late twelfth-century church built above it, so that the apparent anomalies to be found in the twelfth-century east end—the varying sizes of the radiating chapels and the irregular spacing of columns—may be attributed to the existence of the underlying crypt.

Seldom did the Gothic architect have the opportunity to build on an unencumbered site, and the reconstruction of an existing cathedral might be a long, drawn-out process, as finances permitted or as other circumstances dictated. In situations such as these, where the old and new works were expected to coexist for some time, the character of the former would inevitably affect that of the latter.

It is evident that when the eastern arm of Canterbury Cathedral was rebuilt between 1175 and 1185, following a devastating fire in 1174, the project was not envisaged as the first phase of a more general reconstruction of the cathedral but instead as an end in itself to work alongside the older sections. At Canterbury, then, the new eastern arm had to be structurally compatible with the older western arm, which was not rebuilt for another 200 years. This may be the reason that the eastern arm of Canterbury, despite being designed by a French master mason, does not emulate more closely the greater height of French cathedrals.

There was even less room for innovation in the late fourteenth-century reconstruction of the nave of Westminster Abbey. Here, the eastern arm, transepts, and eastern bays of the nave had been rebuilt under Henry III between 1245 and 1272. When the western bays of the nave came to be rebuilt more than 100 years later, the master mason responsible, Henry Yevele, adhered faithfully to the design of the earlier work, so that only minor differences—the molding profiles, for example—distinguish the two periods.

Rebuilding the Nave

The nave of St. Peter's Cathedral, York (York Minster), was built between ca. 1291 and 1360. The view given here is from the east, looking toward the great west window with its curvilinear tracery containing a heart-shaped centerpiece. The size of the Gothic nave was very much determined by that of its Norman predecessor, and the arcades separating the nave from the aisles were built on the stumps of the eleventh-century outer walls.

Planning the Aisles

The aisles were a highly significant element of cathedral planning, widely used in promoting efficient spatial management. Aisles facilitated communication within the building by providing the means to perambulate the entire perimeter without interrupting the services within the main body. It was an important factor to take into account in approaching the design of great churches, such as Sigüenza, Spain, which encompassed numerous peripheral buildings and areas devoted to different activities. Here, we see the south aisle looking east.

DEVISING THE PLAN

The Master Builders

Although in many instances the architects of the great cathedrals are shadowy figures about whom we know little or nothing, there is no doubt regarding their central role and high status. These attributes are implicit in the numerous pictorial references to master masons that survive from the Middle Ages. Of particular interest is the medieval labyrinth formerly set into the floor of Reims Cathedral nave—each of the four polygonal corner projections depicts the four master masons involved in the construction of the cathedral between 1212 and 1290. Chartres and Amiens both had labyrinths that also seem to have been intended to celebrate the names of the master masons.

THE MASON'S TOOLS
This nineteenth-century illustration of a medieval master mason was used by the eminent French architect Eugène Viollet le Duc as the frontispiece to his Dictionnaire Raisonné de L'Architecture Française. *Here, in reference to his depiction in medieval illustrations, the master mason is identified by his compasses.*

SQUARE AND COMPASS
A figure on one of the vaulting bosses on the south side of the church of Semur en Auxois is probably to be identified as an architect by the square and compasses that he holds, tools that are associated with the profession of mason.

KING AND
MASTER MASON
This depiction of the construction of St. Alban's Abbey, from Matthew Paris's thirteenth-century work Lives of the Offas, *shows the king and his master mason. The latter is distinguishable by the tools of his profession, the compasses and square. Further indications of his superior status are to be found in his depiction at the same scale as the king and in his elegant robe, which contrasts with the poorer garb of the manual workers.*

GRAVE SLAB OF
HUGUES LIBERGIER
(Right) Hugues Libergier (d. 1263) was the designer of the church of St. Nicaise in Reims (begun in 1231 but destroyed in the eighteenth century). His grave slab, originally in St. Nicaise but now in Reims Cathedral, shows him holding his measuring staff and a model of the church, while at his feet are his mason's square and a pair of calipers.

DEVISING THE PLAN

Ground Plans

Most medieval cathedrals were cruciform in plan, a highly symbolic form that evoked Christ's Crucifixion (a central tenet of Christianity) and which has an architectural pedigree extending back into the late Roman period. The four main components were the nave to the west, the eastern arm or choir, and a pair of transepts extending to the north and south; the point of intersection for these elements is known as the crossing. This general concept was widely adopted, although the manner in which the cruciform plan was interpreted was by no means standard, and the proportions and form of the different elements display marked variations, often denoting distinct regional practices.

One example of such regional differentiation is that in France transepts tend to be short, whereas in England they project much more boldly. This distinction is related to the English practice of accommodating chapels on the eastern side of the transepts instead of concentrating them at the east end of the building, which was the norm in France and other European countries. The architectural prominence accorded to transepts in England extended in some cathedrals to the provision of an additional pair. At Salisbury and Lincoln, transepts extended from both the crossing and the choir; in an unusual arrangement at Durham, a transept extends across the east end of the building.

Although the cruciform plan might have been the one most commonly used, it was not the only option, and it is clear from the noncruciform plan of Bourges (ca. 1195–1275), one of the greatest of French cathedrals, that transepts were not always considered necessary. Here, the pursuit of a unified architectural effect took precedence over symbolism, yet the plan of Bourges is to a considerable degree still derived from that of a cruciform church—Notre-Dame de Paris. At Paris, however, the transepts barely extend beyond the aisles, so that the cruciform character of the church is not so obvious from the ground plan.

While the high altar and presbytery were always contained within the eastern arm of the church, the position of the liturgical choir varied; sometimes it, too, was housed entirely within the eastern arm (Ely is one example of this), but sometimes it extended into the crossing (as at Winchester) and occasionally into the nave (St. Albans). In Spanish cathedrals, the usual position for the liturgical choir (or, to give it its Spanish name, *coro*) was at the east end of the western arm, an arrangement that greatly reduced the length of the nave and so diminished its architectural impact.

An English Cruciform Plan

York Minster has a plain, but emphatic cruciform plan, with eastern and western arms of the same length, and a typically English square east end with integral Lady chapel. Rebuilding of the Norman church commenced with the transepts (ca. 1225–55), then chapter house (ca. 1280–90), nave (ca. 1291–1360), Lady chapel (1361–73), and choir (1394–1407).

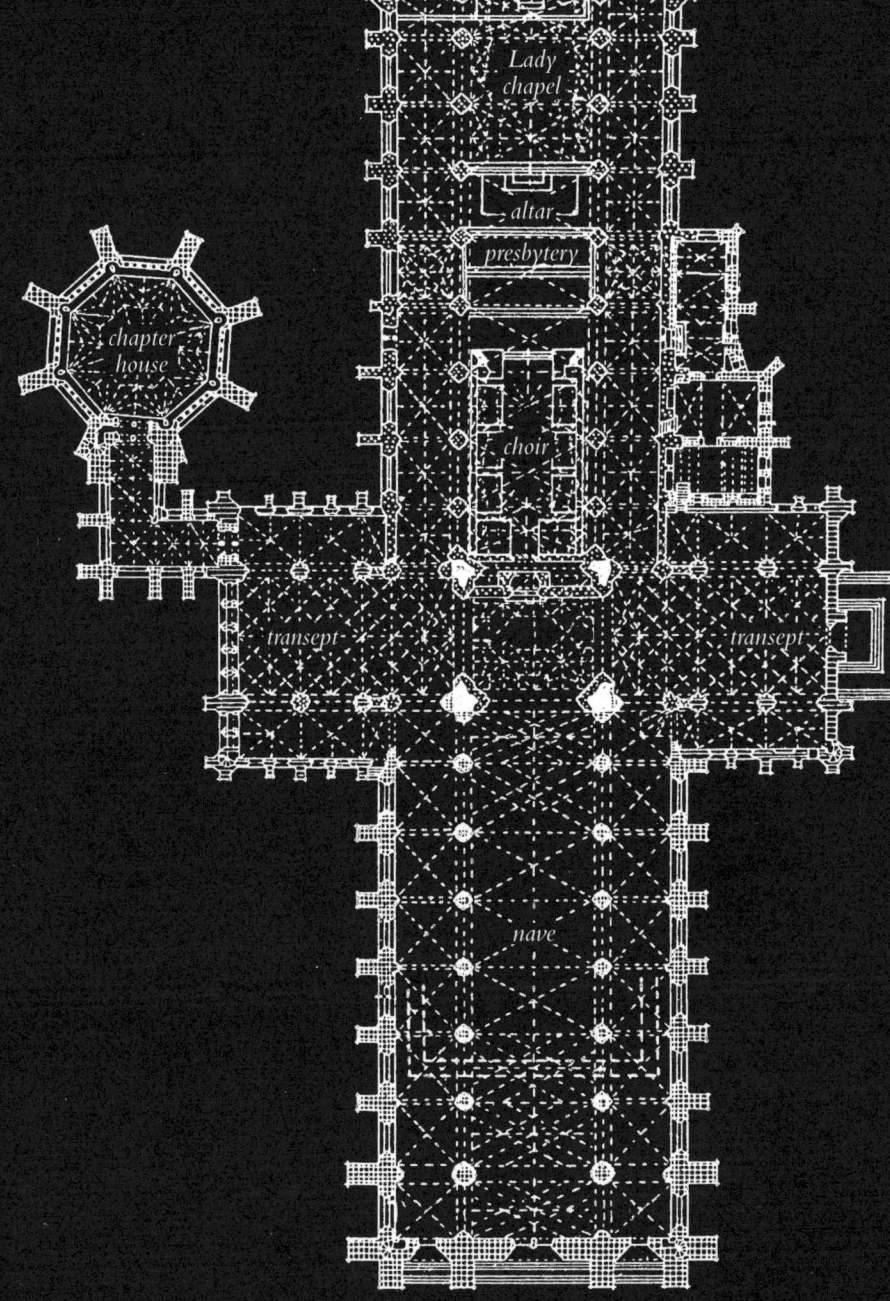

A French Cruciform Plan

Amiens, which has the largest ground plan of all French cathedrals, is also typical of French cruciform in having transepts of short projection and an apsidal east end with radiating chapels. The church was begun in 1220 under the direction of Robert de Luzarches. Unusually, the nave came first, then the choir (1236–70), followed by the transepts. Later work included the upper stages of the west front, including the towers (1366–1420).

The east ends of most French and Spanish cathedrals are apsidal (semicircular) in form. Apsidal east ends are usually provided with a series of projecting apsidal chapels, which formed an architectural feature known as a chevet (see pages 24–25). This provides a striking contrast with architectural practice in England during the Gothic period, where, although some great churches were given apsidal east ends—Canterbury and Westminster are examples of this, both, tellingly, buildings with strong French influence—the overwhelming majority are square ended, a convention that was probably derived from the austere nature of Cistercian architecture.

While the eastern terminations of English cathedrals may be less ornate than their Continental counterparts, greater emphasis was placed on the length of the eastern arm. English choirs regularly exceed 150 feet (46 m) in length (Ely, Lichfield, Salisbury, and Worcester), some (Exeter, Lincoln, and York) exceed 200 feet (61 m), while the eastern arm of Canterbury is approximately 300 feet (91 m). French cathedrals are not so ambitious in this respect. The eastern arm of Amiens, the largest French cathedral, is approximately 170 feet (52 m) long; that of Cologne, the largest German cathedral, approximately 165 feet (50 m); and Toledo, one of the larger Spanish cathedrals, approximately 150 feet (46 m).

This English emphasis on length extends to the ground plan in general. The great Gothic churches of continental Europe are regularly matched and often exceeded in length by those of England. Amiens and Cologne are both approximately 475 feet (145 m) long, while Seville, the largest cathedral in Spain, measures approximately 433 feet (132 m). In contrast, some English cathedrals, including Canterbury and York, exceed 500 feet (152 m) in length. Winchester, at 558 feet (170 m), is the longest medieval cathedral in England.

Both the nave and eastern arm were usually provided with a single pair of aisles, although sometimes, particularly in continental Europe (Notre-Dame de Paris, Bourges, Milan, and Toledo are examples), two pairs of aisles were built. Within the eastern arm, the aisles extended around the east end to form an ambulatory. Transepts might also be provided with aisles, something that was particularly important in England, where eastern aisles were used to accommodate chapels. Sometimes, where the transepts were a particularly important feature, they might be provided with two aisles (as at Wells, Winchester, and York). Aisles were both architectural devices to enhance the grandeur of a church and a practical means of communication within the building. In some cathedrals (Bourges, Paris, and Rouen), they provided access to a series of lateral chapels situated around the perimeter of the nave and choir. While this was not an English trait, the practice was introduced into Scotland from France (Melrose Abbey is one example).

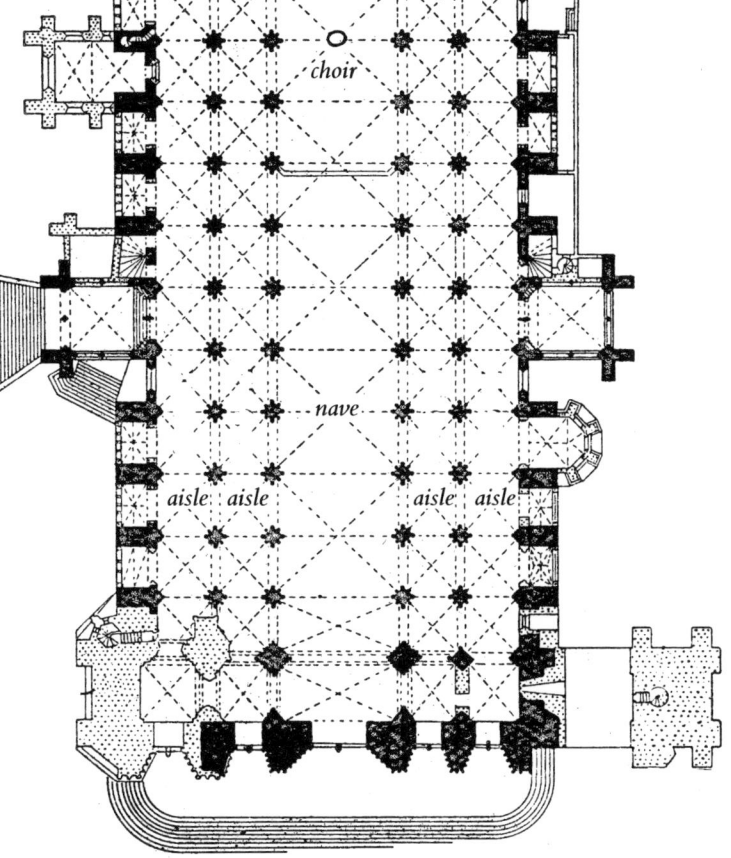

A Noncruciform Design

(Left) The Cathedral of St. Etienne, Bourges, which was begun ca. 1195 and completed by ca. 1275, is, like Notre-Dame de Paris, to whose plan it bears a superficial resemblance, a double-aisle building with apsidal east end. The ambulatory around the apse gives access to a number of small apsidal chapels.

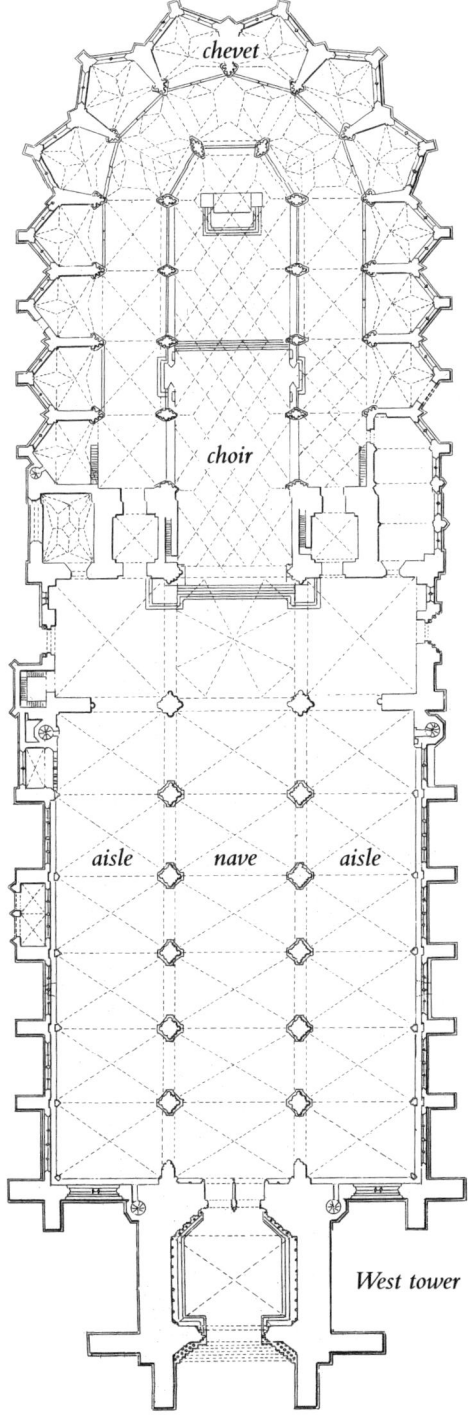

A Quasi Noncruciform Plan

(Right) Freiburg-im-Breisgau Minster, in Bavaria, comprises a thirteenth-century crossing, aisled nave, and west tower, and a late fifteenth-century choir with a chevet of polygonal chapels extending all around the choir. Although the ground plan gives no indication, the building has a pair of short transepts, but they don't project beyond the aisles. The single, centrally placed west tower is a German trait.

DEVISING THE PLAN

Chapels, Chevets & Transepts

The many subsidiary chapels found in cathedrals and monastic churches (see page 14) were accommodated in a number of different ways. In continental Europe, where apsidal east ends were the norm, chapels projected from the perimeter of the apse to form a feature known as a chevet. In England, where apsidal east ends were rare, chapels tended to be housed in the eastern aisles of transepts; this is one reason for the greater architectural significance accorded to transepts in England.

HEREFORD LADY CHAPEL
Dating from around 1220, the Lady chapel of Hereford Cathedral, like many English Lady chapels, is an eastward extension of the choir and, typically, has a square end. Lady chapels had a special prominence in England, where the cult of the Virgin Mary was particularly strong.

ÁVILA AMBULATORY
The ambulatory around the apsidal east end of a cathedral was a continuation of the aisles and gave access to the chapels of the chevet. This example at Ávila Cathedral, Spain (ca. 1160), was probably modeled on Abbot Suger's St. Denis.

TOLEDO CHAPELS OF THE CHEVET
This shows two of the chapels of the chevet at Toledo Cathedral (1227–38), built under the direction of the mason Martín. The cathedral was to a large extent based on the French cathedral of Bourges (ca. 1195–1275).

DURHAM CHAPEL OF THE NINE ALTARS
Begun in 1242 to accommodate the shrine of St. Cuthbert, the Chapel of the Nine Altars is a transept that extends across the east end of Durham Cathedral. It was modeled on the early thirteenth-century Chapel of the Nine Altars at Fountains Abbey in Yorkshire.

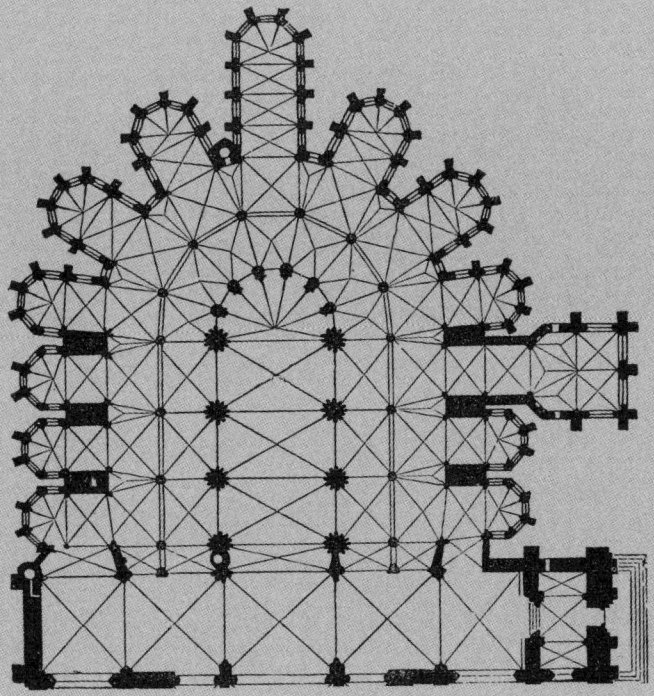

AN EXTENDED CHEVET
The chevet at Le Mans Cathedral (begun 1218) is remarkable in that it was not confined to the apse but extended along the sides of the choir as far as the transepts. The elongated form of the chapels themselves reflects the plan of the choir rather than simply that of the apse.

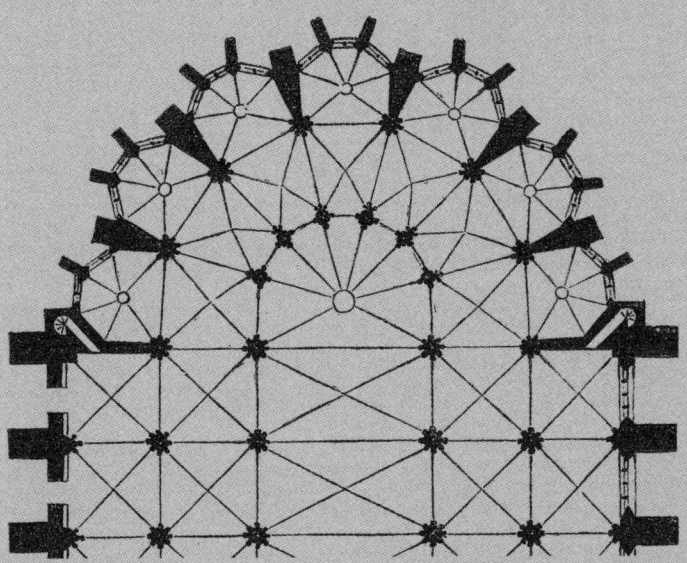

FIVE-CHAPEL CHEVET
(Below) Destruction by fire led to the rebuilding of Reims Cathedral from 1211. The design of the chevet must be attributed to the master mason Jean d'Orbais, who began the construction of the choir. The chevet comprises a series of five tightly packed chapels.

SEVEN-CHAPEL CHEVET
(Above) Begun in 1248 by a Master Gerhard, the choir of Cologne Cathedral was based on French models, notably Amiens (see page 21) and Reims. The chevet, like that of Amiens, incorporates seven chapels, but here all are of equal size.

Abbot Suger

Suger (1081–1151), Abbot of the Benedictine monastery of St. Denis, near Paris, was one of the outstanding figures of early twelfth-century France and is widely regarded as having played a key role in the adoption of the Gothic style of architecture there. Suger's association with the abbey of St. Denis began in 1091, and in 1122 he was elected abbot. A friend and advisor of King Louis VI, he was also an influential aide to his successor, Louis VII.

From the 1130s, he began the reconstruction of St. Denis Abbey church, starting with the west front and then moving on to the choir, which was dedicated in 1144. The choir is generally thought of as the first substantial Gothic work and was highly important as a model for the style. Suger championed the use of costly materials and decoration as a means of advancing spiritual enlightenment and was deeply interested in the quality of light in church buildings.

DEVISING THE PLAN
Profiles

Just as there is considerable diversity in medieval cathedral ground plan design within certain prescribed parameters, so too is there a wide degree of variation in their sectional profiles. Generally, the sectional division comprised a tall central nave and considerably lower side aisles, each of the three vessels being roofed separately. Light was brought into the central vessel by clerestory windows that pierced the side walls of the nave above the level of the aisle roofs. In double-aisle buildings, such as the cathedrals of Bourges and Paris, the outer aisles were lower than the inner aisles so that a clerestory arrangement might also be employed here.

In France, it was height that was the important factor. One aspect of the development of twelfth- and thirteenth-century Gothic architecture in France concerns the increasingly ambitious approach to the vault over the main body of the church. Comparing the nave profiles of the great cathedrals of northern France shows a trend over time of steadily increasing height: Paris 111 feet (34 m), Chartres 121 feet (37 m), Reims 124 feet (38 m), Amiens 138 feet (42 m), and Beauvais 157 feet (48 m). In contrast, the tallest English nave is that of Westminster Abbey at only 102 feet (31 m).

The soaring verticality of Gothic architecture that was such a feature of the cathedrals of northern Europe, particularly those of France, was not a quality that was much sought after in Italy. Here, where classical civilization had stamped its mark so deeply, Roman architecture was too potent an influence to be supplanted, and in the medieval cathedrals of Italy the style is moderated by native tradition. Even Milan Cathedral (ca. 1385–1485), which is a building with a good deal of northern influence and one with vaults that rival those of the northern French cathedrals in height (148 feet/45 m), appears comparatively squat in profile (see page 31).

In Germany, a distinct regional type of profile developed, in which the nave and aisles are approximately the same height, a design that results in a very open and perhaps architecturally less interesting interior with very tall arcades between the nave and aisles. Known as the *Hallenkirche*, or hall church, this is the type that was adopted at the cathedral church of St. Stephen in Vienna (1300–1510), where nave and aisles are set under a very steeply pitched single-span roof. Hall churches do exist outside Germany, although the only example of such an arrangement being adopted for an English cathedral is at Bristol, specifically the choir, which was built between 1306 and 1332.

High-Vaulted French Naves

This section through the nave of Reims Cathedral (1211–90) demonstrates the typical French characteristics of great verticality, high vaults, and bold flying buttresses. At 124 feet (38 m) from floor to vault, Reims is not the highest of French cathedrals (Beauvais is the highest at 157 feet 6 inches/48 m), but it dwarfs the highest of England's great churches (Westminster at 102 feet/31 m).

The Hall Church

The Church of St. Elizabeth, Marburg, Germany, which dates from ca. 1257–83, is a *Hallenkirche*, or hall church, a distinct regional type largely associated with Germany, although examples do occur in other countries. In this type of building, the nave and aisles are of equal height, so that the triforium and clerestory are eliminated and lateral illumination is only from the aisles.

DEVISING THE PLAN
Architectural Drawings

Draftsmanship was one of the key skills in the medieval master mason's repertoire, being widely used in the design process as a means of conveying an impression of an intended building to a patron and providing a useful method of recording the details of existing buildings for future reference. Architectural drawings are known to have been in use from the mid-thirteenth century, the date of the earliest surviving examples. Here are two thirteenth-century drawings of recently constructed buildings from the portfolio of Villard de Honnecourt (see panel opposite) and a fifteenth-century German plan.

DESIGN FOR ULM MINSTER
A design of ca. 1470 for the tower of Ulm Minster, Germany, attributed to the master mason Moritz Ensinger. Work on the tower had begun in the 1370s under the then master, Ulrich von Ensingen, but work progressed slowly and, indeed, the spire was not completed until the nineteenth century. This drawing is probably related to the construction of the third story of the building.

DESIGN FOR REIMS CATHEDRAL
A section through the flying buttresses (above) of Reims Cathedral by Villard de Honnecourt and an engraving of the finished construction (right). Reims was rebuilt from 1211, and Villard de Honnecourt was probably active in the 1220s and 1230s.

TOWER AT LAON CATHEDRAL
Villard de Honnecourt's drawing (above) of one of the western towers of Laon Cathedral, built between 1160 and 1225, and Viollet le Duc's nineteenth-century rendition of the same perspective (left). The west towers of the cathedral would have been only recently completed when Villard made his sketch.

The Portfolio of Villard de Honnecourt

The portfolio of Villard de Honnecourt, which dates from the first half of the thirteenth century, comprises a remarkable collection of drawings and commentary. For a long time believed to be the compilation of a peripatetic master mason, it is now considered that it might instead be the work of a widely traveled layman. Far from indicating an aesthete, however, the portfolio suggests a man with a deep interest in the scope and process of architectural practice. The material includes architectural elevations, plans, and details of known buildings, aspects of masonry and carpentry, examples of practical geometry, designs for machines (including lifting devices), and studies of human and animal forms. It seems an eclectic collection, but most of the subjects in Villard's portfolio, which range from art to engineering, are items that fall within the medieval architect's ambit, and there is no doubt that the portfolio would have proved to be of interest to a member of the profession.

DEVISING THE PLAN

Proportions & Practical Geometry

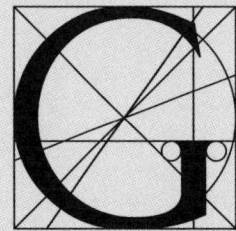eometry lay at the very heart of medieval cathedral design. Plans, profiles, and facades were all based on proportions that had been derived from geometrical constructions. Even details, such as finials, window tracery, and moldings, would have been based on geometrical figures and drawn up with a pair of compasses and a square.

Geometry was the source of the proportional systems of measurement that were commonly employed in designing the general layout of church. The most popular was 1:√2 (1:1.41), which, in practical terms, represents the ratio of the side of a square to its diagonal and was, therefore, easy to remember and construct. Other proportions are only slightly more complex. One of them—1:√3 (1:1.73)—was derived from the equilateral triangle and denotes the relationship between half the length of one side of the triangle and its height. Another proportion (1:1.62), which was known as the golden section (also called golden cut, proportion, ratio, etc.), could also be derived from the square.

The square and the triangle also formed the basis of two of the most important geometrical systems in use for designing the profile of a great church: *ad quadratum*, which was based on the square, and *ad triangulum* which was based on the equilateral triangle. Where the base of the figure represented the width of the building, the "correct" height of the nave could be calculated from that of the figure. *Ad quadratum*, which resulted in a taller building in relation to its width, was more popular with the architects of Gothic cathedrals, who valued height, although it is worth mentioning that the profile of Bourges, one of the most significant Gothic cathedrals in France, was based on the triangle.

Ad triangulum found particular favor in Italy, perhaps because it produced buildings with proportions that were closer to those of classical convention. It was a modified version of this system that was eventually chosen for determining the height of Milan Cathedral (begun ca. 1385), the most Gothic in character of the great churches of Italy, but only after a debate in which *ad quadratum* was also considered.

The adherence to geometrically based plans indicates a demand for rules of design, or principles to follow, as a measure of professional competence and as a means of attaining a quantifiable architectural correctness. In the case of Milan Cathedral, where the native masons were building in an unfamiliar idiom, numerous foreign architects were consulted. The result was a clash of building traditions that highlighted the fact that there were no universal rules and that the adoption of particular tenets derived from regional practice and personal experience.

Ad Triangulum Design

Ultimately derived from the equilateral triangle, the final profile of Milan Cathedral (begun ca. 1385) is the result of modifications and adjustments, which had the effect of reducing the height of the church. The result is a low building comparative to its width, but one that in this respect sits well with the Italian tradition.

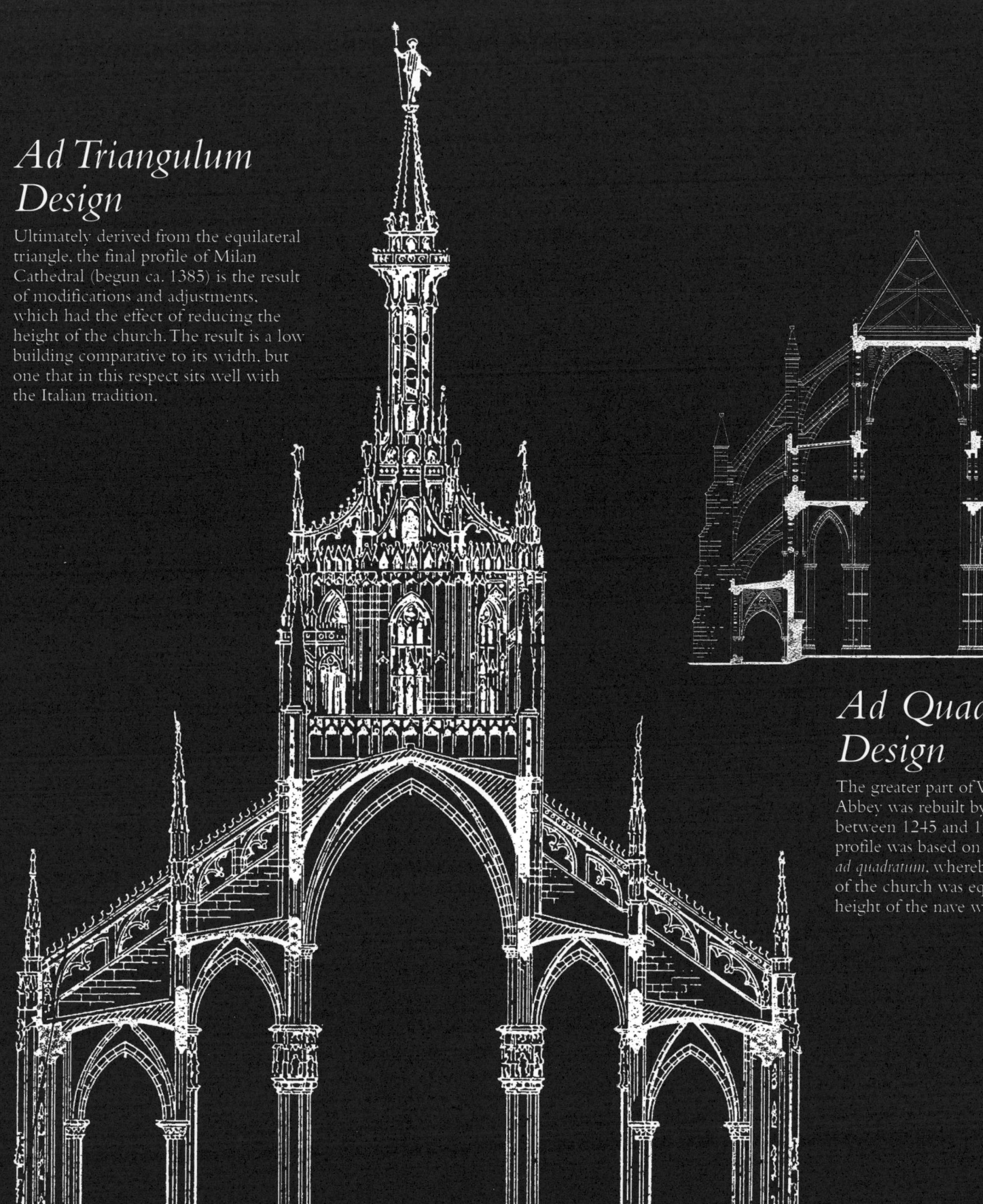

Ad Quadratum Design

The greater part of Westminster Abbey was rebuilt by Henry III between 1245 and 1272. The profile was based on a version of *ad quadratum*, whereby the width of the church was equal to the height of the nave walls.

While there are some instances of geometrical constructions in Villard de Honnecourt's portfolio, it was not until close to the end of the medieval period that much effort was made to record some of these traditional masonic methods in a permanent form. This occurred in southern Germany, where a series of texts appeared in the late fifteenth and early sixteenth centuries. Among these were two works by Mathes Roriczer of Regensburg—*Buchlein von der Fialen Gerechtigkeit* (*Booklet on the Correct Design of Pinnacles*) of 1486 and *Geometria Deutsch* (*Geometry [in] German*) of 1487—another booklet on pinnacles (*Fialenbuchlein*) of ca. 1487 by Hans Schmuttermayer of Nuremberg, and the *Unterweisung* (*Instruction*) of 1516 by Lorenz Lechler.

These documents provide us with insights into the medieval master mason's methods in applying geometry to architectural design, although it has to be remembered that while they might represent aspects of southern German practice in the late Middle Ages, they do not show the full picture and must be taken as only an indicative sample. What they do suggest is a repertoire of purely practical knowledge, not an academic understanding of mathematical principles. It was sufficient that geometrical construction techniques could be applied in carefully prescribed steps to achieve the required ends.

One such technique that appears in both Villard de Honnecourt's portfolio and Roriczer's *Buchlein* is that of the rotated square, in which a smaller square can be created from a larger one or vice versa. The method is to construct the second square at a 45-degree angle to the first and then rotate it so that the two are concentric. Roriczer used it in the design of a pinnacle, the starting point for the whole construction being the square that was used as the outline plan of the base. All measurements were derived from this square by geometrical construction.

This technique is characteristic of the manner in which medieval architects approached design, whereby the proportions of medieval buildings were often based upon a single module, so that the plan, elevations, and other details could be worked out through a series of manipulations of geometrical figures. A similar methodology is also evident in Lechler's *Unterweisung*, where, for example, the dimensions of the window mullions, vault ribs, vault shafts, and capitals were derived from the thickness of the choir wall. Apart from endowing the process of architectural design with a practical logic, there is no doubt that such a system was also a powerful tool in persuading practitioners and laymen alike of the authority of the mason's craft.

The Rotated Square

In this construction, a square of one size can be derived from one of a different size. In the first example (1–2), a smaller square is obtained from a larger, and in the second example (3–4), a larger from a smaller.

Proportional Systems

The instructions are given here for constructing rectangles using three different proportional systems of measurement.

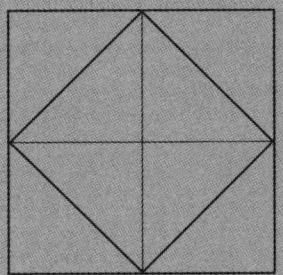 

SMALLER SQUARE FROM A LARGER

1. Draw a square.

2. Draw a smaller square at a 45-degree angle within it by joining the center points of the sides.

3. Rotate the smaller square so that it is concentric with the larger square.

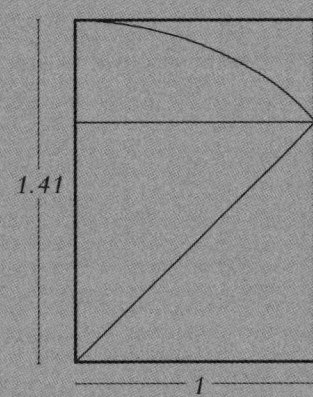

ONE TO THE SQUARE ROOT OF TWO
$1:\sqrt{2}$ (1:1.41)

1. Draw a square of suitable size.

2. Draw a line between two opposite corners.

3. Use the length of this diagonal line as a radius to determine the length of the rectangle.

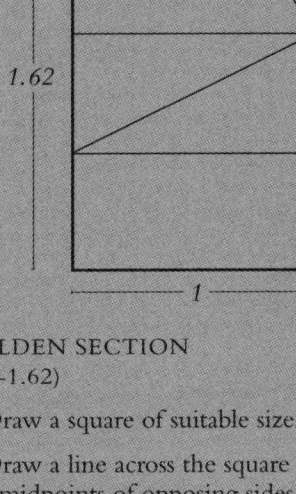

GOLDEN SECTION
(1:~1.62)

1. Draw a square of suitable size.

2. Draw a line across the square between the midpoints of opposing sides.

3. Draw a diagonal between opposite corners of one of the resulting halves of the figure.

4. Use this diagonal as a radius to calculate the length of the rectangle.

LARGER SQUARE FROM A SMALLER

1. Draw a square.

2. Using the diagonal of the square as one of the sides, draw a larger square at a 45-degree angle to the first.

3. Rotate the larger square so that it is concentric with the smaller square.

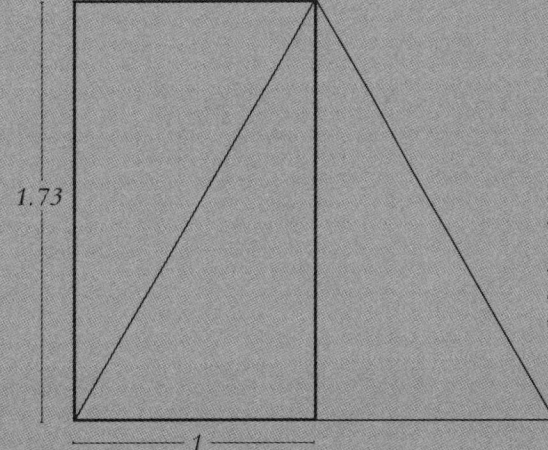

ONE TO THE SQUARE ROOT OF THREE
$1:\sqrt{3}$ (1.73)

1. Draw an equilateral triangle of suitable size.

2. Draw a perpendicular from the center of the base to the apex.

3. One half of the base equals the short side of the rectangle, and the perpendicular equals the long side.

BUILDING SALISBURY CATHEDRAL

Planning & Foundations

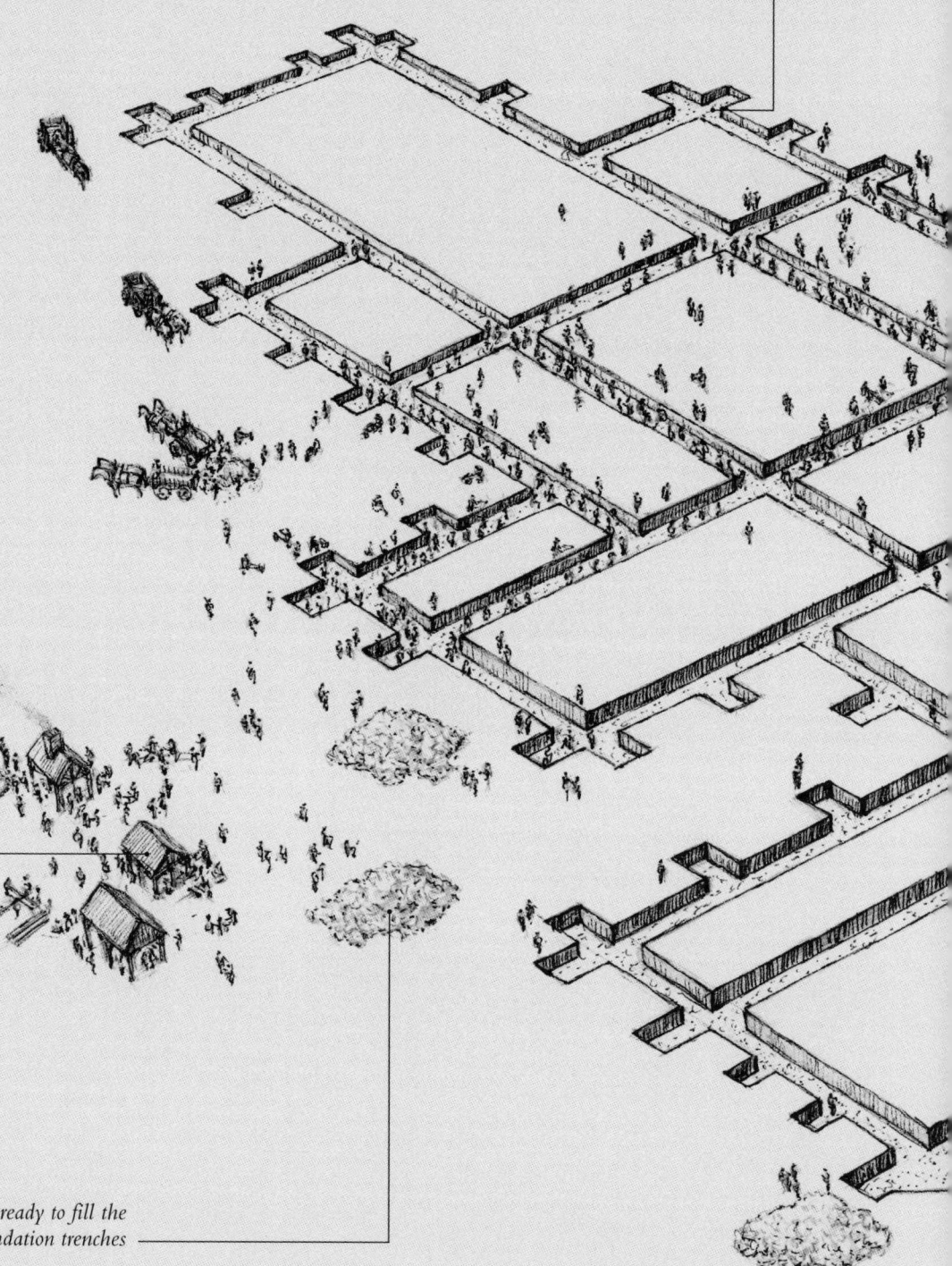

The bottoms of the foundation trenches of the three eastern chapels have been filled with mortar and rubble

Workshops

Piles of rubble ready to fill the foundation trenches

The year is 1219, and work has started on the construction of the cathedral at Salisbury, which is to form the focus of a new city to be raised on an undeveloped site some 2½ miles (4 km) south of the existing cathedral at what is now Old Sarum. The virgin site meant that for once the architect encountered no major difficulties in setting out the plan and in ensuring the symmetry of his design.

Foundation trenches have been dug for the eastern arm, the transepts, crossing, the first two bays of the nave, and at the eastern end of the cathedral, and work has already commenced on filling the bottoms of the trenches with the rubble-and-mortar mix that will form the bed of the foundations. However, the greater part of the western arm is still demarcated with only cords and pegs. This part of the church is not a priority for the moment and will only be commenced once the foundations of the eastern part have been prepared.

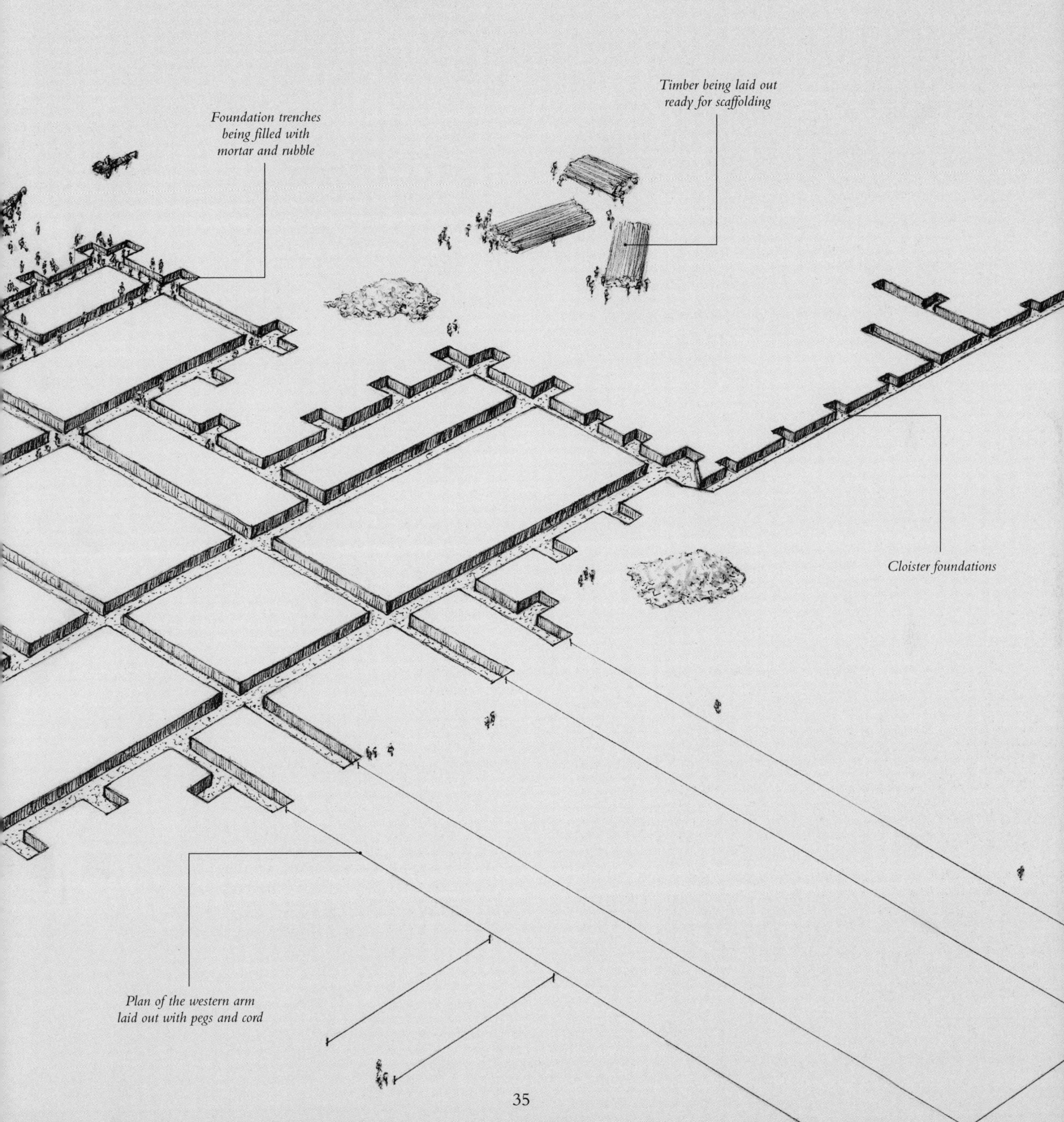

uilding
the Walls

BUILDING THE WALLS

Introduction

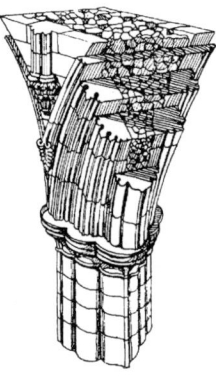

ONCE THE BUILDING had been set out on the ground, the construction work could begin. However, a good deal of preparatory work was essential before one stone could be laid upon another, including the recruitment of personnel and the procurement and preparation of materials. Stone was the principal building material used in wall construction. High-quality stone that could be finely dressed (freestone) was used for wall facings and molded and sculptured details, while a good deal of lesser-quality rubble was used for less visible parts of the structure. Generally, rubble was sourced locally, but not all sites were close to a source of freestone, and the stone often had to be imported from a considerable distance away.

The sources of building materials, especially stone, were an important logistical consideration because the cost of transport was extremely high. At Vale Royal Abbey in Cheshire, where between 1278 and 1280 some 35,000 loads of stone were carted from the quarry to the site—a distance of approximately 4 or 5 miles (6.5–8 km)—it cost more than three times as much to transport the stone than it did to quarry it. While carting—powered by teams of horses or oxen—was an essential element of the transport chain, it was slow and expensive and was avoided if any faster and less costly method was available; generally, this meant water transport. It was entirely feasible, for example, for the master mason William of Sens to import stone from the quarries of Caen in Normandy in France, for the works at Canterbury in southern England, because the greater part of the journey was by water.

Canterbury had the advantage of being situated on a navigable river, but at Rievaulx Abbey in Yorkshire in northern England, where the remoteness of the site meant that there was little in the way of an existing infrastructure, a purpose-built canal was created in order to facilitate the transport process of building materials. Here, as well as on natural waterways that served other cathedral sites, special wharfs were constructed to which the stone was transported by land and then loaded onto barges.

Nevertheless, even where water conveyance played a large part in the logistics of supply, transport was still a major part of the expenditure. It was, therefore, expedient that every effort be made to lessen the bulk and weight that had to be carried. To this end, freestone was at least scappled, or roughly dressed, with an ax at the quarry. While this would have been standard practice, it is also clear that, in some instances at least, finished building stones, or ashlars, were also supplied from the quarry already prepared.

Introduction

While stone was the primary building material, mortar was its essential companion. Medieval mortar was made from a mixture of lime, sand, and water. The preparation of lime for building work was a specialty industrial activity involving the burning of chalk or limestone rubble in a kiln to produce quicklime. The process was either carried out on site, in kilns built for the purpose, or the lime could be purchased already prepared from manufacturers, such as Agnes, the lime burner of London, who supplied the works at Westminster Abbey in the 1250s. Quicklime was slaked with water in order to produce lime putty and then mixed with sand to produce mortar.

The mortarmen who prepared the material were just one of the categories of specialty building workers who assembled at the start of a project. Others included masons, carpenters, and smiths; laborers were also required for various roles, including the excavation of the foundation trenches and the various on-site logistical tasks that ensured the efficient progress of a building project. It was the masons, however, who were central to the task of raising the walls. There were several categories of mason, differentiated by the tasks they performed. The main division was between the cutters, or freemasons, who carved the stones to shape, and the layers, or roughmasons, who placed them in position. Scapplers, who cut the newly quarried stone to shape with an ax, formed another category, but this operation could have been carried out by both freemasons and roughmasons and is unlikely to have been a specific trade. Another class, the setters, who seem to have been employed in assembling window tracery and other molded and sculpted elements, were highly skilled technicians capable of making adjustments to components where necessary, and they would have been drawn from the ranks of the freemasons.

The arrival of the workers at a building site necessitated the provision of workshops and, at the more remote sites, living accommodation as well. These were usually temporary buildings made from timber. The masons' lodge was essentially a workshop in which the freemasons prepared fine-quality masonry, and where their tools were stored; they might also take their meal breaks there. A building contract of 1421/22 for the construction of a bridge over the River Swale at Catterick in Yorkshire stipulates that the clients should provide a wooden lodge at the site for the masons to work in. Occasionally, the lodge is depicted in illustrations of building sites as an unremarkable structure that could be used to allow masons to continue working during periods of inclement weather.

BUILDING THE WALLS

Preparing the Foundations

he process of excavating foundation trenches was an exploratory one, the object of the task being to find firm ground, preferably bedrock, on which to build. After the collapse of the central tower of Ely Cathedral in 1321, the sacrist, Alan of Walsingham, who was in charge of the rebuilding work, ensured foundation pits were excavated for the supporting columns of the replacement structure "until he found solid ground on which the foundations of the work could be safely laid." Archaeological evidence for such geotechnical test pits was found alongside the foundation trenches for the Anglo-Norman Cathedral at York during the excavations of the 1960s and 1970s. It is reasonable to suppose that an examination of the building propensities of the site would have been carried out in most cases.

The excavations at York provided a rare opportunity to examine a cathedral's foundations in detail. Here, the builders excavated a continuous foundation trench 6 feet (1.8 m) deep with sloping sides. It has been estimated that a team of thirty diggers could have completed the task within one month. The bottom of the trench was filled with a layer of mortared rubble 2 feet 6 inches (760 mm) thick, after which a grid of timber beams was laid on top. Then two-coursed rubble retaining walls were erected, one on each side of the trench, within which the timberwork was contained to a height slightly below ground level. The entire space between them was filled with more mortared rubble, an act that buried the timberwork, which may have been included for the purpose of countering uneven settlement of the mortar mixture as it set.

Foundations could be of considerable depth, depending upon the nature of the site: William Worcester recorded a depth of 31 feet (9.5 m) below ground level for the foundations of the late fifteenth-century tower of the church of St. Stephen in Bristol, and on soft or marshy terrain wooden piles might have to be driven into the ground to provide sufficient stability on which to build. In some cases, however, the sound geology of the site and the proportions of the planned building obviated the need for deep foundations. The new cathedral that was begun at Salisbury in 1218 was built on a well-drained, gravel terrace that offered ideal conditions for building. Here, it was only necessary to take the foundations down to a depth of 4 feet (1.2 m) before stable ground was reached. At this level, a 2-foot (610-mm) deep bed of rammed rubble and lime mortar was laid down, and then two courses of masonry were set on top; these were the extent of the foundations.

Laying the Foundations

(Right) Here, the foundations are in the process of being constructed. A mortar bed has been spread over the bottom of the trench. On top of this the sides have been built up with large stone blocks and the space between then filled with a mixture of mortar and rubble. The masons are now constructing the upper part of the foundation, lowering the blocks into position with a crane.

3 courses of sandstone

1 course of stone

14 courses of rubble blocks

Mortar bed

The Foundations at Amiens

(Left) This shows the foundations of Amiens Cathedral as recorded by Viollet le Duc in the nineteenth century. The predecessor to the present church was destroyed by fire in 1218. Unusually, work began with the nave, the foundation stone being laid in 1220. Approximately 28 feet (8.5 m) deep, these footings were based on a bed of mortar 16 inches (400 mm) thick laid on top of the clay subsoil. Above this were fourteen 12–16 inch (300–400 mm) courses of rubble blocks comprising hard silica-filled chalk from Bavelincourt, 9 miles (14.5 km) northwest of Amiens, then a course of stone from Croissy-sur-Celle, some 13 miles (21 km) to the south of Amiens, and, finally, three courses of sandstone up to ground level. These materials formed the facing; the core was made up of rubble from the Bavelincourt and Croissy quarries mixed with mortar.

BUILDING THE WALLS

Constructing the Walls

ollowing the establishment of the foundations, work could start on the walls. In the case of cathedrals, it was normal to use high-quality ashlar masonry for the inner and outer facings, and, depending on the thickness of the walls, to then infill the cavity with a mixture of rubble and mortar. At Notre-Dame de Paris, where the nave walls are only 3 feet (915 mm) thick, they are almost entirely of ashlar. Worked stones would be cut to size and shape in the masons' lodge using wooden templates supplied by the master mason; they were then transported to their allotted places, where they would be mortared into position by the layers. Medieval illustrations (see pages 134 and 136) show individual stones being carried on manual and wheeled biers and sometimes on the shoulder. Mortar was carried to the layers manually in buckets, hods, and bowls. The layers used pointing trowels and were responsible for maintaining horizontal and vertical accuracy of the walls using plumb lines.

Walls could be raised to approximately 4 feet (1.2 m) in height above ground level before scaffolding had to be employed. Contemporary illustrations show various types of wooden scaffolding in use. The main scaffold frames were, as a rule, partially supported by the building, with earthbound verticals, the horizontals resting on the tops of the walls or fitted into square putlog holes deliberately incorporated into the fabric for this purpose. Ropes or withies (willow branches) were used to tie together the vertical and horizontal members, and withies were also used in the manufacture of hurdles (rectangular panels), which often acted as the working platforms. In some cases, scaffolding might be entirely supported by the building itself, the outer ends of the horizontals being carried on brackets. Runged ladders were in use (see pages 130, 135, and 136), but so too were inclined walkways made of hurdles (see page 13).

Even before the walls were high enough to require scaffolding, the heavy and unwieldy nature of many stone building blocks meant that manhandling them into position was not always feasible, and it is probable that mechanical lifting devices came into use almost as soon as the masonry work began. Cranes frequently appear in medieval illustrations (see pages 134–135), equipped with a windlass (turning mechanism) for hoisting and lowering, and an iron scissorlike attachment that picked up individual stones in a pincer grip. An alternative was the lewis, a metal attachment that fitted into a specially made hole in the surface of the stone, and which gripped the sides of the hole firmly when tension was applied by hoisting, allowing it to be lifted. Slings were also used for lifting stones.

Wall Construction

Viollet le Duc's reconstruction drawing of a section of wall shows the composite nature of construction in major medieval churches. Here, in keeping with medieval practice and for reasons of economy, the cavity between two ashlar-faced skins is filled with a core of rubble mixed with lime mortar. The wooden beam shown here, embedded within the mortar mix inside the cavity, is a reminder that timber lacing was often used in early medieval construction to help in tying-in the walls.

Masons at Work

This is a section of stained glass from the thirteenth-century St. Chéron window, in one of the eastern chapels of Chartres Cathedral, showing four masons at work. On the right-hand side are two freemasons working on carved stones; one (left) wields a mason's ax, the other (right) a mallet and chisel. At the foot of each man there is a mason's square, and above them, under the right-hand arch, two molding templates and a pair of compasses are depicted. On the left-hand side, another freemason (right) works at a bank, or bench, with a mason's ax; a fourth (hooded) figure (left), probably a layer, who is engaged in building a tower, uses a weighted plumb line to check the verticality of the wall.

BUILDING THE WALLS
Constructing the Arches

Arches were drawn up at full size using a pair of compasses, and then each arc was divided into segments. This design formed the patterns for the individual stones, or voussoirs, that made up the arch, and wooden templates could be prepared for the instruction of the stonecutters. Structural character varied: some pointed arches had a keystone at the apex; others had a vertical joint in this position; some smaller archways were monolithic or composed of no more than two stones. Where an arch was made up of voussoirs, during the construction process, it would have to be supported on some kind of centering—a temporary wooden structure reflecting the finished form of the arch.

Medieval stone walls often appear to have been raised comparatively slowly; average construction rates in the region of between 10 and 12 feet (3–3.5 m) per annum have been calculated for medieval towers. In the case of Henry III's reconstruction of Westminster Abbey, the walls of which rose to a height of approximately 100 feet (30.5 m), the first phase, which included the eastern arm, transepts, crossing, and chapter house, was probably completed in its entirety, including foundations and roofs, over a period of thirteen years (1246–59). Work seems to have been carried on fairly continuously, although cash-flow problems more than once led to walkouts by the workmen. Indeed, the availability of funds was often the factor behind the slow progress of some medieval cathedrals. Following the completion of the first phase of Westminster, the next, which comprised only the four eastern bays of the nave, was carried out on at a more leisurely pace, lasting from 1260 until ca. 1269. However, it took from 1375 to 1506 to complete the western bays of the nave.

In a discussion on the rate of progress, it has to be remembered that the construction year was curtailed by the onset of winter, during which, due in part to the reduced hours of daylight, operations would be considerably reduced, or in some cases cease altogether. Some tasks, such as stone cutting and scappling, could be continued throughout the winter, but wall construction would be particularly affected. Frost damage was a threat to newly laid mortar, and in medieval buildings, where the wall core consisted of heavily mortared rubble, the long setting time of lime mortar necessitated a staged approach. The winter season provided the opportunity to allow for the mortar to dry. When the building season came to an end in the fall, the uncapped walls were covered in straw to prevent water penetration and to provide insulation from the frost.

Arch Construction

This illustration depicts the structural character of the choir arcade of Whitby Abbey, a construction dating from ca. 1220. The innermost order of the arch would have been built on wooden centering and would then itself have served as part of the centering for the second order. While the innermost order is completely of ashlar, in the subsequent work the ashlar is confined to the outer faces, the interior being filled with rubble and mortar.

Wooden Centering

The nave arcade of Beverley Minster in Yorkshire was built between ca. 1310 and 1349. The individual arches would have been raised on wooden centering, as depicted in this conjectural reconstruction, which could be moved from one bay to another.

BUILDING THE WALLS

Masons' Marks

Of the frequently encountered marks inscribed by masons on fine-quality stonework, some were aids to construction: setting out lines, keying marks, or positioning marks to denote the place in which a particular stone was to be set. Others, however, were, to all intents and purposes, signatures and guarantees of authenticity, and there is little doubt that in many cases they were used in quality control or for the calculation of piecework wages. References in building accounts to payments for work completed "at task" show that many masons were paid according to incentive plans instead of at a day rate; the labeling of their work would have reduced the possibility of administrative errors.

Many masons' marks are simple in form and widely used, and while it is today difficult to read much significance into the designs, there is no doubt that some of the patterns are very ancient indeed and may, in earlier times, have been endowed with religious, ritual, or apotropaic (helping to ward off evil) qualities. One of these is the swastika, a not uncommon form of mark in both its clockwise and counterclockwise forms. The swastika is one of several types of crosses used as masons' marks, some of which may have had a religious significance for an individual, although others were no doubt adopted for their simplicity of execution and recall.

Other widely used types of mark include the dart, or V shape, and the star, such as the asterisk and a five-pointed figure composed of three darts; there are also designs based on arrows, uncomplicated linear patterns, and on the triangle, from which was derived the popular hourglass shape. The frequency with which some marks are encountered over time and geographical area suggests that they were in use by more than one practitioner at any one time. Such duplication of common marks at a single site could have presented administrative problems, and it is probable that, in some instances at least, a mason might have been only temporarily associated with a particular mark, perhaps just as long as a specific job lasted.

It is unusual to find masons' marks on all the finely dressed stone within a building. It may be that some marks face inward, and are, therefore, hidden, but a general absence of masons' marks would suggest that they were not always deemed necessary. The limited number of craftsmen in small-scale works, for instance, might be easily overseen by the master mason, but where large numbers of masons were employed from different parts of the country, or where the stone was obtained from the quarries already dressed, they may have been considered essential aids to traceability and successful supervision.

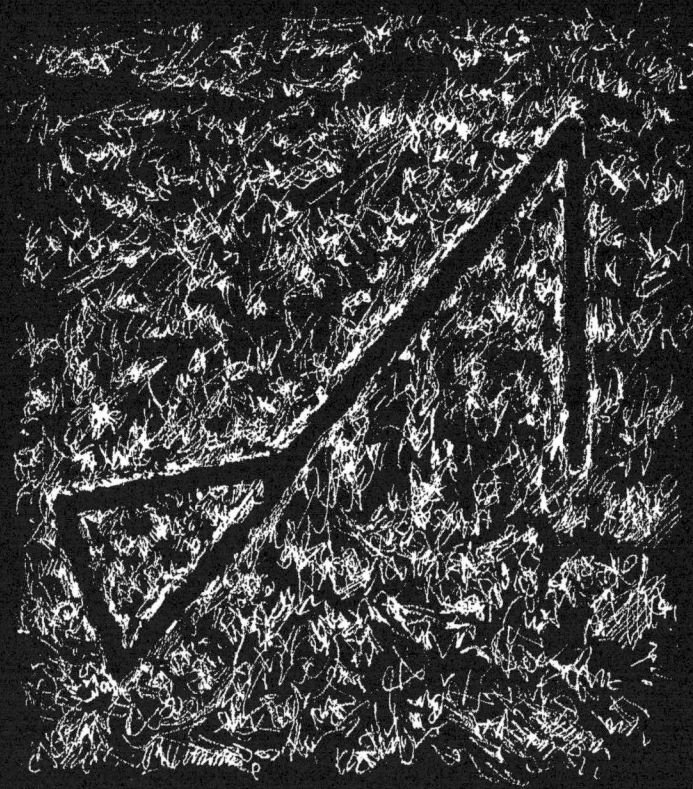

A BANKER MARK
This illustration shows a rubbing of a fourteenth-century "banker" mark from a site in Yorkshire. Banker marks are so called from the practice of cutting fine-quality masonry on stone benches, or banks. Once a stone had been finished, the mason would identify it as his work by cutting his mark on it. Only then would it be placed in position by the layers or setters. This particular mark is a variant of the popular "hourglass" pattern.

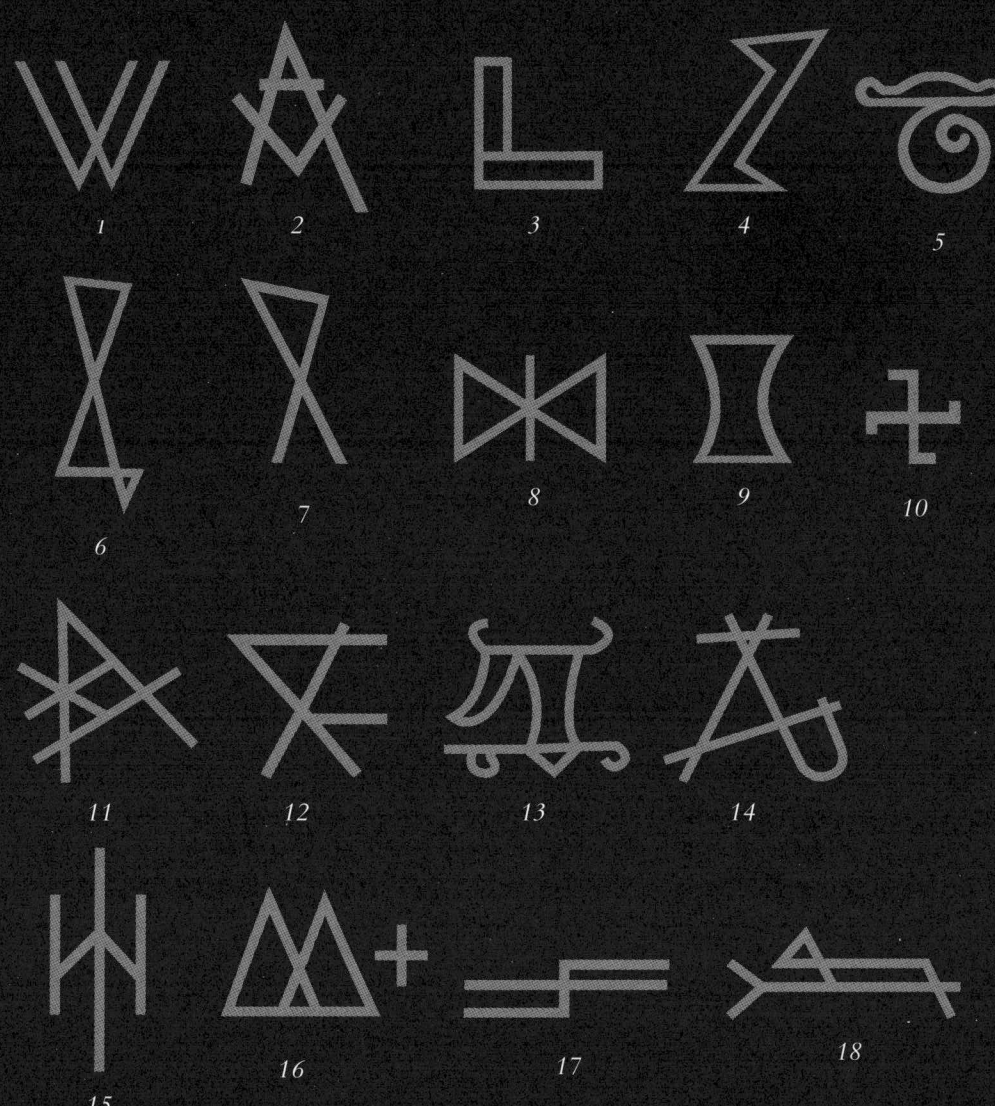

A SELECTION OF MASONS' MARKS
The selected masons' marks depicted here have been recorded from various thirteenth- and fourteenth-century buildings. Some of the less abstract marks seem to represent masons' tools, including the square (3), hammer, pair of compasses (2), and double-headed ax (8). Others were clearly intended to represent initial letters and may have been related to the mason's name. Many of this type date from the later Middle Ages and may reflect an increase in literacy among the workforce. W (1) and R are both found fairly frequently, and may perhaps denote the many common names beginning with those letters: William, Walter, Ralph, Richard, Robert, and Roger. T (5), which is also found occasionally, may represent Thomas. It is more difficult to read a significance into some other marks, although they might, of course, have meant something to their makers.

BUILDING THE WALLS

Vertical Articulation & Column Construction

The internal elevations of a great church are divided into a series of bays based on the divisions of the main arcades. These divisions are continued upward by wall shafts extending from the main piers, and then by the transverse arches of the vault. The task of the Gothic cathedral architect was to create a design that expressed these stages as a continuum and that thereby emphasized the verticality of the building.

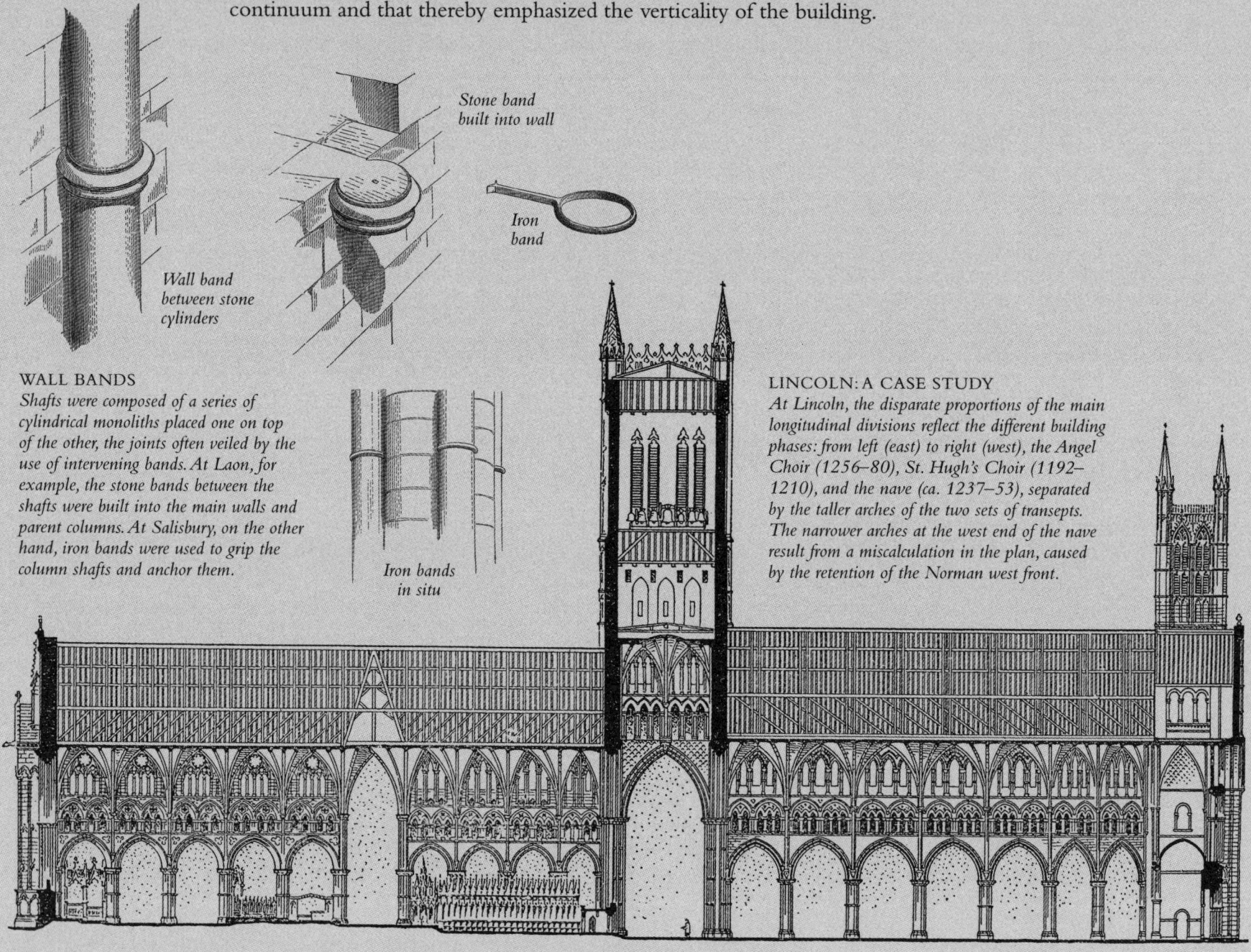

Stone band built into wall

Iron band

Wall band between stone cylinders

WALL BANDS
Shafts were composed of a series of cylindrical monoliths placed one on top of the other, the joints often veiled by the use of intervening bands. At Laon, for example, the stone bands between the shafts were built into the main walls and parent columns. At Salisbury, on the other hand, iron bands were used to grip the column shafts and anchor them.

Iron bands in situ

LINCOLN: A CASE STUDY
At Lincoln, the disparate proportions of the main longitudinal divisions reflect the different building phases: from left (east) to right (west), the Angel Choir (1256–80), St. Hugh's Choir (1192–1210), and the nave (ca. 1237–53), separated by the taller arches of the two sets of transepts. The narrower arches at the west end of the nave result from a miscalculation in the plan, caused by the retention of the Norman west front.

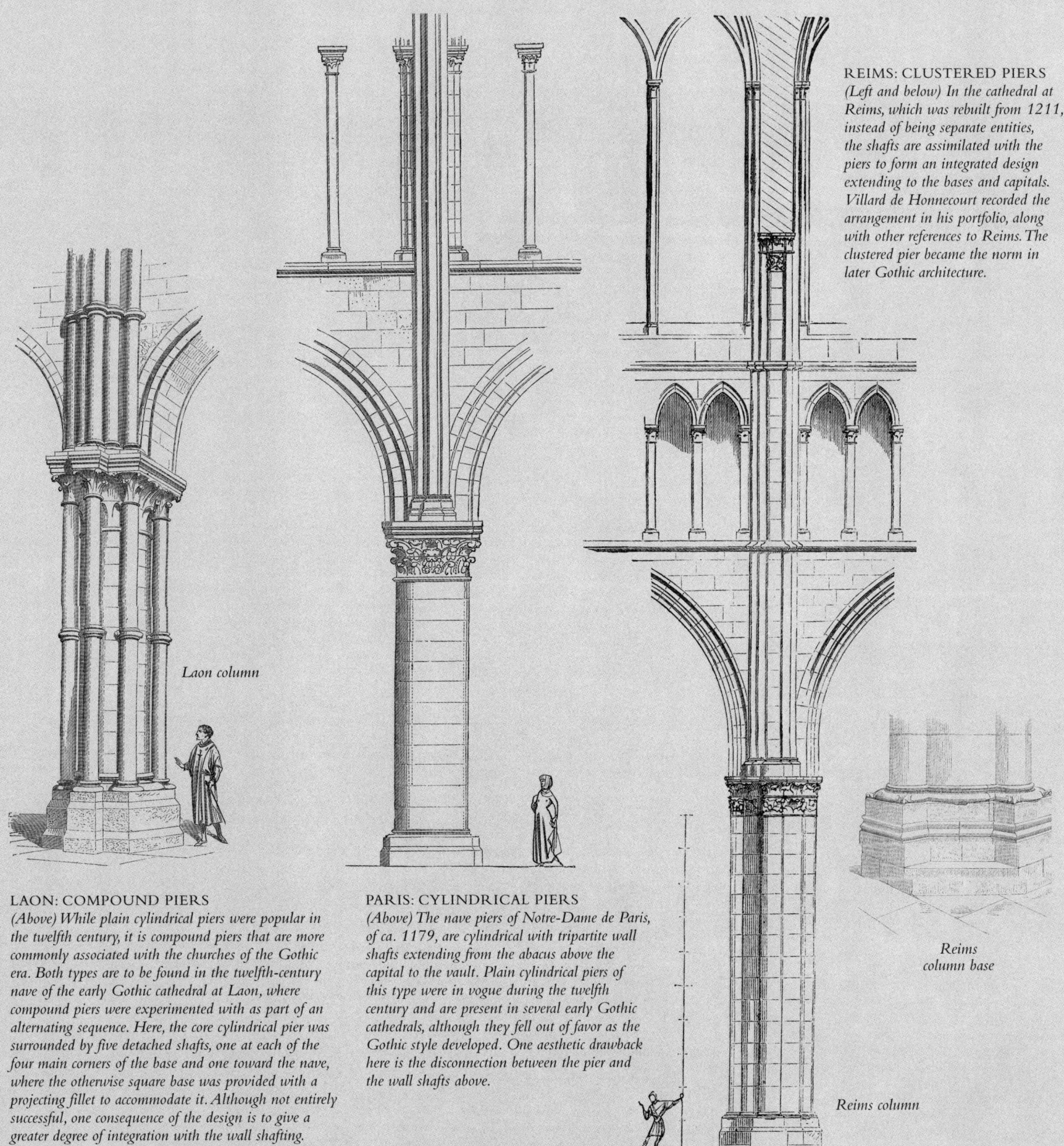

Laon column

Reims column base

Reims column

REIMS: CLUSTERED PIERS
(Left and below) In the cathedral at Reims, which was rebuilt from 1211, instead of being separate entities, the shafts are assimilated with the piers to form an integrated design extending to the bases and capitals. Villard de Honnecourt recorded the arrangement in his portfolio, along with other references to Reims. The clustered pier became the norm in later Gothic architecture.

LAON: COMPOUND PIERS
(Above) While plain cylindrical piers were popular in the twelfth century, it is compound piers that are more commonly associated with the churches of the Gothic era. Both types are to be found in the twelfth-century nave of the early Gothic cathedral at Laon, where compound piers were experimented with as part of an alternating sequence. Here, the core cylindrical pier was surrounded by five detached shafts, one at each of the four main corners of the base and one toward the nave, where the otherwise square base was provided with a projecting fillet to accommodate it. Although not entirely successful, one consequence of the design is to give a greater degree of integration with the wall shafting.

PARIS: CYLINDRICAL PIERS
(Above) The nave piers of Notre-Dame de Paris, of ca. 1179, are cylindrical with tripartite wall shafts extending from the abacus above the capital to the vault. Plain cylindrical piers of this type were in vogue during the twelfth century and are present in several early Gothic cathedrals, although they fell out of favor as the Gothic style developed. One aesthetic drawback here is the disconnection between the pier and the wall shafts above.

49

BUILDING THE WALLS

Horizontal Articulation

While the main vessel of a great church is essentially a single-story structure, its vast height and the existence in most cases of side aisles results in a number of horizontal divisions, or stories. At ground-floor level is the arcade, a series of open arches supported on columns or piers, which allows for access to the aisles. If an aisle is a two-story structure, the upper story is generally called a gallery (also tribune, tribune gallery, or—incorrectly—triforium). The gallery is usually glazed on the exterior wall and has corresponding openings toward the nave in order to help illuminate the central vessel. The aisle roof, which was usually a lean-to structure, created an area of walling within the nave that could not itself be fenestrated. This part of the internal elevation was used to house the triforium, an arcaded wall passage without external illumination. The nave walls above the level of the aisle roof—the clerestory—contain the highest tier of fenestration and light the uppermost part of the nave.

These four stories formed the basis of the nave elevation, but there was no standard pattern, so that one of the truly interesting elements of cathedral architecture is in appreciating the plans that different Gothic masters devised for arranging the horizontal articulation. Not all great churches aspired to four stories, but even in the larger ones there was a tendency to reduce the number of stories by dispensing with either the gallery (as at Chartres and Amiens) or the triforium (Lincoln and Westminster, for example). Galleried aisles, which had been a recurring feature of large Romanesque churches, adding to the apparent solidity of such structures, did not necessarily sit well with the aesthetic and structural ethos behind many Gothic great churches, and although they remained in the cathedral-builder's repertoire, they largely disappeared from the nave elevations.

In the later Middle Ages, there was a trend to integrate the two upper tiers of the nave elevation in order to create a composition consisting of only two stories of equal height—an arcade, and a clerestory with blind arcading and tracery beneath it. While the two essential components, in the case of a church with independently roofed aisles, were the arcade and clerestory, even the clerestory was obviated in the German *Hallenkirchen* (see page 27), in which, due to the unusual design whereby the nave aisles were of the same height, the nave elevation consisted simply of an arcade, and the all lateral illumination was by way of the aisle windows.

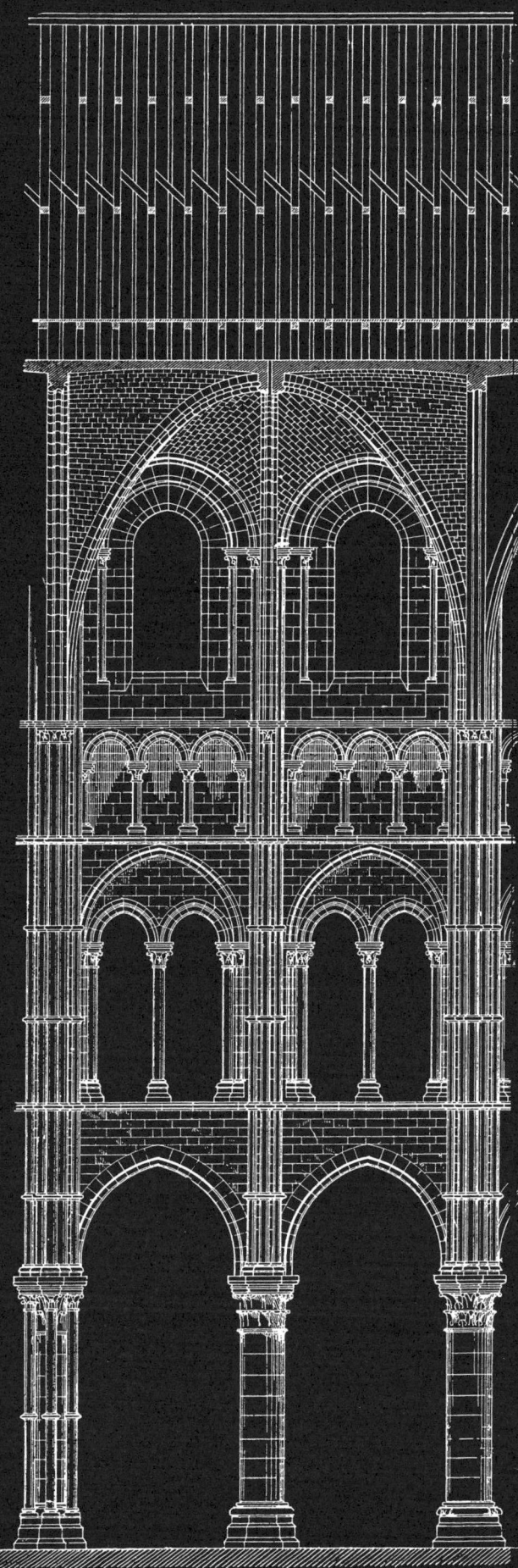

The clerestory is the upper part of the nave, its windows providing illumination above the level of the aisle roof.

The triforium is a wall passage corresponding with the position of an aisle roof.

The gallery forms an upper story of an aisle; it fell out of favor in the later Gothic period.

The arcade is the constant factor in aisled churches, supporting the walls of the nave while allowing access to the aisles.

A Four-Story Design

The rebuilding of the cathedral at Laon in the Gothic style began between 1155 and 1160. The four-story internal elevation comprised arcade, gallery, triforium, and clerestory, the divisions between the tiers being clearly defined by stringcourses—horizontal banding across the facade.

BUILDING THE WALLS
Wall Treatment

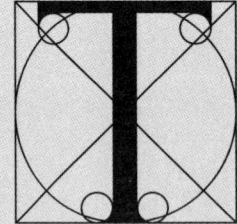To the Gothic cathedral builders, large expanses of plain masonry were an undesirable trait, and the external wall surfaces of a great church were broken up in diverting fashions by plinths, stringcourses (horizontal banding), paneling, and wall-head decoration. West fronts were particular areas of attention (see pages 56–57), but other parts of the church were far from neglected. At York Minster, for example, the elevations of the mid-thirteenth-century transepts were embellished with lancet arcading, reflecting the fenestration pattern. The wall of the late fourteenth-century east end of the cathedral was covered with trefoil-headed paneling, a motif that is repeated in the late medieval openwork parapet of the cathedral. Most elaborate of all, perhaps, is the traceried openwork stone screen that was built over the west front of Strasbourg Cathedral that partly obscured the main aisle windows.

The lower walls of Salisbury Cathedral are embellished with a set of twelve consecration crosses, three to each of the four main sides, which probably date from 1220. Consecration crosses were commonly displayed on the inside and outside of a church, often in paint, but the ones at Salisbury are unusually elaborate and permanent. Each one consists of a stone disk 2 feet (610 mm) in diameter tightly joined into the surrounding ashlar; the surrounding borders (a quatrefoil set within a circle) are raised prominently above the wall face. Within the quatrefoil is the indent for the brass cross that formerly served as the centerpiece of the composition.

Corresponding brass crosses on the internal walls were surrounded by painted decoration, exemplifying the very rich use of paint to ornament the interior. One common form of painted decoration was to imitate the underlying ashlar surface by applying a whitewash or colorwash and then marking out a pattern in red to suggest ashlar blocks. Such a pattern was used in the thirteenth century at Salisbury, both on the walls and on the vaulting. Indeed, most of the cathedral's interior appears to have been painted to some degree, although the richest decoration was reserved for the choir and transepts.

At Westminster Abbey, thirteenth-century paintings of biblical scenes survive within the blind arcading panels that line the walls of the south transept. Such blind arcading, which was frequently used to decorate the lower walls of a church, presented useful frames for pictorial representations. At Westminster, this type of arcading is of lancet form (see pages 150–151) with Purbeck marble shafts and foliated capitals and arches. The spandrels (see page 174) are completely covered with carved diaper-patterned stonework, an extravagant surface treatment that extends to the spandrels of the nave arcades and galleries.

Parapet Decoration

The upper wall and parapet of the choir of the church of St. Urbain de Troyes, which dates from between 1290 and 1310, is a richly decorated affair. The windows are provided with traceried gables from which finials rise through and above the projecting openwork parapets. The spandrels between the window gables are divided by vertical members, which also extend through the parapet and end in finials. On each side of this division is a roundel containing foliate decoration. The whole arrangement resembles a traceried grid covering the plain ashlar of the walls.

Wall Arcading

The south aisle of St. Hugh's Choir in Lincoln Cathedral, of ca. 1200, where the treatment of the walls is symptomatic of the astonishing originality of the cathedral's first Gothic master, who was in charge of the rebuilding from 1192. Here, an outer arcade of pointed trefoil arches is superimposed upon a two-centered inner arcade. While the concept owes something to Romanesque intersecting motifs, its alternation of forms and pronounced three-dimensionality transform it into a highly innovative design. The shafts are of Alwalton marble, one of the English hard limestones that can be worked to a highly polished finish.

BUILDING THE WALLS

Approaches to Bay Design

While cathedral bay design was undertaken within formulaic parameters, there were wide variations. From our retrospective viewpoint, this is partly a result of chronological factors, where changing fashion and technological improvements have left an evolutionary trail. To the master mason and his client, however, it was a question of what kind of effect they wanted to achieve, and under what constraints they had to labor. Existing models were studied for their innovations, but also for their shortcomings. Behind every great church, however, there was an original mind working to stamp its personality on the design.

PARIS
Dating from ca. 1160, the initial Gothic design for Notre-Dame de Paris included a four-story elevation comprising arcade, gallery, oculus (circular window), and clerestory, as depicted here in the restoration by Viollet le Duc. This was modified from ca. 1220, when the third-story oculi (round windows) were removed, so that the clerestory could be enlarged and remodeled in the fashion of Chartres and Reims.

BOURGES
The apparent five-story nave elevation is something of an optical illusion, due to its double-aisle plan. The first three stories are the arcade, gallery, and clerestory of the inner aisle, with the outer aisle window visible at ground-floor level through the arcade. However, these are seen through the very high nave arcade, above which are the nave triforium and clerestory. Bourges Cathedral was built from between ca. 1195 and 1285.

CHARTRES
In planning the nave elevation of Chartres Cathedral, of ca. 1195–1220, the architect created a radically different design by omitting the gallery, a very important component of both Laon and Notre-Dame de Paris. Instead, far greater prominence was given to the clerestory, which incorporated plate-traceried roses (see pages 152–153), and which was here the dominating element of the composition.

LINCOLN
St. Hugh's Choir of 1192–1200 at Lincoln Cathedral has a three-story elevation comprising arcade, gallery, and clerestory. In dispensing with the triforium instead of the gallery, the middle story makes a greater architectural impact than it does at the contemporary Chartres. Lincoln's is a much richer and three-dimensional design, deeper perspective being provided by the multiple-shafted and plate-traceried gallery openings and the triple-lancet screen to the rear of the clerestory windows.

SÉEZ CATHEDRAL
This reconstruction of the thirteenth-century west front of Séez Cathedral in Normandy gives an impression of the intentions of the medieval architect that have since become obscured by alterations. Work began on the western arm ca. 1240 but the design of the west front is largely devoid of window tracery, and is, instead, reliant upon the lancet window. Lancets have, indeed, been used to considerable effect in the creation of this very vertical composition, which is only restrained by the blind arcade to either side of the central portal, and by the banding at the bottom of the twin towers and central gable. The crowning of the towers with stone spires is the logical climax to the erect character of the design.

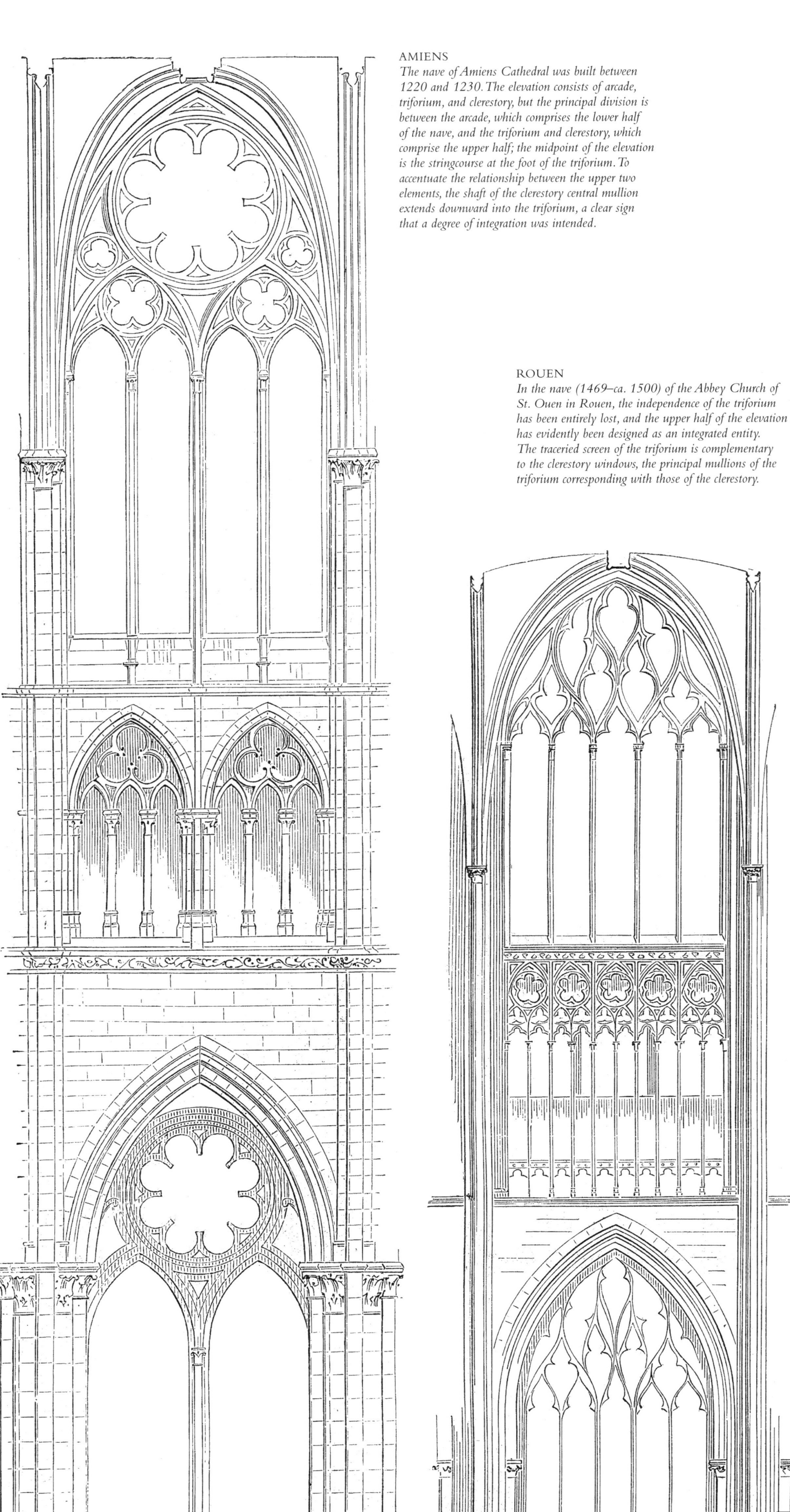

AMIENS
The nave of Amiens Cathedral was built between 1220 and 1230. The elevation consists of arcade, triforium, and clerestory, but the principal division is between the arcade, which comprises the lower half of the nave, and the triforium and clerestory, which comprise the upper half; the midpoint of the elevation is the stringcourse at the foot of the triforium. To accentuate the relationship between the upper two elements, the shaft of the clerestory central mullion extends downward into the triforium, a clear sign that a degree of integration was intended.

ROUEN
In the nave (1469–ca. 1500) of the Abbey Church of St. Ouen in Rouen, the independence of the triforium has been entirely lost, and the upper half of the elevation has evidently been designed as an integrated entity. The traceried screen of the triforium is complementary to the clerestory windows, the principal mullions of the triforium corresponding with those of the clerestory.

BUILDING THE WALLS

Approaches to Facade Design

Gothic cathedrals were, on the whole, inward-looking buildings, with conscious architectural effects being concentrated on the interior. The principal exception is the west front, the public face of the church housing the main ceremonial entrances. In France, the west front often reflected the interior arrangement; the emphasis was on a tripartite arrangement of portals (with windows above) denoting the positions of the nave and side aisles, a pair of towers being placed over the western bays of the aisles. In England, due to the development of the screen front, this relationship between the interior and exterior is not generally so marked; the portals are less important and the overall surface treatment is more significant.

LICHFIELD
The west front of Lichfield Cathedral was probably begun in the 1280s, and the spires of the western towers, as well as that of the central tower, were probably complete by the 1320s. An example of an English screen front, the facade was designed to accommodate several tiers of figure sculpture, most of which were destroyed during the English Civil War. Now, the main impact of the Lichfield front comes from its twin spires and their visual relationship with their counterpart spire over the crossing tower.

LINCOLN
The Gothic facade of Lincoln Cathedral represents a remodeling of the Norman west front, which survives as the central component of the later composition. Its three high portals still dominate the facade, albeit modified by the addition of Gothic details. The lower stages of the twin towers are also Norman and stand over the western bays of the aisles. It was probably during the second quarter of the thirteenth century that the west front was lengthened into a screen wall and provided with tiers of niches for statuary; the central portal was provided with a pointed arch. The western towers were heightened in the late fourteenth century.

BUILDING SALISBURY CATHEDRAL
Raising the Walls

It is around 1226, and the three eastern chapels have been completed and consecrated and are now in use, with temporary partitions having been constructed between them and the choir on which work is continuing. The masons have now completed the arcades of the choir, transepts, and two easternmost bays of the nave and have established working platforms on the tie beams of the aisles preparatory to beginning the construction of the gallery. Conveniently, spiral staircases built into the fabric of the four transepts give the masons access to these platforms and will subsequently extend to the higher levels. In addition to progress on the eastern arm, the lower courses of the walls of the western arm have also been built so that the entire footprint of the cathedral is now in place.

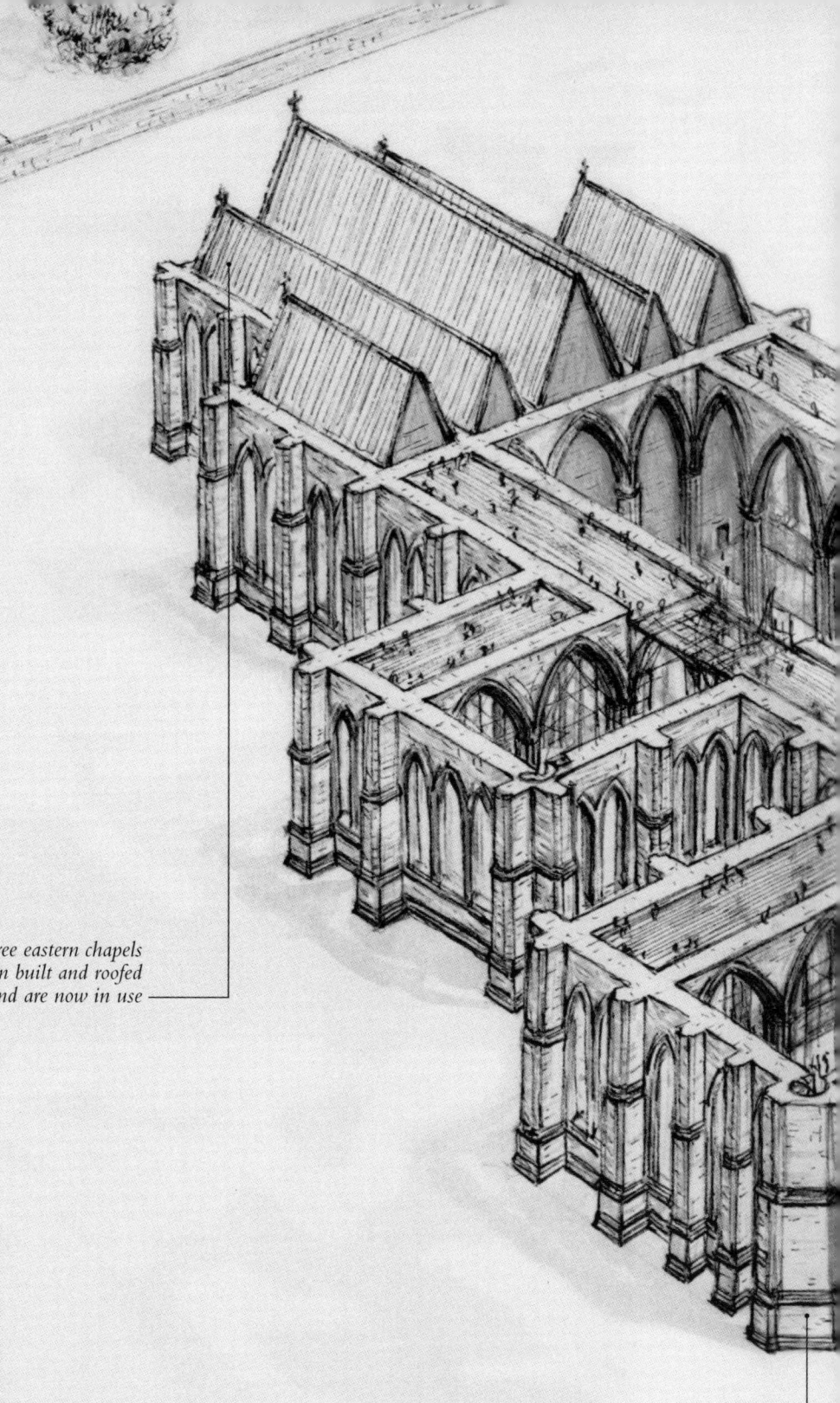

The three eastern chapels have been built and roofed and are now in use

Stair turret

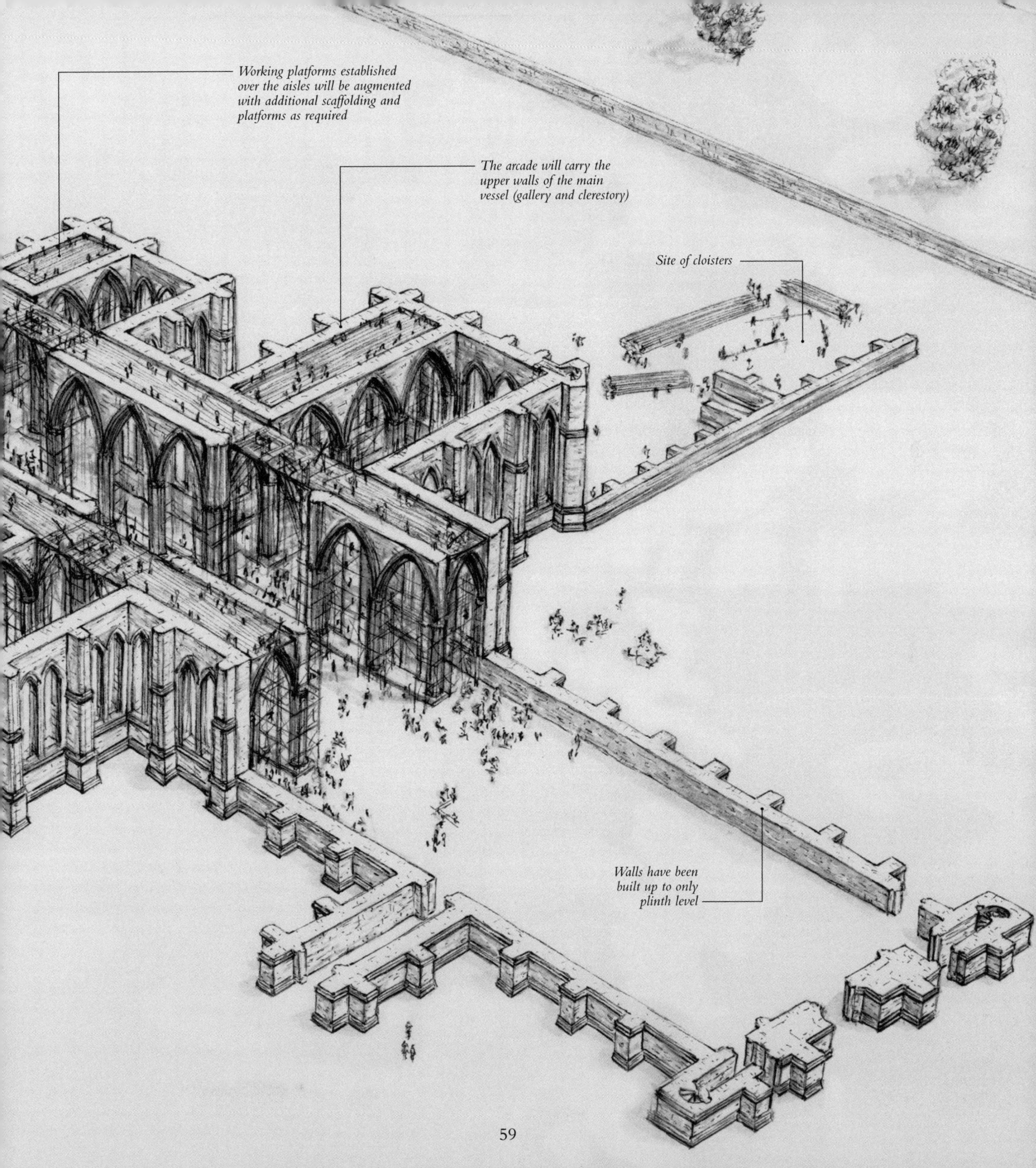

aking the Strain

TAKING THE STRAIN
Introduction

IN STRUCTURAL THEORY, the thrust line is the path taken by the vertical thrust of a load from the top of a structure to its foot. In a freestanding wall or column of simple and regular character, this should pass down the center of the structure so that the thrust is applied symmetrically, and no part of the structure is subjected to undue stress. However, in most buildings, the walls will be exposed to lateral stress from the roof members and, in the case of vaulted buildings, from the vault as well. The effect of lateral stress on the walls is to distort the thrust line so that it runs obliquely instead of vertically. If the thrust line diverges sufficiently from the center to reach the outer face of the wall, cracks could develop and the structure fail.

The medieval builder grasped something of this—although his understanding might have been based on bitter experience instead of an abstract knowledge of structural theory—and countermeasures were taken to combat the danger posed. One method of counteracting lateral thrust was to add extra weight to the top of the wall; this had the effect of lessening the degree of deflection caused to the line of thrust. At the Abbey Church of Cluny, in Burgundy, where the church was rebuilt from 1089 with pointed barrel vaults, the walls of the nave were extended high above the clerestory in order to provide the additional mass that was deemed necessary to ensure the building's structural stability. A similar effect could be achieved by filling the void behind the springing of the vault with mortared rubble, a practice that continued to be followed throughout the Gothic period (see page 67).

In the Romanesque churches of Normandy and England, any deflection of the thrust line caused by the lateral load of the roof and vaults was to some extent offset by the substantial thickness of the walls. Buttressing amounted to no more than a localized thickening of the wall to correspond with the positions of the transverse ribs that formed the structural framework of the vault. In other instances, bracing of the nave might be provided beneath the roofs of the flanking galleries (see page 65). This might take the form of quadrant vaults, whereby the whole length of the upper nave wall was abutted. An alternative system that was more economical in materials involved the use of quadrant arches, which, instead of abutting the entire length of the nave, instead targeted the positions from which the rib vaults sprang.

Introduction

The aesthetic character of Gothic cathedral architecture is underpinned and determined by a structural system, the principles of which are profoundly different from the Romanesque that preceded it. Whereas the Romanesque architect relied on solidity of construction to ensure the structural integrity of his works, his Gothic counterpart espoused a more rational approach in which the emphasis was not on the strength of the walls but instead on the creation of a mechanically stable framework formed by columns, vaults, and buttresses. The stability of such a system is dependent on the interaction of force and counterforce to achieve a self-preserving equilibrium. The stone skeleton that formed the basis of the Gothic great church reduced the structural significance of the walls and, thus, allowed for the great expansion of the fenestrated area that characterized the development of the Gothic.

The buttress, therefore, is a highly important component of the Gothic cathedral, and its design and construction was taken very seriously indeed. Failure of the buttresses would result in the failure of the vaults and, thereby, lead to disaster. It is this mechanical significance that gives the buttress, notably the flying buttress, such a high profile in Gothic architecture. Not only was the flying buttress an invention that made Gothic architecture possible, it is also one of the defining features of the style, instantly recognizable in the highly visible displays around many of the great churches of the period.

The ordinary buttress was designed in a simple way to brace the wall against the lateral forces of the vault, but the flying buttress was a far more involved and crucial piece of engineering that had to be much more skillfully applied in order to be effective. The flyer had to meet the nave wall at the vital point at which the lateral thrust exerted itself—that is to say, at the springing of the vault—and was designed not to buttress the walls so much as to divert the forces exerted by the vault away from the walls to the buttress pier.

The flying buttress achieved the peak of sophistication in France, where the emphasis on height amplified its structural significance and visual impact. It is no coincidence that in England, where nave vaults were generally much lower than those of their French counterparts, flying buttresses were far less elaborate or evident. While in France early flying buttresses are highly visible, in England they were slow to make an impact, and it was only during the rebuilding by William of Sens of the eastern arm of Canterbury from 1174 that external flying buttress were introduced.

TAKING THE STRAIN

Origins of the Flying Buttress

The principle of the flying buttress was known to the Byzantines certainly by the tenth century, when several were added to the west face of the fifth-century cathedral of Hagia Sophia in Constantinople. Hagia Sophia was well known in the West by the time that the flying buttress came to be developed there, but it is arguable as to whether the technique was borrowed from this particular source or whether it developed independently in western Europe. Many Romanesque churches, for example, used related systems of nave abutment, hidden beneath the gallery roofs. In these instances, quadrant vaults or quadrant arches extended from the tops of the aisle walls to the face of the nave wall, where they countered the thrust from the vault. The structural principle is similar to that of the flying buttress. Quadrant arches were in use by the late eleventh century at Durham (see opposite) and other English cathedrals.

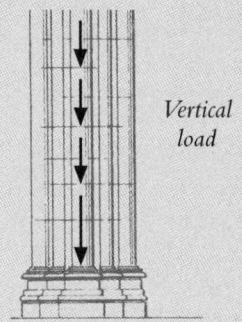

Vertical load

These two diagrams depict the thrust line in a structure in which the load is applied directly from above (top) and the effect on the thrust line from the application of oblique pressure from the roof or vault (bottom).

These demonstrate that there was a Western building tradition in existence from which the flying buttress of the Gothic period might have been derived. However, proper external flying buttresses did not appear until the twelfth century, although the destruction of much of the evidence makes it hard to pinpoint a precise date. Arched buttresses were added to the Abbey Church of Cluny in response to the collapse of the nave vault ca. 1125. These were akin to gallery arches, but instead of being hidden, they were highly visible external structures. One of the earliest examples of a systematic deployment of flying buttresses in a new structure may have been the new choir of the Abbey Church of St. Denis, near Paris, of 1140–44. St. Denis is generally considered to be the earliest of the great churches in the Gothic style; it was a seminal building, rapidly becoming an exemplar for a new kind of architecture. Later twelfth-century flying buttress systems include those at the cathedrals of Laon (begun 1155–60) and Notre-Dame de Paris (begun ca. 1160), although the earliest to survive intact is at the Church of St. Remi, Reims, of ca. 1170 (see page 68).

Thrust from roof

By the time that the cathedrals at Chartres and Bourges came to be rebuilt from the 1190s, the flying buttress system was an essential and familiar component of any Gothic great church. By this time, instead of having remained a purely structural element, the flying buttress had begun to take on the aesthetic qualities that were to contribute to its secondary role as a powerful symbol of the theories and principles behind the formulation of the Gothic style.

Transverse Arches

The galleries of the choir of Durham Cathedral, which was built between 1093 and 1099, are spanned by semicircular transverse arches. These stone arches corresponded with the ribs of the high vault over the central vessel of the choir, a construction that was replaced in the thirteenth century by the pointed vault seen today. Their function must have been to counter the lateral thrust of the main vault while allowing uninterrupted access within the galleries.

Quadrant Arches

In the nave of Durham, constructed between 1099 and 1128, the galleries are still spanned by arches that correspond to the ribs of the high vault over the nave. In this instance, however, the semicircular arches of the choir galleries have been replaced by quadrant arches. Although they are hidden within the aisles, to all intents and purposes, these are flying buttresses, countering the lateral thrust of the vault ribs where they meet the walls of the nave.

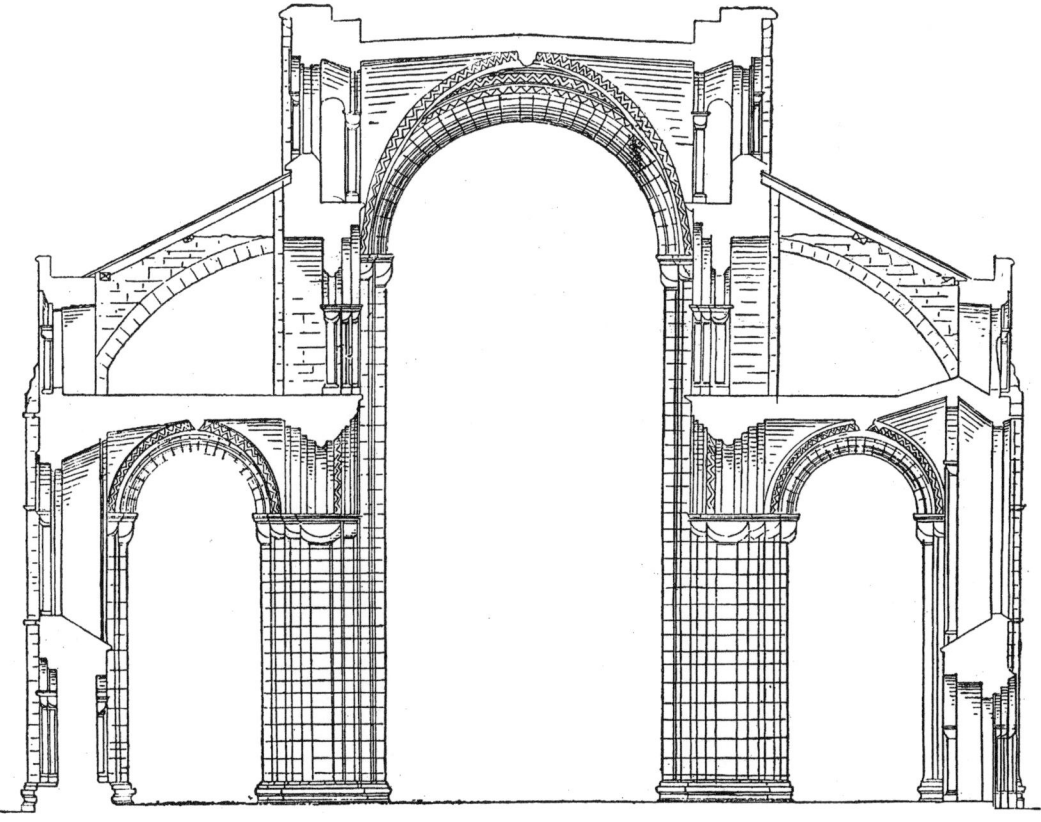

TAKING THE STRAIN

Flying Buttress Construction

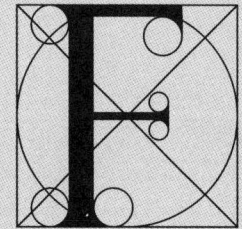lying-buttress piers were generally incorporated into the walls of the aisles, and would have been constructed in concert with them. When the masons had reached the roof level of the aisle, they would probably have established working platforms between the tops of the aisle walls and the arcades (see pages 58–59). These would have provided secure bases on which to continue operations, not only on the buttresses but also on the walls of the central vessel, or aisle, above the arcades. Lifting equipment, probably in the form of hand-operated windlasses, would have been established on the working platforms and materials hauled up to the platform from the aisle floor.

Because the buttress piers usually rose higher than the aisle walls, they and the walls of the main vessel would now be built in isolation, making use of individual scaffolds and of platforms at even higher levels. When the buttresses had reached the point from which the flyers were to spring, and the walls had reached the height at which the flyers were to abut, the wooden centerings on which the flyers were to be supported during their construction could be placed in position.

These centerings, which replicated the curve of the flyer, would have been prepared by the carpenters, assembled on the ground, and their dimensions and forms checked. It is not clear whether they would then have been lifted into position in one piece or whether they would then have been disassembled, raised element by element, and reassembled at the height at which they were to be used. There would seem to be advantages and disadvantages to both methods, although, for reasons of accessibility, the former process would have to have been carried out before the aisle roof went on, and it would have been necessary to use a substantial lifting device, which, in the case of the centering for the upper flyer, would need to have been situated at a level not far below that of the nave roof.

From St. Remi onward, flying buttresses usually had two flyers, the lower of which was obviously situated to counter the thrust from the vault. The upper flyer, however, which is generally positioned high above the springing point of the vault, abutting the wall head, is evidently capable of no such thing. It is probable that its function was to counter wind thrust and to give the walls greater stability.

Once in position, the centering would serve an additional structural purpose by tying the buttress pier to the nave wall and so providing temporary stiffening, thus lessening the chance of instability arising in these otherwise exposed components.

The Buttress System

This drawing shows a section through the chevet of Amiens Cathedral, of 1236–69, and depicts the buttress system and its relationship with the church wall. The lower flyer arch springs from the split buttress pier to the right and abuts the wall at the bottom of the vault. It is supported on a column at clerestory level, and this is itself carried on a ledge supported from beneath by the outer wall of the triforium. Also shown here is the medieval technique of filling the vaulting void with mortar and rubble in order to offset the lateral thrust from the vault and to take the pressure away from the walls. Another effect of this practice was to counteract any distortion of the thrust line within the vault ribs.

TAKING THE STRAIN
Development of the Flying Buttress

Between the late twelfth century and the early thirteenth century, the flying buttress underwent rapid development, because the structural issues encountered during the great sequence of Gothic cathedral building in France caused the master builders to consider and refine its design. During these years, the flying buttress evolved from a heavy built but imperfectly understood abutment, to a more carefully targeted construction, efficient in its disposition and use of materials.

CHARTRES
(Below) At Chartres, dating from ca. 1195–1220, there are no galleries, and the lower flyers meet the wall at the springing of the vault in order to fulfill the main function of the buttress system in a more efficient manner than at St. Remi. The massive lower flyers are, in fact, two-tiered, each comprising two flyers, the space between them being filled by an open arcade, complete with capitaled columns, which extends the design of columnar supports to the flyers at the point at which they abut the church wall.

ST. REMI, REIMS
The Church of St. Remi in Reims, which was begun ca. 1170, incorporates one of the earliest examples of an external flying-buttress system to survive, although older designs formerly existed at Notre-Dame de Paris and Laon. Keynotes of this early form are the wide piers and flyers, and the plain functional nature of the design. In this section through the choir of St. Remi, the upper flyer abuts the church just below the wall head of the main vessel, and the lower flyer at the head of the gallery wall. The design is, therefore, flawed, because the thrust of the vault is not countered directly, that is, at the springing of the vault. Where the upper flyer meets the wall, it is supported on a fluted column with Corinthian capital, which is itself carried by a corbel table at the height of the clerestory window sills (see detail above right).

AMIENS
(Below) The extravagantly engineered design of the main flyer of Chartres was not repeated in its thirteenth-century successors, and by the time Amiens Cathedral came to be built (from 1220), flying buttresses were being constructed with far greater economy and efficiency. Here, the lower flyer, which meets the nave wall at the most crucial position for countering the lateral thrust from the vault, is a far more focused piece of engineering than its counterpart at Chartres.

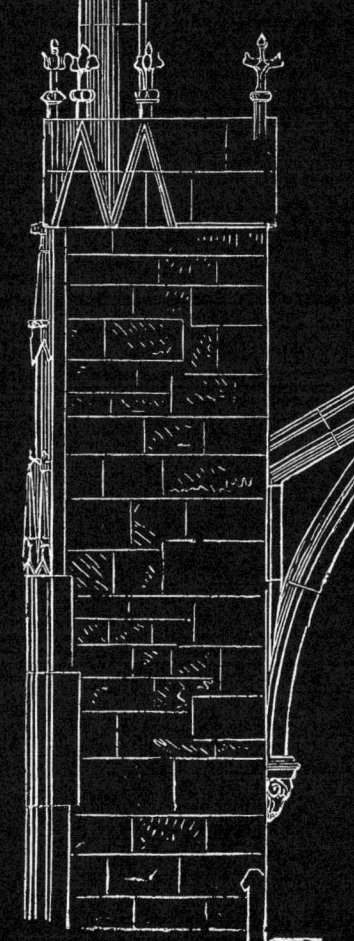

ST. URBAIN DE TROYES
In the Collegiate Church of St. Urbain de Troyes, which was begun in 1262, the structural character of the flyers was of extreme delicacy. The principle of two-tiered flyers adopted at Chartres is still apparent, but here the two components have each been reduced to a single course of stonework, an economy of materials symptomatic of the thirteenth-century approach to great church architecture.

Henry III

King Henry III of England, who reigned between 1216 and 1272, was a noted patron of the arts and is particularly linked with the reconstruction of Westminster Abbey between 1245 and 1272. It is clear that Henry had strong aesthetic sensibilities and a profound interest in architecture. Westminster Abbey was rebuilt through his personal intervention, and he provided the finance and motivational force; it is no coincidence that the project came to a standstill on his death. His inspiration for Westminster Abbey came from France, and his intention was to emulate not only the architecture of the great Gothic churches that were being raised there, but also the spiritual associations that the French monarchy enjoyed. In the years preceding the commencement of operations at Westminster, three French churches with strong royal associations (St. Denis Abbey, Reims Cathedral, and the Ste.-Chapelle, Paris) had been under construction. Westminster, the coronation church, royal sepulchre, and resting place of England's national saint, was Henry's response.

TAKING THE STRAIN

Pinnacles

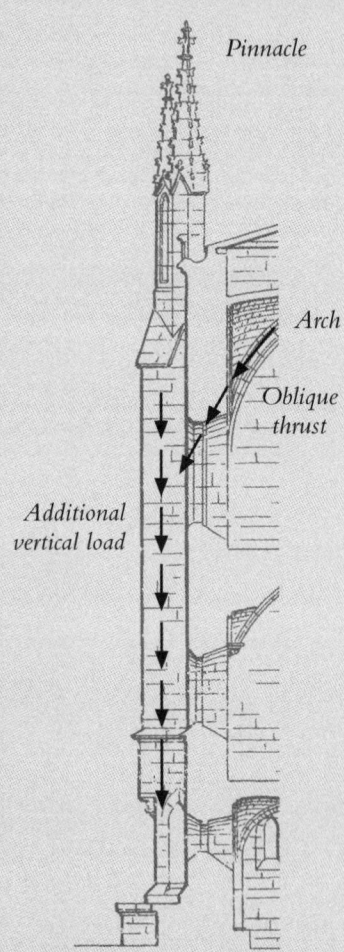

Pinnacle

Arch

Oblique thrust

Additional vertical load

This diagram shows the countermanding effect of the extra load represented by the pinnacle on the deflection of the thrust line caused by lateral forces from the vault.

While pinnacles were much used by Romanesque builders in order to weight the corners of buildings, their employment in association with buttresses was slow to take hold. In early flying buttresses, the flyer was attached to the head of the pier (for example, St. Remi, Reims, and Chartres—see page 68). This was an unsatisfactory structural arrangement because, although the lateral thrust from the vault was conveyed away from the nave wall by the flyer, it caused a deflection of the line of thrust within the pier, thereby placing it under stress.

An improvement was devised by drawing on the experience of the Romanesque builders, who loaded the tops of nave walls with extra weight in order to counter the thrust from the vaults. This technique was applied to the buttress pier by extending it upward from the point at which it received the flyer. Such was the method adopted by the builders of Canterbury Cathedral during the reconstruction of the choir following the fire of 1174 and also by the builders of Soissons Cathedral, ca. 1200 (see opposite).

It was not, however, until the early thirteenth century, that this principle was developed to include the use of the pinnacle. Reims Cathedral, which was rebuilt from 1211, is the earliest great church to weight its flying-buttress piers with pinnacles. While their principal purpose was to act as counterweights to the lateral thrusts of the vault, the opportunity was taken to disguise the function of the design by creating an emphatic decorative feature (see opposite).

An idea of the building sequence might be reflected in the nave of York Minster of ca. 1291–1360, where the buttresses to the aisles were capped with tall and elaborate pinnacles, even though the absence of a stone vault means that the scale at which they were built was quite unnecessary. It is evident that a stone vault and a flying-buttress system were planned but never built, and that the pinnacles were raised before the decision to abandon such a design was taken.

Most pinnacles were richly molded or sculptured, and each individual stone would have been crafted with precision so that at the assembly stage it could be fitted accurately into its allotted position with the minimum of redressing. These were considerable structures; the Reims pinnacles were over 30 feet (9 m) high from the top of the buttress to the top of the finial, and those of Amiens, of the 1220s, only a little shorter. The assembly of each would have necessitated its own individual scaffolding system.

Buttresses without Pinnacles

The choir of Soissons Cathedral, which was begun ca. 1200 and dedicated in 1212, was built with flying buttresses. The buttress piers do not bear pinnacles, but the fact that they rise above the level of the flyers suggests that the builder was aware of the structural principle behind the adoption of the pinnacle. The piers and their upward extensions are surmounted by pitched caps with finials at the gabled ends, a detail that relieves the tendency toward an otherwise rather stolid functionality.

Decorated Pinnacles

At Reims Cathedral, the tops of the buttress piers comprise columned aedicules (columned openings) containing sculptures of angels. These elements are capped with pinnacles of octagonal plan rising to foliated finials. The angles are decorated with crockets (projecting leaf-shaped decorations), a form that replicates that of the steeple, and one that accords well with the essential verticality of the Gothic style.

TAKING THE STRAIN

Buttress System Case Studies

The case studies of buttress systems given here illustrate two aspects of design. The first is that although the flying buttress system worked in most cases, if the building formula was varied without the structural principles being fully understood, then the master builder could make himself vulnerable to miscalculations. Such a miscalculation seems to have occurred at Beauvais. The second is that not all cathedrals used the flying buttress system; a case in point being Albi Cathedral, which was quite differently designed due to the specific circumstances of its construction.

BEAUVAIS CATHEDRAL

In 1284, disaster struck the Cathedral of St. Pierre, in the northern French town of Beauvais, when a structural collapse brought down part of the vault. By that time, little more than a decade after the completion of the eastern arm, the cathedral was probably already famous for the audacity of its design. At 157 feet 6 inches (48 m) above the floor of the church, the stone vault is the highest of any cathedral in Europe. We do not know if contemporaries believed the disaster to be a judgment on a Babel-like hubris, but in more recent times the collapse is sometimes thought of as having brought a cataclysmic end to the thirteenth-century trend toward ever-increasing height.

Construction of the cathedral had begun, ca. 1225, with the choir to the east of the Romanesque church known as the Basse Oeuvre, which the cathedral was intended to replace, but which still occupies the intended site of the nave. Almost immediately (in 1225) there was a structural collapse, not thought to have been serious but which proved an inauspicious start to an ill-fated building project that was never brought to fruition.

The disaster of 1284 stemmed from the empirically led approach to building design and construction that characterized the medieval period. A number of design features contributed toward the failure, but the immediate cause was probably a collapse of some of the buttresses, which were insufficiently well conceived to take the weight of the high vault. It is an episode that heavily underscores the importance of the flying buttress to the Gothic cathedral.

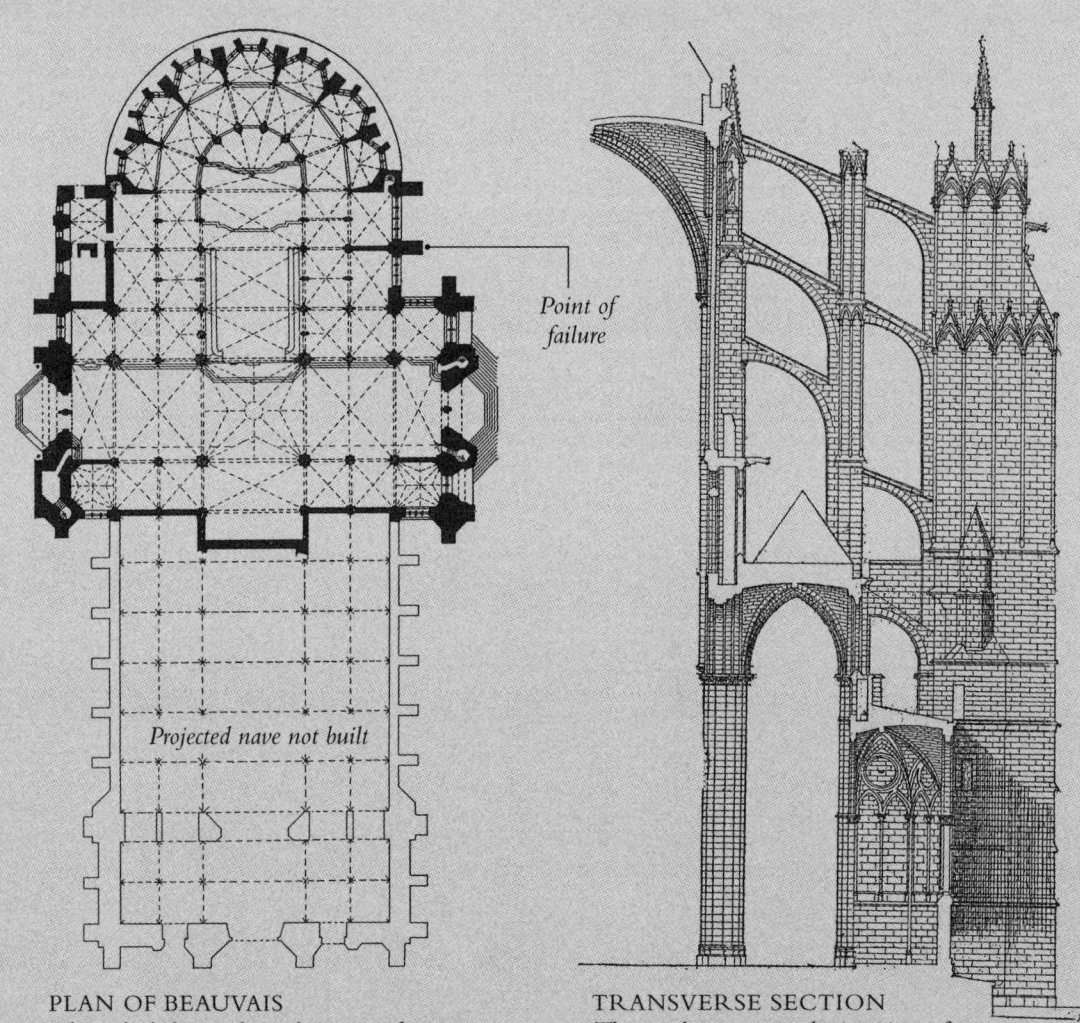

Point of failure

Projected nave not built

PLAN OF BEAUVAIS
The cathedral was planned as a cruciform church, but only the eastern arm was built during the medieval period. This has an apsidal end and a chevet (see pages 24–25) in the manner of Reims and Amiens. The collapse seems to have concentrated on the center of the straight-sided section of the eastern arm, at the point where the heaviest section of the high vault was exerting pressure upon the weakest element of the buttress system.

TRANSVERSE SECTION
The two buttresses at the junctions of the straight-side element of the eastern arm and the chevet (which did not fail) were extravagantly engineered structures that incorporated three tiers of flyers, in deference, no doubt, to the unprecedented height of the building. The inner buttress pier is partly carried on the vaulting of the ambulatory, but there is a fourth flyer buttressing the ambulatory vault.

ALBI CATHEDRAL

Shortly before the catastrophe at Beauvais, work began on a new cathedral at Albi in the south of France at the instigation of Bishop Bernard de Castanet. Dedicated to St. Cécile, it was built between 1282 and 1390, in a region that had, in the early years of the century, formed the epicenter of the Albigensian Heresy, a religious unorthodoxy that had provoked a twenty-year war, or "crusade" (1209–29). While the King of France and the Catholic Church had triumphed and imposed their joint hegemony over Languedoc, the legacy of violence and mistrust remained. Bishop de Castanet was neither liked nor trusted, and it may be for this reason that Albi is unusual among French cathedrals in having been conceived as much as a fortress as a church, and there is no doubt that defense and defiance were contributory factors in the formulation of its idiosyncratic design. In keeping with the unconventional character of the cathedral, the buttress system is an unusual one.

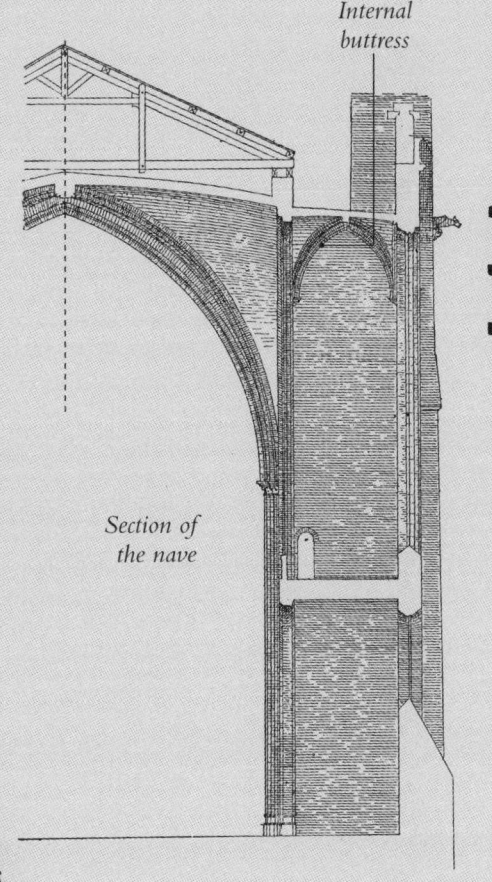

Section of the nave — *Internal buttress*

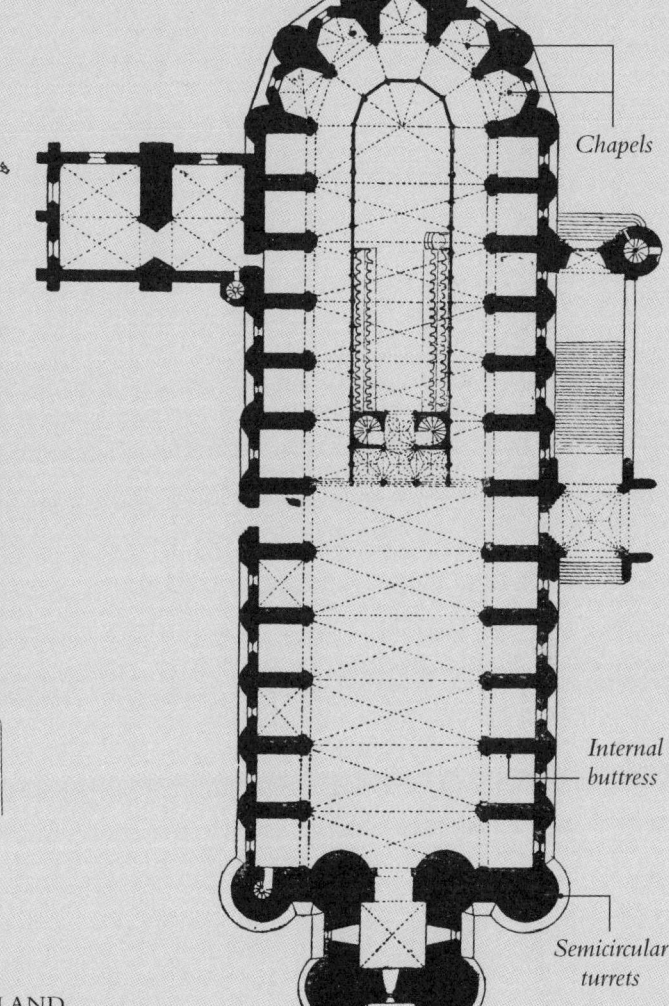

Chapels — *Internal buttress* — *Semicircular turrets*

PLAN AND SECTION OF ALBI
(Above and above right) At Albi, instead of aisles there are only lateral chapels extending around the apsidal east end as a chevet; these are situated between internal buttresses of immense width, which counter the thrust of the nave vault and extend beyond the external walls as semicircular turrets.

FORTRESS CATHEDRAL
Outwardly, the cathedral has something of the nature of a fortress and borrows extensively from the repertoire of the military engineer. The deep plinth rises sheer to a steep batter (inclined face of the wall). Rising from the plinth and so protected by it, are the external faces of the buttresses, which are disguised as semicircular turrets. The windows are cautiously narrow, and a machicolated parapet (one that projects out from the walls on brackets) provides additional protection.

TAKING THE STRAIN

Embellishment & Architectural Effect

While buttresses evolved through structural necessity, they soon graduated from being mere functional appendages to being largely decorative features, and so they became significant contributors to the overall architectural impact.

REIMS AND ROUEN
(Right and below right) Not only were the flyers objects for ornamentation, the buttress piers themselves were equally incorporated into the decorative plans presenting a setting for sculpture. The thirteenth-century flying-buttress piers of the cathedrals of both Reims and Rouen incorporate columned aedicules containing statues.

AMIENS
(Above) This shows the buttressing at the east end of the choir of Amiens Cathedral, which was rebuilt between 1236 and 1269. The two-tier flyer incorporates an openwork arcade as at Chartres (see page 68). At Amiens, however, the ponderousness of Chartres has been replaced by an elegant traceried design.

WESTMINSTER
Here, we see the buttressing at Henry VII's chapel of 1506 at Westminster Abbey. In keeping with the extravagantly decorated interior, both elements of the flying buttresses are highly ornate in character. Two sets of double-tiered flyers are integrated into a single entity by the incorporation of traceried roundels, while the pier is provided with canopied niches, for the display of sculpture, and an ogee-domed pinnacle.

PALMA
One of the tallest great churches in Europe, Palma Cathedral on the island of Mallorca was rebuilt from 1306 at the behest of Jaime II, King of Mallorca. Here, the buttressing of the south front, toward the harbor, has been used to create a profound and deliberate architectural effect. The lower tier of buttresses relates to the tall lateral chapels; the taller buttresses, which abut the nave, are upward extensions of the side walls of the chapels, and this accounts for their great width.

LE MANS
Around the choir of Le Mans Cathedral, which was begun in 1218, a spectacular effect is created by the flying-buttress system. An unusual aspect of the design is the configuration of the buttresses supporting the angles of the polygonal east end. Two tiers of flyers reach from each angle to a pier on the line of the inner ambulatory arcade; from here additional flyers extend in two directions to obliquely set twin buttresses positioned on the line of the outer ambulatory wall between the projecting chapels of the chevet (see page 25 for a plan of the Le Mans chevet). The whole arrangement forms a Y-shaped configuration that is reflected in the floor plan of the cathedral.

Henry de Reyns

Master Henry de Reyns (fl. 1243–50) was the mason in charge of Henry III's rebuilding of Westminster Abbey from 1245 until ca. 1253 and is credited with the introduction into England of some of the ideas used by the thirteenth-century architects of the great churches of France, notably Reims, Amiens, and the Ste.-Chapelle in Paris. Documentary evidence describes his place of origin as "Reynes," thus giving rise to conjecture that he was a French architect. However, although Westminster Abbey is one of the most French of English churches in general concept, the execution of the details suggests that it was masterminded by someone with a grounding in English building practices. In consequence, Henry de Reyns is now thought of as an Englishman, either from the village of Rayne in Essex, or one who took his name from a sojourn in the cathedral city of Reims in Champagne.

BUILDING SALISBURY CATHEDRAL

Buttress Construction

It is now 1245. Since the consecration of the eastern chapels twenty years before, the project has moved on apace. Now the entire eastern arm, both sets of transepts, and the eastern bays of the nave have been completed, as well as a short tower over the crossing. Services are being carried on in the choir, and all the efforts of the builders are now being concentrated on the western arm. While the eastern end of the nave has been roofed, the corresponding parts of the aisles are still open to the elements, although work has begun on the flying buttresses, which at Salisbury are concealed beneath the aisle roofs. At the first three bay divisions, the flying-buttress centering is in place, and a fourth piece of centering is being prepared on the ground. Until the flyers have been constructed, these centerings will act as temporary flyers and conduct the thrust of the vault to the buttress piers incorporated into the aisle walls.

Both sets of transepts and entire eastern arm complete

Stair turret

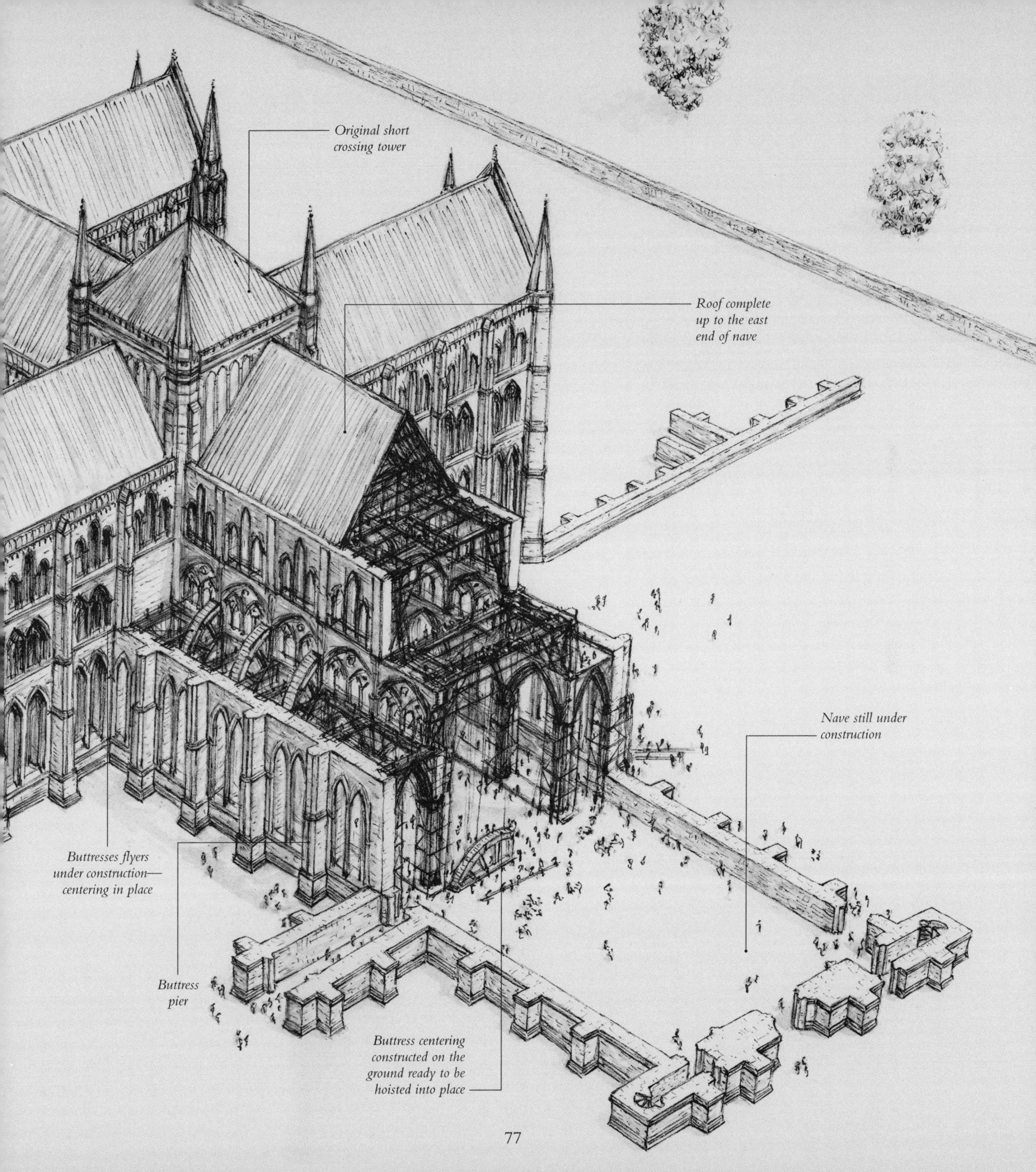

aising
the Roof

RAISING THE ROOF

Introduction

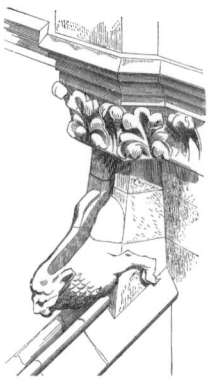

THE RAISING OF THE ROOF was an episode of particular significance in the progress of a cathedral construction project. It marked a crucial stage whereby hitherto exposed and precarious-looking walls were linked and the stability of the building was to a great extent assured. Once the roof was on, work could proceed apace within a sheltered environment. This was one practical aspect of roofing a great church; another concerned the aesthetic quality of the interior. There are very few cathedrals that are open to the roof, and it was usual practice in great church architecture to conceal the roof timbers with a vault or a ceiling.

The roofs of Gothic cathedrals are impressive constructions that reach immense heights and that play an important part in the overall architectural impact of a great church. These structures are also pure works of engineering, which, due to the fact that they were seldom intended to be seen, are untrammeled by the decorative elements that were worked into most structural masonry. The cathedral roof is one of the few reminders of the contribution of the carpenters to the construction such buildings. They were important in facilitating the work of the masons through the manufacture of centering and other formwork, but much of their output was by its very nature ephemeral. Surviving cathedral roofs are among the few permanent relics of the carpenters' craft and a measure of the skill that they brought to a project. That several medieval cathedral roofs should have survived, the earliest dating back to the twelfth century, is a testament to the excellence of their construction.

Many others, however, have long since disappeared, and there is no doubt that the roof was a weak spot in one particular respect. Fire, which was an ever-present danger to the great church, struck cathedrals far too frequently, with devastating consequences, and often provided the impetus for extensive or complete rebuilding. The construction of numerous Gothic cathedrals, including Chartres, Reims, Amiens, and Regensburg, began because their predecessors had been destroyed by fire, and it was often in the roof that the conflagration started. In 1113, the entire roof of Worcester Cathedral was burned down, and the fire of 1174 that gutted the choir of Canterbury Cathedral started in the roof. Sometimes the disaster occurred due to natural forces, as when the bell tower of Durham Cathedral was struck by lightning in 1429; in other instances, it was human agency that was the cause, and the negligence of workmen was often considered the source of the trouble.

Introduction

The susceptibility to fire of timber roofs may be one reason for the widespread use of stone vaulting. While stone vaults were, in some measure, a safety feature, once the decorative propensities of vaulting had been appreciated, developments were concerned with style, and the vault became an integral part of the interior design. Initially, however, it was the technicalities of vault construction and the problems of adapting an ancient form to the needs of the Middle Ages that exercised the minds of the master builders.

Gothic vaulting was ultimately derived from the simple Roman barrel vault of semicircular section, but more directly from a derivative form that resulted from the intersection of two barrel vaults at right angles to one another. At the points where the two vaults met, an arris, or groin, was formed, which followed a line at a 45-degree angle to the axes of the two vaults. If the arrangement at the intersection were to be reproduced in isolation, it created a square compartment, or groined vault, in which the weight of the vault was carried on the four groins, and, if it were multiplied, it could be utilized in vaulting an elongated space, such as a church aisle in a series of compartments.

Accordingly, in Romanesque churches, the groined vault was a common method of covering the aisles and was usually reinforced by the construction of transverse arches between the cells as at, for example, Gloucester Abbey (now Cathedral) choir aisle and ambulatory of 1089–1100. One of the drawbacks to groin vaulting was that each compartment had to be constructed in a single operation using extensive centering. This was perhaps not such a great problem in respect of the aisles, but the high vaults of the wider central vessel presented a far greater challenge. Even so, groined vaults were successfully raised over the naves of a number of churches, including Speyer Cathedral in Germany (ca. 1090) and Vézelay Abbey in Burgundy, France (ca. 1120).

The rib vault, which was one of the hallmarks of the Gothic style, developed from groined vaults after it was understood that the supportive function of the groins could, instead, be fulfilled by stone arches, or ribs, similar to the transverse arches that were already being used to divide the vaulting bays. Whether the step was taken for aesthetic, engineering, or economic reasons is uncertain, but this advance changed the entire structural character of the vault so that it was transformed from the solid mass of masonry and mortar that characterized the groin vault to a skeleton of ribs infilled with panels or webs of stone and/or mortar.

RAISING THE ROOF
Early Rib Vaulting

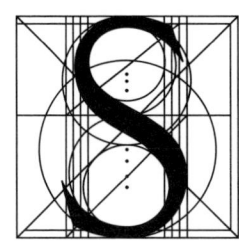

Some of the earliest surviving rib vaults in Europe are those that are located over the choir aisles of Durham Cathedral of 1093–1104. At Durham, the choir aisle vaults are based on a framework of transverse arches (which divide the vaulting bays) and diagonal arches (which span from one corner of the bay to another). This is known as a quadripartite vault because the diagonal ribs divide the vaulting bay into four sections. Such a system (replaced in the thirteenth century) was also used over the central vessel of the choir, and in this, Durham was again in the front line of architectural development, because rib vaulting was more slowly adopted for central aisles than it was for side aisles.

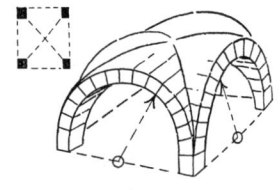

Groin vault over a square bay with semicircular arches of equal diameter.

One of the main problems that Romanesque architects struggled with in designing early rib vaulting was that of reconciling the use of the round arch with a horizontal ridge. In a square bay, the arches at the sides of the vault on the one hand, and the diagonals on the other, span different widths, so that if all the arches were semicircular, then the diagonal required an arch with a greater diameter than those of the side arches. In that case, the vault would take on a domical form, and indeed domical rib vaults were constructed in some parts of Europe, notably much of France. In Normandy and England, however, the preference was for the horizontal ridge, and in order to achieve this, either the side arches had to be raised on stilts to match the height of the diagonals or the height of the diagonals had to be depressed by using a segmental arch.

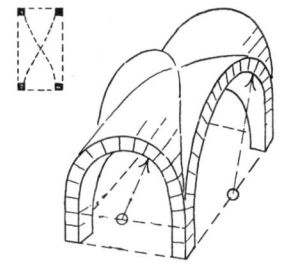

Groin vault over an oblong bay with semicircular arches of different diameters springing from different heights so that the smaller arch is stilted.

Vaulting oblong bays was more difficult, because there were three different spans to take into account (lateral, longitudinal, and diagonal), but where the vaulting of both nave and aisles was contemplated, it was inevitable that oblong bays would have to be used, for even if the aisle bays were square, then the nave bays would have to be oblong due to the greater width of the nave. The compromises made to address the issue of the horizontal ridge gave aesthetically flawed results, and the use of the segmental arch over a long reach produced weaker diagonals. The solution came with the introduction of the pointed arch, the profile and span of which could be varied without weakening the vault. In addition, all the arches could spring from the same level to present a more pleasing appearance. Here, again, it was Durham that led the way in introducing the pointed arch to the high vault over the nave.

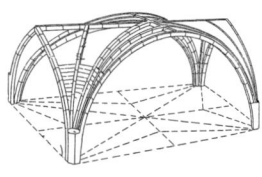

Rib vault over an oblong bay with semicircular arch at the long side and pointed arch at the short side, both springing from the same height.

Durham Rib-Vaulted Nave

The interest of the nave of Durham Cathedral (ca. 1115–30) is that it is the earliest surviving example of a rib-vaulted nave, and the oldest rib vault in Europe to use the pointed arch in its construction. Rib vaults had also been used in the choir (ca. 1104) and in the transepts (ca. 1110), but in these locations the architect had used the rounded arch, whereas in the nave the transverse arches were pointed. The introduction of pointed rib vaults at Durham was an outstanding technical development that had profound repercussions for the development of twelfth-century architecture, and it seems to have been achieved independently here in northern England instead of being an import from the Continent.

RAISING THE ROOF

Rib Construction

Like other arches, vault ribs were constructed on wooden centering and were composed of a series of accurately cut stone voussoirs. As in the case of flying buttresses, the early functionality of these structures was soon overshadowed by increasingly elaborate decorative elements that contributed to the aesthetic appeal of the interior.

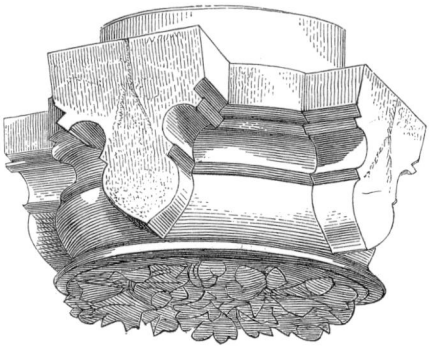

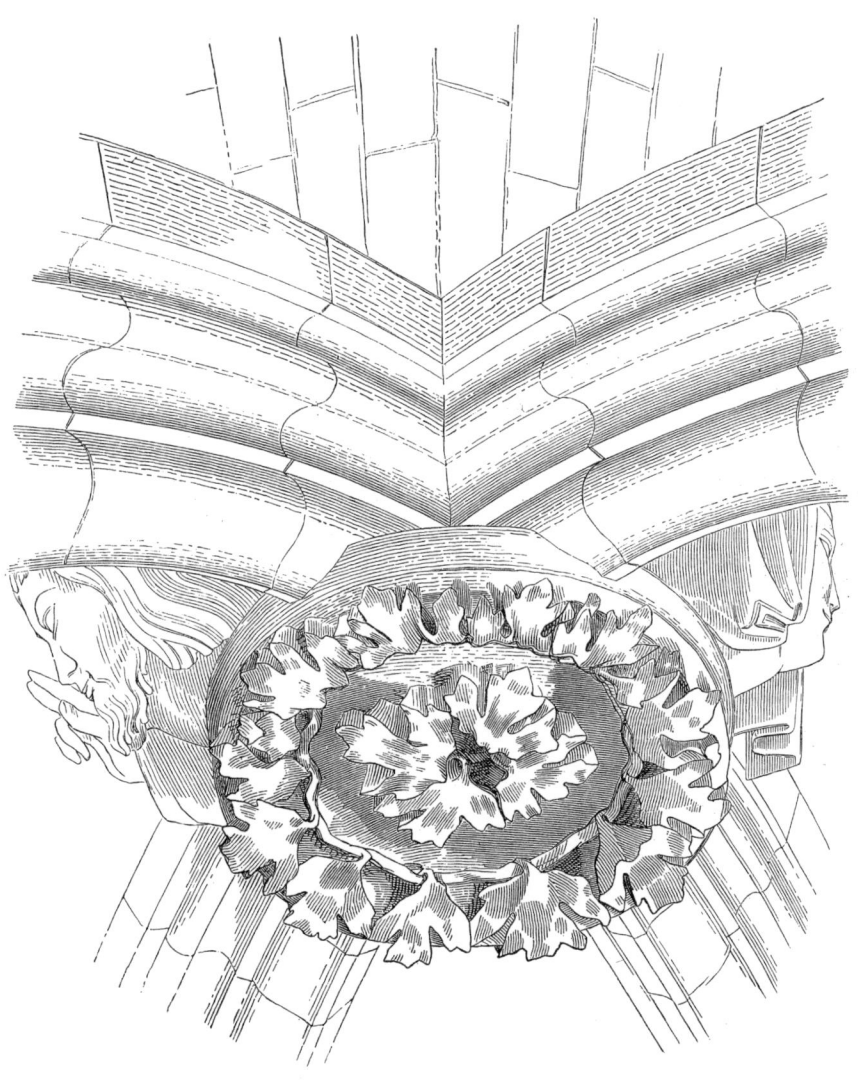

THE KEYSTONE
The keystone is the voussoir at the apex of the vault that holds the whole construction together. It is the common element where two or more ribs intersect. This ex situ example (above) is for a quadripartite vault and displays the molded stubs extending from it that are designed to meet the four diagonal ribs. The presence of the keystone at an intersection of the vault ribs presented an opportunity for embellishment, and it was often provided with a sculptured design that transformed it into an emphatic boss. In England in particular, where vaulting ribs proliferated in the later medieval period, thereby increasing the number of intersections, the carved boss became a very significant element of the overall decorative effect. In this early fourteenth-century example (left) from Carcassonne Cathedral in southwest France, not only is the soffit (underside) of the boss covered with a foliate design, but protruding from the sides are two sculptured heads of Christ and the Virgin.

THE EVOLUTION OF PROFILES

Vault ribs were jigsaws of individual components, each designed and cut to take its particular place within the arch. Early vault ribs had been purely functional, but the massive plain ribs of the Romanesque soon gave way to elegantly molded profiles more appropriate to the Gothic aesthetic, in which lightness of appearance and mass played an important role. The effect was to increase the degree of proficiency required to cut each voussoir, which in turn necessitated an increase in the number of highly skilled stonecutters.

These examples of rib profiles show something of the increasing enrichment that evolved during the Gothic era. At St. Pierre Abbey Church, Chartres, the profile is confined to chamfers (where the edges have been cut away) and simple rolls, the flat soffit providing a link with the square character of early ribs. The slightly later profile from Nevers Cathedral is not dissimilar in general structure, but a filleted roll molding has been substituted for the flat soffit to create a more stylish design. In the two fourteenth-century examples, the stones forming the inner orders are daintier, more deeply cut, and more elaborately molded.

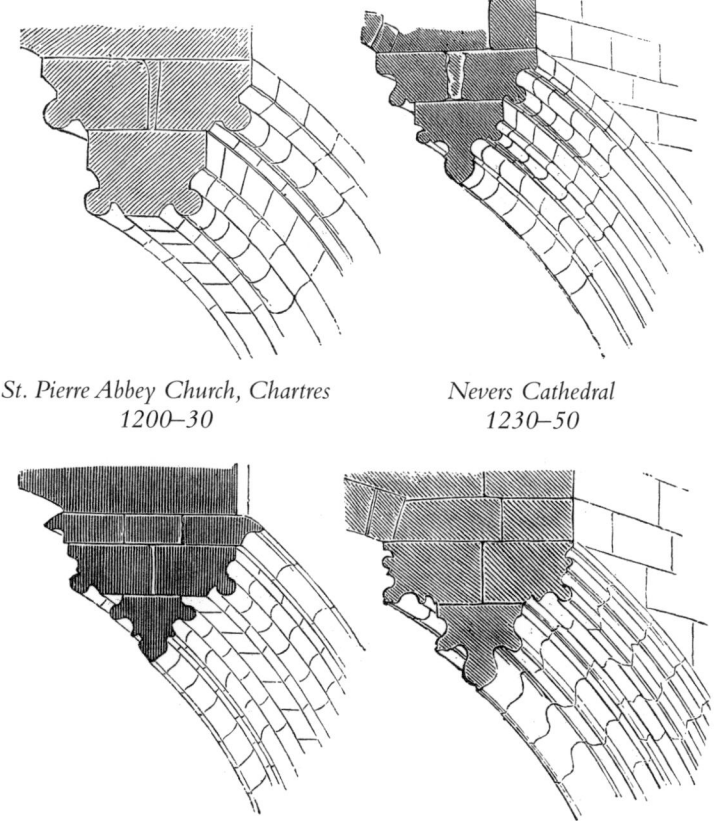

St. Pierre Abbey Church, Chartres
1200–30

Nevers Cathedral
1230–50

Paris Cathedral
1320–30

Narbonne Cathedral
ca. 1340

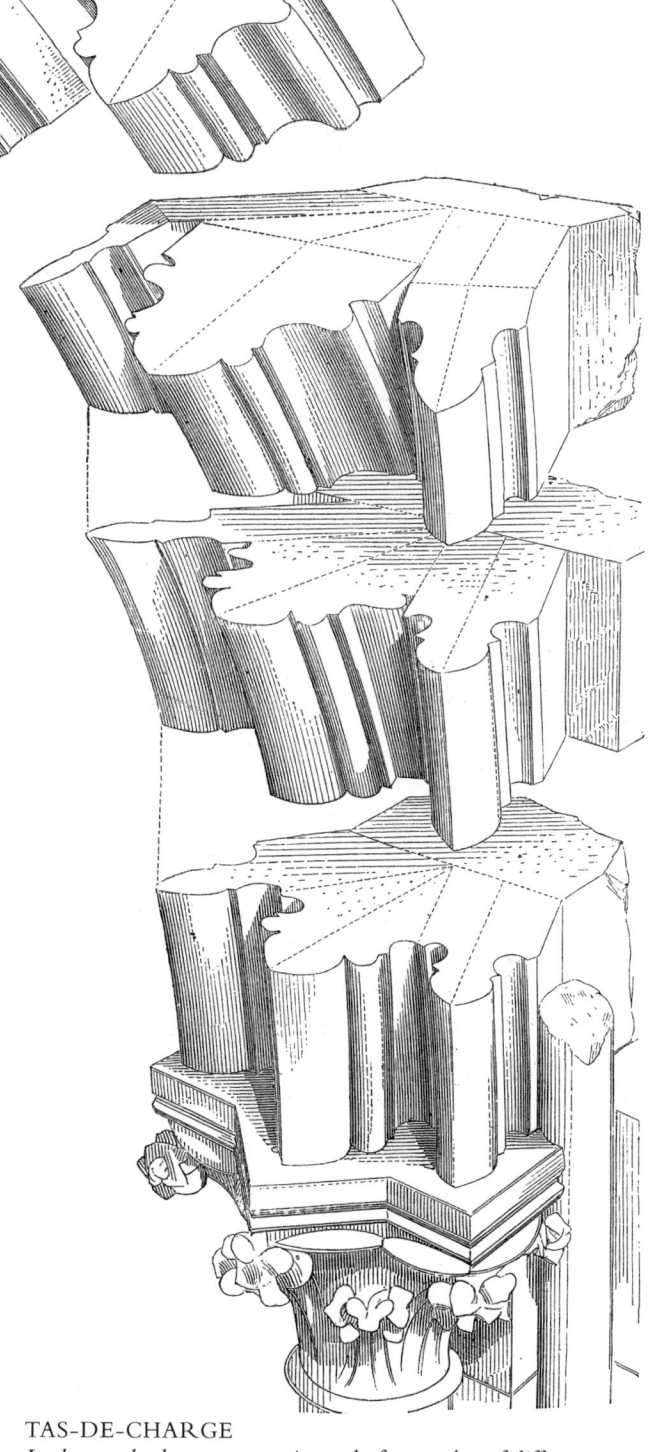

TAS-DE-CHARGE

In the tas-de-charge system, instead of a number of different ribs springing independently from the same point, the lower courses of the ribs are fused within a series of horizontally coursed blocks that form part of the wall. As the drawing shows, the molded-rib element of the blocks is inclined as it begins to form the arch, while the backs of the blocks remain vertical, anchored within the wall. Only when the assembly reaches a certain height do the ribs continue as independent voussoirs. The tas-de-charge technique gives greater stability to the construction; it seems to be a development of the late twelfth century, with one of the earliest examples being seen at Chartres Cathedral.

RAISING THE ROOF

Infill Panels

The transition from groin vaulting to rib-vault construction amounted to a sizeable technological change. Instead of the solid construction of the former, rib vaults represented a framed construction in which the spaces between ribs were filled in with stone and/or mortar webs. Although early rib-vault builders did not always avail themselves of this opportunity, the form lent itself to a much more economical use of materials and, thus, had considerable potential to assist in minimizing the lateral forces exerted by the vault. In Gothic architecture this was a very important consideration.

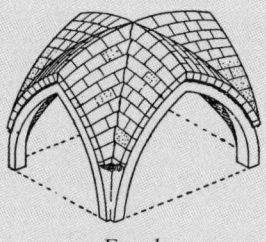

French

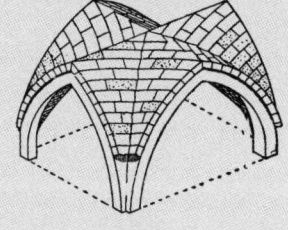

English

While the infilling of rib-vault cells with a mortar mix remained an option that was sometimes adopted, it is also true that from the twelfth century onward Gothic builders were constructing bowed vaulting webs of comparatively thin stone courses. The webs were filled in one by one, starting at the springing of the ribs, and then continuing course by course up to the ridge. These stone courses would have been laid on shaped wooden centering that bridged the gaps between the rib centering. Rib vaulting, unlike groin vaulting, gave the medieval builder the flexibility of being able to infill the cells one by one instead of having to complete the task in a single operation.

Two principal methods of web construction evolved, which were based on the regional masonic practices of the Île de France and England. In the French system, the stones of which the web was constructed—the voûtains—were laid in tapering courses, with the final objective of creating a straight joint at the ridge. In English practice, however, the courses were laid parallel with one another, so that as work proceeded there was a progressive deflection of the coursing away from the ridge. Thus, by the time the ridge was reached, the web coursing was entirely out of line with it, and adjacent sections of webbing met each other along the ridgeline at an angle.

These two drawings show the distinction between the French (top) and English (bottom) techniques of constructing infill panels for rib vaulting. In the French method, the tapering of the stone courses results in a well-fitting joint at the ridge, whereas in the English method, in which the courses were not tapered, the result is an oblique and irregular joint.

Aesthetically, the French method obtained the best result, but it was more time consuming because each voûtain had to be trimmed to an individual shape and size before it could be placed in position. The English method, therefore, was more economical, because the work progressed more rapidly. There was a certain amount of geographical overlap in these techniques, the French method occasionally being used in England and the English method also being found in France, notably in the English sphere of influence in the southwest. In at least one instance, the church at Mouliherne, near Saumur, the two techniques are found side by side in the same vault.

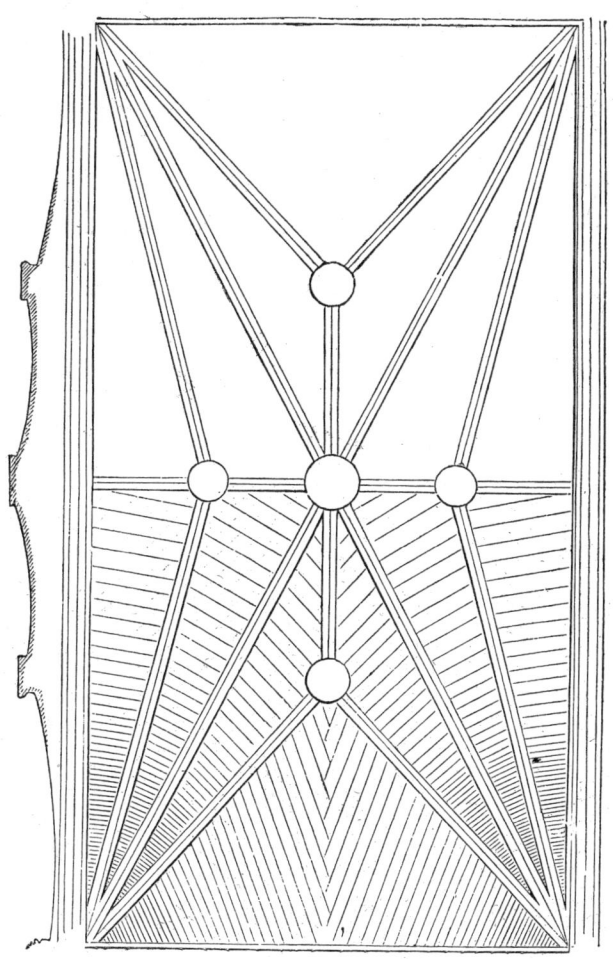

Web Coursing at Ely

The presbytery of Ely Cathedral, which was built between 1239 and 1250, is covered by a tierceron vault (see page 88) in which the vault bays are divided into a number of triangular sections by the rib pattern. The webbing within these sections has been constructed in the English fashion, in which the stone courses of adjacent sections of webbing meet at the ridge obliquely. This is particularly evident in the bottom triangle of the plan. The perspective drawing to the right shows the springing of the vault next to one of the clerestory windows, which is of tripartite lancet form and which is framed within a wall rib.

RAISING THE ROOF

The Development of Vaulting

As we have seen, early rib vaulting was based on lateral, transverse, and diagonal ribs. Ridge ribs were introduced later, both as a decorative feature and as a strengthening measure. Ridge ribs are both longitudinal and transverse, the former extending all the way along the axis of the building. The ridge rib is a more significant feature in England than in France and may have been introduced to mask and/or strengthen the oblique joints between adjacent sections of English-style webbing. In England, where the practice was to construct the longitudinal ridge rib in a horizontal plane, it was continuous throughout the main body of the church and formed a conspicuous feature of the vaulting system, thereby giving it great unity. In France, however, where the longitudinal ridge tended to be arched, ribs in this position were not usual because there was no pressing structural need for them.

The ridge rib became a fundamental part of the English high vault during the construction of St. Hugh's Choir at Lincoln Cathedral of 1192–1200. The architect of the choir had a highly original and innovative approach, and the ridge rib played an important role in his design for the high vault. Here, although the vault has a ridge rib, there are no diagonals. Instead, the master mason introduced intermediate ribs, known as tiercerons, a type that was to become an essential element of the English vault. In the Lincoln choir, they were deployed in a very singular and asymmetrical fashion that produced no imitators, although the tierceron itself was used in the later work at the same building.

Tiercerons were designed to strengthen the ridge rib by providing support between the intersection with the diagonal ribs and the ends of the bay. Arrangements vary, but in the nave of Lincoln, where the vault is of ca. 1235–40, in addition to the two diagonal ribs and the longitudinal ridge rib, there is a short transverse ridge rib as well as eight additional tiercerons, all of which extend from the four corners of the vault bay. Four of these meet the longitudinal ridge rib at a point midway between the center of the bay and its sides. The other four rise to the ends of the transverse ridge rib.

The next innovation was the introduction of a subsidiary rib known as the lierne, from the French *lier*, meaning "to tie, bind, or link." The lierne spanned the gaps between adjacent ribs, further breaking down the web compartments. Liernes are largely decorative in function and were deployed to create increasingly elaborate vaulting patterns.

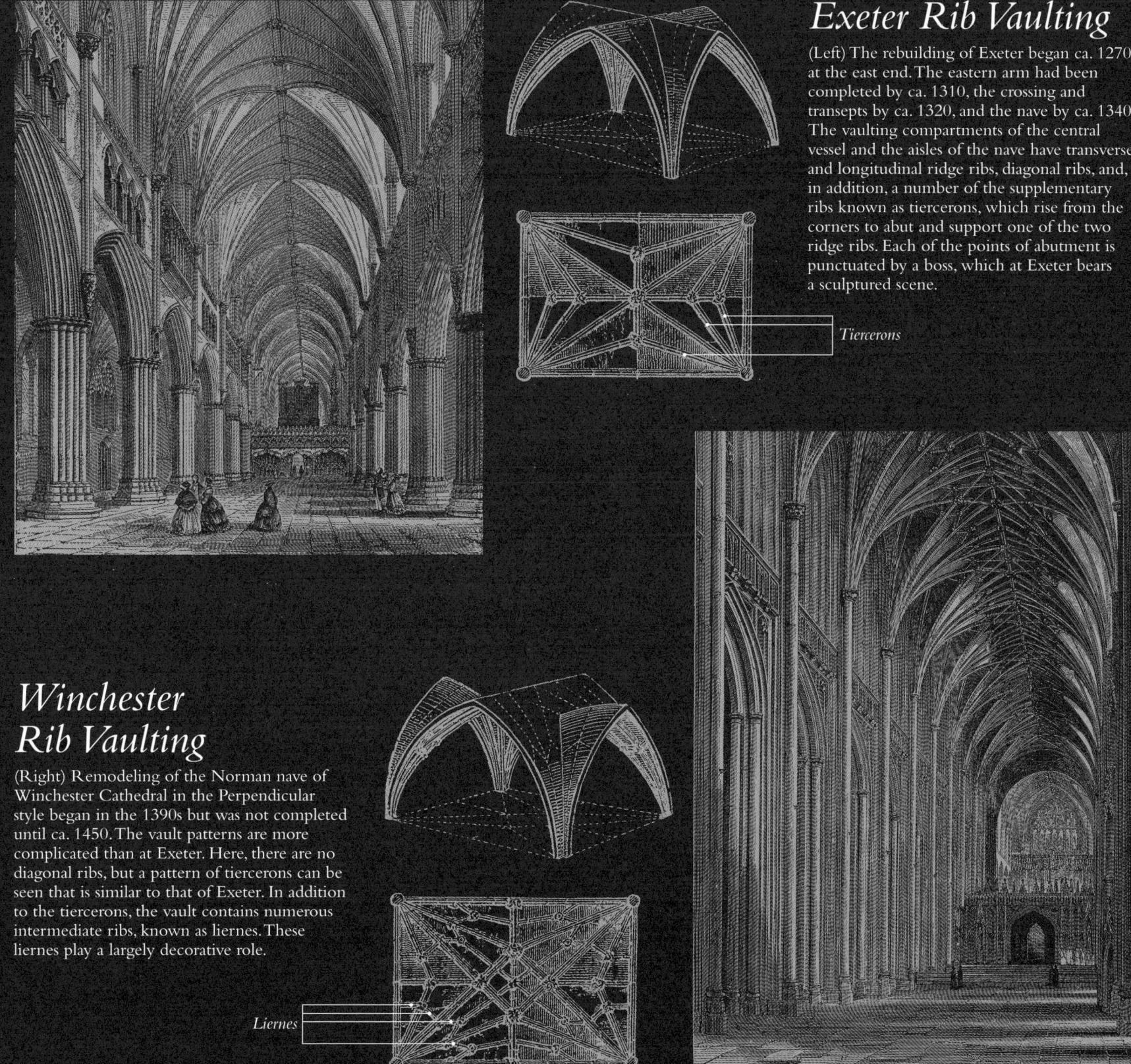

Exeter Rib Vaulting

(Left) The rebuilding of Exeter began ca. 1270 at the east end. The eastern arm had been completed by ca. 1310, the crossing and transepts by ca. 1320, and the nave by ca. 1340. The vaulting compartments of the central vessel and the aisles of the nave have transverse and longitudinal ridge ribs, diagonal ribs, and, in addition, a number of the supplementary ribs known as tiercerons, which rise from the corners to abut and support one of the two ridge ribs. Each of the points of abutment is punctuated by a boss, which at Exeter bears a sculptured scene.

Tiercerons

Winchester Rib Vaulting

(Right) Remodeling of the Norman nave of Winchester Cathedral in the Perpendicular style began in the 1390s but was not completed until ca. 1450. The vault patterns are more complicated than at Exeter. Here, there are no diagonal ribs, but a pattern of tiercerons can be seen that is similar to that of Exeter. In addition to the tiercerons, the vault contains numerous intermediate ribs, known as liernes. These liernes play a largely decorative role.

Liernes

RAISING THE ROOF

Late Medieval Vaulting

The evolution of later medieval vaulting in England is characterized by increasingly elaborate decorative features—particularly in the development of the fan vault. This architectural technique, which was inspired by sculptural forms, spanned a period of over 150 years, reaching its height right at the end of the medieval period.

GLOUCESTER FAN VAULTING
Begun in the 1350s, the cloisters of St. Peter's Abbey, Gloucester (now the cathedral) are covered with the earliest surviving example of fan vaulting in England. The fan vault represents a development of the lierne vault, but the sense of a structural framework of principal ribs that had hitherto been evident in Gothic vaulting is no longer apparent. Instead, the ribs have been subsumed within an overall surface treatment of traceried panels in which the most notable features are the trumpetlike inverted cones that give rise to the name. The remodeling of Gloucester, which began with the south transept in the 1330s before moving on to the eastern arm (ca. 1337–60) and then the north transept (1368–73), was a highly important stage in the development of the Perpendicular style. The architect behind the fan vaulting of the cloisters is unknown, although royal masons are considered to have been responsible for the remodeling of the church.

PETERBOROUGH FAN VAULTING
At Peterborough Abbey, between 1496 and 1509, Abbot Kirton commissioned the construction of a "New Building," extending from the east end of what is now the cathedral. This retro-choir (between the high altar and the eastern chapel), which enclosed the Norman apse, was covered with a much loftier example of fan vaulting than at Gloucester. There is little doubt that the work was carried out by the master mason John Wastell, one of the high-ranking English architects of the late medieval period, who subsequently went on to design the vaults of King's College Chapel at Cambridge (1508–15).

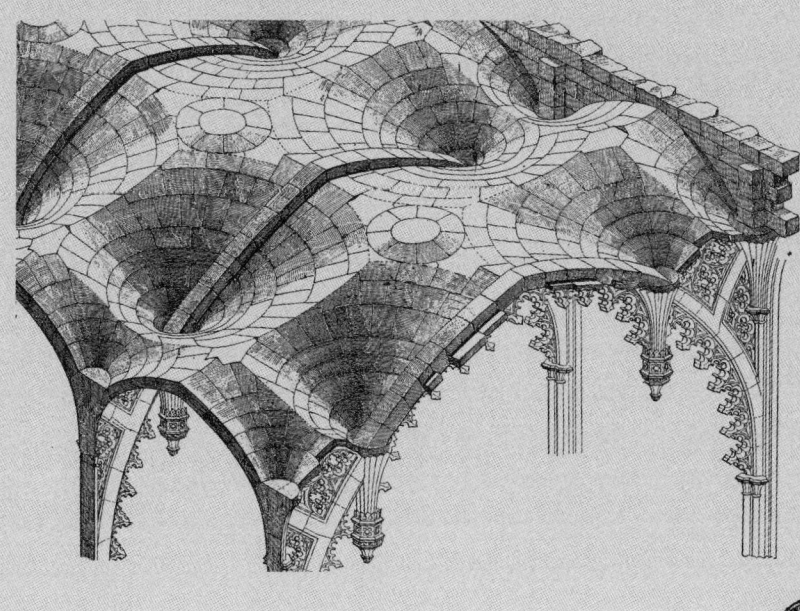

WESTMINSTER VAULT CONSTRUCTION
(Above) One of the most distinguished examples of English church vaulting, also one of the latest, was created over Henry VII's chapel at Westminster Abbey between 1503 and 1509. This view of the vault from above shows that it is based on a number of transverse arches, the lower parts of which are clearly visible within the chapel, although the upper parts, which lie above the vault, cannot be seen from below. These, however, are the only ribs in the construction, the rest of it being made up of traceried panels. The pendants are suspended from the transverse ribs, and the cone-shaped fans built up on top of them. The skill that must have been required in creating the design, cutting and carving the stones to shape and size, and fitting them together is nothing short of astonishing.

WESTMINSTER VAULT INTERIOR
Henry VII's chapel at Westminster Abbey is one of the most extravagantly detailed Gothic buildings of the Middle Ages, this opulence extending to the elaborate pendant vault that forms one of its most spectacular features, and the effect of which is one of gravity-defying virtuosity. The building was masterminded by the brothers Robert and William Vertue, although Robert died in 1506, leaving William to bring the project to fruition. William Vertue, the King's master mason, was the last great proponent of the Gothic style.

Constructing the Roof

Although the vault sits beneath the roof, it was usually the roof that was constructed first, both to provide protection from the inclement weather that might otherwise hamper the work but also, for structural reasons, to tie the walls together, thus giving the whole structure a much greater degree of stability. There are exceptions to this sequence of construction, but in these cases there must have been some kind of temporary roofing to protect the vaults.

It was during the raising of the roof that the carpenters came into their own, temporarily eclipsing the masons in the building workers' hierarchy. There is, however, cause to suppose that the master mason would have had a reasonable understanding of carpentry and might have taken a major role in the design process. Something of this is hinted at in the case of William of Sens (see pages 12–13) who was familiar with timber technology, including the construction of lifting engines.

The great scale at which cathedrals were built required timber of commensurate dimensions. Suger's account of the construction of the choir of St. Denis Abbey of ca. 1140 hints at the difficulties that might be encountered in obtaining suitable material in certain areas, although in this particular instance the story had a happy ending, and the twelve oaks needed for St. Denis came from the forest of Yvelines on conventual lands only some 25 miles (40 km) southwest of the abbey. The timber for the roofs of Lincoln Cathedral (1192–1280) was obtained from the royal forest of Sherwood, which was at a similar distance. There are numerous references in the English royal records to grants of oaks in connection with great church building enterprises, for it was in the royal forests, which had been protected since the Norman Conquest of 1066, that the great oaks necessary for such major carpentry constructions survived.

Cathedral roofs were of timber-frame construction, the individual components of the roof frames being manufactured separately according the master carpenter's plan. Following their completion, they were assembled on the ground in a designated framing place. This would require a considerable area to be set aside, because a roof truss for a major cathedral could measure more than 50 feet (15 m) high (Chartres, Lincoln, and Reims, for example) and nearly as much across. The joints would be fitted together and adjusted where necessary, and the individual timbers inscribed with a carpenter's mark in order to identify them as belonging to that particular frame. The frame would then be disassembled and stored ready for hoisting into position. This manufacturing process would be carried out some time in advance.

Cross Frame   Longitudinal Section

TIMBER CATHEDRAL ROOF
These drawings illustrate the character of the fifteenth-century timber roof over the nave of Reims Cathedral, as recorded by Viollet le Duc in the nineteenth century. They show one of the cross frames as well as part of the long section (C, taken on the center of the truss, and A–B, taken on the dotted line). This structure dates from after 1481, when a fire, caused by the carelessness of some roofing workers, destroyed the thirteenth-century roof. This replacement was itself destroyed during World War I. The roof was approximately 51 feet (15.5 m) high and 47 feet (14.4 m) wide.

RAISING THE ROOF

The Roof of Notre-Dame Choir

These drawings of the roof over the late twelfth-century choir of Notre-Dame de Paris include the plan of the apsidal east end, the transverse (north–south) section, depicting the most easterly of the timber roof trusses, and the longitudinal (east–west) section viewed from the south.

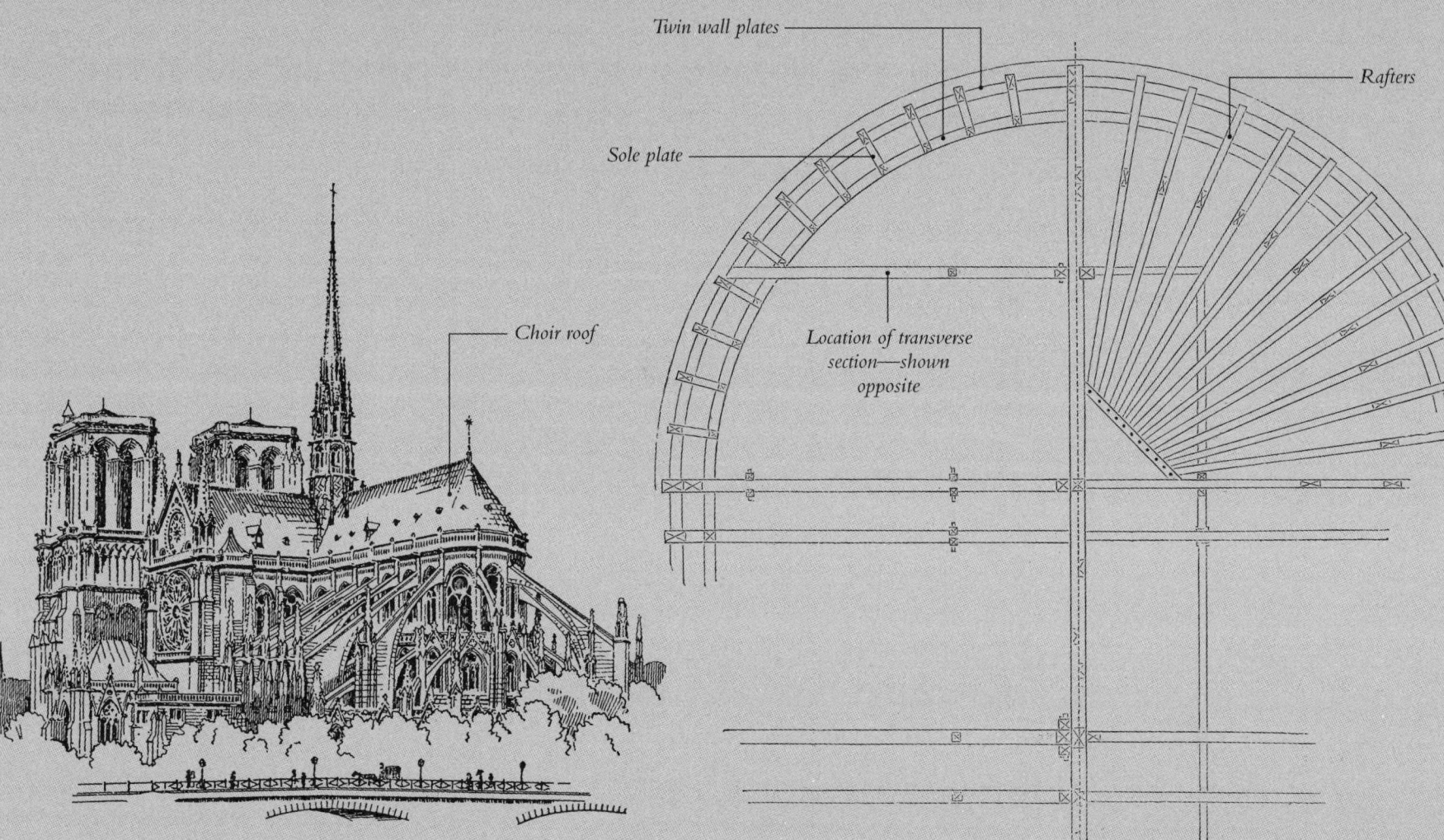

THE CHOIR FROM THE SOUTHEAST
Construction began on the choir of Notre-Dame ca. 1160 and the structure was consecrated in 1182, by which time it was complete. Much of the roof dates from this late twelfth-century phase, although early thirteenth-century modifications are evident. This is the view of the cathedral from the southeast, with the choir in the foreground and the spire or flèche (see pages 116–117) rising above the crossing. The east end of the choir Notre-Dame is apsidal in plan and the roof accordingly ends in a distinctive rounded hip.

PLAN OF APSIDAL EAST END
The stone wall around the apsidal east end of the choir is surmounted by twin wall plates. The left-hand side of the plan shows a sequence of short horizontal timbers known as sole plates fitted over the tops of the wall plates so that the assembly resembles a railroad track. These sole plates support the feet of the rafters, which are fitted into their outer ends, while short vertical timbers known as ashlar pieces, which rise to join the soffits of the rafters, are fitted into their inner ends (see longitudinal section opposite for this arrangement).

94

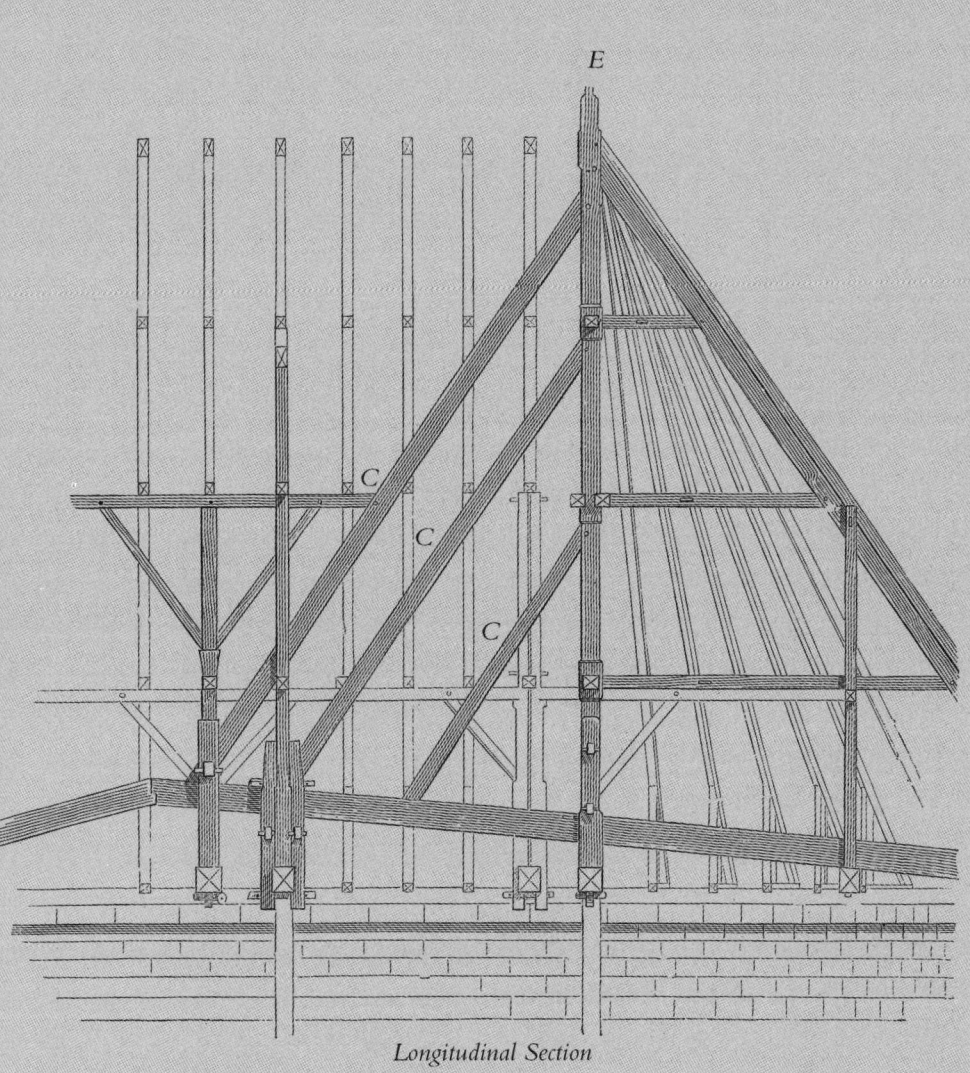
Longitudinal Section

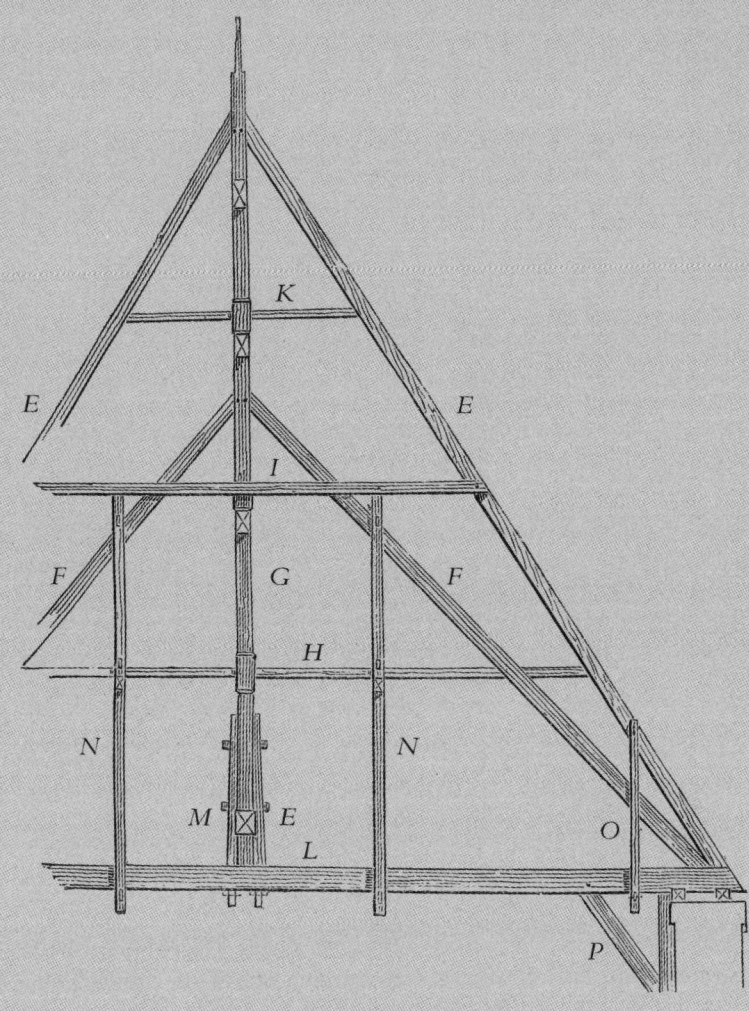
Transverse Section

Carpenters

While the masons might be the senior partners in a cathedral-building project, the carpenters also played a highly significant role. The two crafts worked in close association right from the start of operations, because a good deal of carpentry was used from early in the construction process. Of particular note was the centering for the arcades, doors, windows, and vaults, and first in importance was the fabrication and assembly of the centering for the high vaults, a task that demanded a superior level of skill and application. The roofs were the principal contribution of the carpenters to the fabric of the building itself. These were usually hidden from general view and were, therefore, purely functional in character, but sometimes, as at York Minster, the cathedral might be given a timber vault, and in these circumstances the aesthetic qualities would become important. Timber vaults were made in imitation of their stone counterparts and required finely joined and molded ribs, as well as sculptured bosses, and they illustrate the point that like that of the masons, the carpenters' craft encompassed a wide range of skills and specialisms. The finer side to the carpenters' work is particularly evident in cathedral fittings, including the elaborately decorated choir stalls that still furnish several cathedrals and other churches.

LONGITUDINAL AND TRANSVERSE SECTIONS

The cross frame consists of a tie beam (L), a long king post (G) that rises from the center of the tie beam to the apex of the roof, and a pair of principal rafters (E), which extend from the ends of the tie beam to a point just below the top of the king post. Between the principal rafters and the king post is a pair of interrupted collars (H and K), and a pair of raking lateral braces (F) extends from the ends of the tie beams to the king post; both devices provide lateral stiffening. Longitudinal stiffening is provided by three braces to the west, which are shown in the longitudinal section drawing (C) and by the rafters of the apse to the east. Additional support is given by a number of twinned members (I, M, N, and O), which are not part of the frame proper but which have been secured to both sides of the truss (or in the case of M to the king post) by timber keys.

A roof truss of the form depicted here would likely have been assembled in the following sequence. First of all, the tie beams would have been hauled to the top of the wall, probably by a pair of cranes, one on each side of the building, and then fitted into position over the tops of the wall plates. The tie beams would have provided the basis for a working platform on which the assembly work could have been undertaken more safely. The king post (G) would have been the first of the uprights to be raised into position, probably using a rope-and-pulley system. Next came the raking braces (F) and the king post stiffeners (M), and then the inner ends of the split collars (H and K), which would have been fitted into the king post, ready to receive the principals (E). The construction of the frame would have been completed by the erection of the principals. All the joints were secured by oak pegs.

RAISING THE ROOF

Timber Vaults & Ceilings

While timber provided the essential material for cathedral roofs, its widespread use as an alternative to stone vaults is not always appreciated. Romanesque builders had frequently covered the naves of great churches with timber constructions, but even after the problems that were associated with stone vaulting over wide spans had been solved, timber was often the preferred option. When Henry III of England gave instructions that the new chapel of St. Edward in Windsor Castle was to have a high wooden roof in imitation of stonework, he stipulated that it was to be modeled on a roof in what was described as the "new work" at Lichfield Cathedral, which suggests that the thirteenth-century nave of Lichfield was vaulted in this manner.

The Lichfield vault was destroyed in the seventeenth century, but several other English cathedrals were also given timber vaults instead of stone, some of which have survived. All the major vaults at York Minster were (and still are) in timber, the earliest being over the transepts (ca. 1225–55). Although these are no longer extant, having been replaced twice (in timber), the chapter house vault, of ca. 1290, survives. Later timber vaults at York included those over the nave (1350s), the Lady chapel (ca. 1371), and western choir (ca. 1405). Other timber vaults include the examples raised over the early fourteenth-century choir of St. Albans Abbey (now the cathedral) and over the nave of Winchester Cathedral.

The timber alternative to a vault was to suspend a wooden ceiling beneath the roof. This type of structure must have been more prevalent at one time, but few examples remain, and the only one to survive in an English cathedral is the painted ceiling of 1230–50 over the nave of Peterborough Cathedral (see opposite). A similar construction (no longer in existence) was raised over the choir of Glasgow Cathedral in the thirteenth century, and it is possible that a timber ceiling was planned for the nave roof of 1237–40 at Ely Cathedral, 25 miles (40 km) to the southeast of Peterborough.

The advantages of using timber vaults were, first of all, that they were easier and cheaper to construct, and, second, that they were a lot less heavy than stone vaulting. The principal disadvantage was that timber vaults were more susceptible to fire, a problem that may have encouraged the development of stone vaulting in the first place, and one which has certainly taken its toll in more recent years, notably at York, where fire destroyed the fourteenth-century nave vaulting in 1840, and the fifteenth-century south-transept vaulting in 1984.

Peterborough Nave Ceiling

Unique in England, the painted timber ceiling of Peterborough Cathedral, which covers the nave, dates from the period 1230–50. Dendrochronological analysis suggests a north German provenance for the wood from which the panels were made. Knowledge of this import trade is known from references in building accounts and other documents to "Estland" or "Estriche" boards from the thirteenth century onward. Boards from Baltic countries have been identified in other cathedrals, such as Ely and York, and it is also evident that Baltic boards were often used to produce painted panels. The Peterborough ceiling has a canted profile reflecting the form of the scissor-truss roof to which the panels were secured. Although other ceilings of this type exist in continental Europe, few have survived.

RAISING THE ROOF

Roof Coverings

ead was often the preferred roofing material. Roofing lead was made by being cast on beds of sand into sheets, or tiles, of a manageable size. This process was often carried out on the building site, as at Westminster Palace, in 1259, when the plumbers William of Strand and John Govair were paid for "founding, casting, and laying 8 chars of lead." However, building account entries also show that already prepared lead sheeting was sometimes purchased.

Prior to covering in lead sheeting, the buildings would be roofed with timber boards, which would be nailed to the rafters (see page 133). It was the practice to spread some form of insulation material (clay, sand, or moss) on the boards so that the timber and lead were not in direct contact; this protected the lead from corrosion by acids from the wood and also provided the wood with a measure of defense against the changes in temperature to which the lead covering was subject.

The plumbers laid individual lead sheets in strips, starting at the ridge and extending to the bottom of the roof. Each sheet was held in position at its lower edge by an iron or lead clip, which was itself nailed to the roof boards. The strips of leading were joined together by wrapping the lateral edges around each other, thereby rendering the covering watertight.

The advantages of lead were that it provided a close-fitting watertight surface with fireproof qualities. Moreover, it was easily recycled and had a high salvage value. However, it was an expensive material, which may be the reason why at Wells it was only used to roof the cathedral church, while the ancillary buildings and the cloister were instead roofed in stone slate. Similarly, at Finchale Priory in northern England, lead was being laid on the roof of the choir in 1366, although other buildings within the monastic complex were roofed with stone slates.

Sometimes, however, a cathedral church itself might be roofed in stone, as when, in 1390, the Reims-based slater Jehan Nepveu and his brother Colart, of Troyes, entered into a contract to reroof part of Troyes Cathedral. The slaters undertook to supply both the slates themselves and the nails for securing them. Ceramic tiles were an alternative to stone slates in areas that did not have a ready supply of suitable material. They were used to roof the twelfth-century Abbey Church of Vézelay in Burgundy and part of Sens Cathedral (see opposite). Some roof tiles were highly decorative with crested ridges and glazes of contrasting colors.

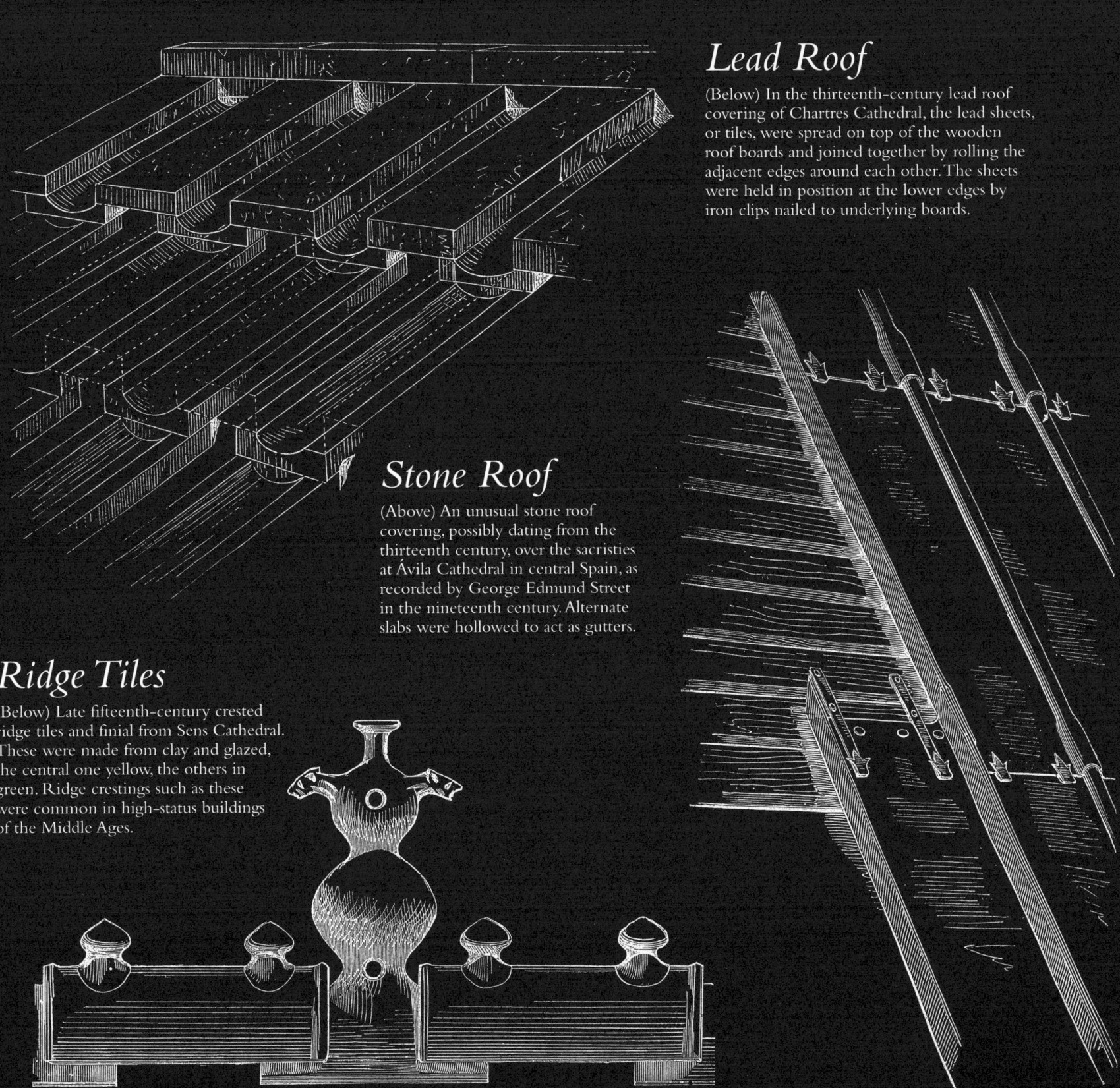

Lead Roof

(Below) In the thirteenth-century lead roof covering of Chartres Cathedral, the lead sheets, or tiles, were spread on top of the wooden roof boards and joined together by rolling the adjacent edges around each other. The sheets were held in position at the lower edges by iron clips nailed to underlying boards.

Stone Roof

(Above) An unusual stone roof covering, possibly dating from the thirteenth century, over the sacristies at Ávila Cathedral in central Spain, as recorded by George Edmund Street in the nineteenth century. Alternate slabs were hollowed to act as gutters.

Ridge Tiles

(Below) Late fifteenth-century crested ridge tiles and finial from Sens Cathedral. These were made from clay and glazed, the central one yellow, the others in green. Ridge crestings such as these were common in high-status buildings of the Middle Ages.

RAISING THE ROOF
Drainage

The high roofs of Gothic cathedrals, combined with the wet northern European climate, rendered it necessary to deal with large amounts of rainwater so that it was kept away from the wall head and windows and maintenance problems were avoided. Accordingly, methods of dealing with rainwater were devised and were often included within the design of the flying buttresses.

St. Urbain de Troyes sectional elevation

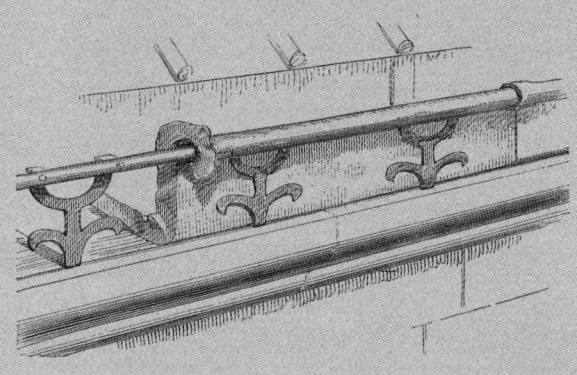

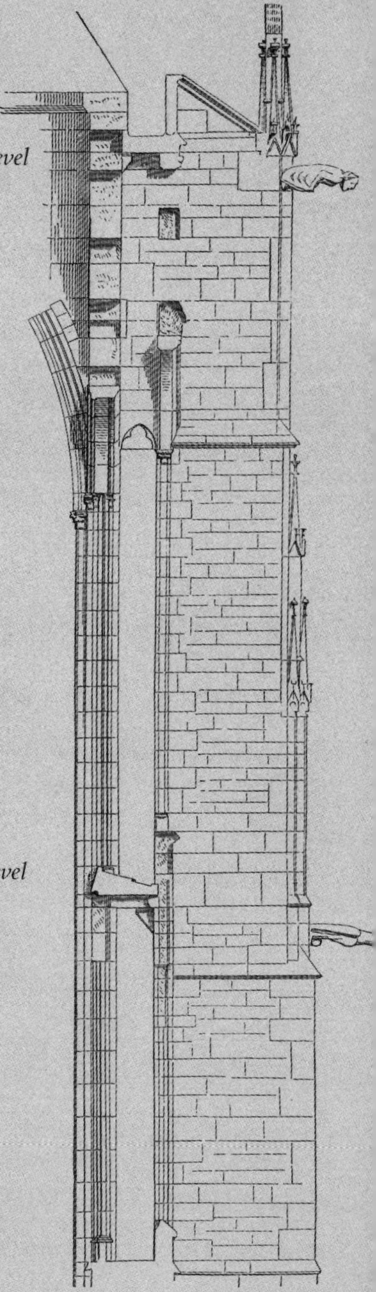

LEAD GUTTERING
(Above) Main roofs were provided with lead guttering. Sometimes this consisted of a lining for a wooden gutter and sometimes, as in this illustration, the lead channel was contained within an iron framework.

WATER CONDUITS
The thirteenth-century church of St. Urbain de Troyes houses water conduits within the buttresses around the apse. These took away the rainwater at two different levels, the uppermost from the roof gutter and the lower from a gallery around the great east window. Both channels discharged through the gargoyles that project from the front of the buttresses.

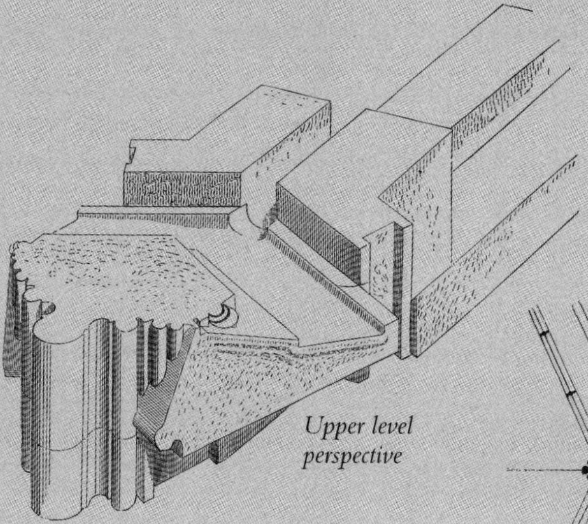

Upper level perspective

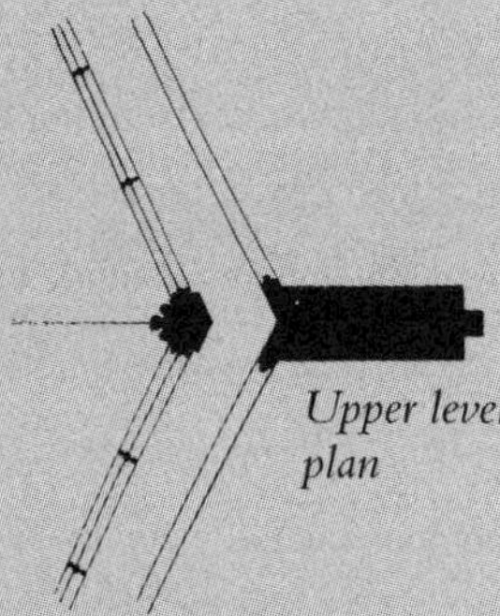

Upper level plan

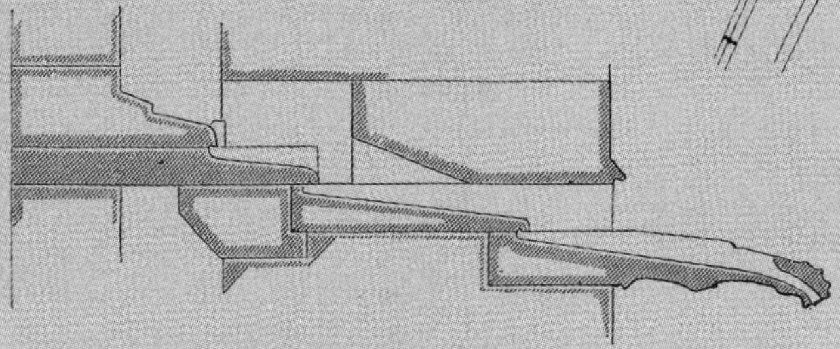

Upper level

Section through lower level

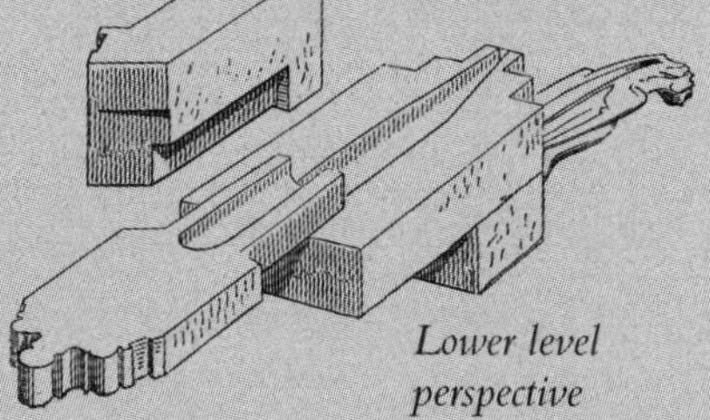

Lower level

Lower level perspective

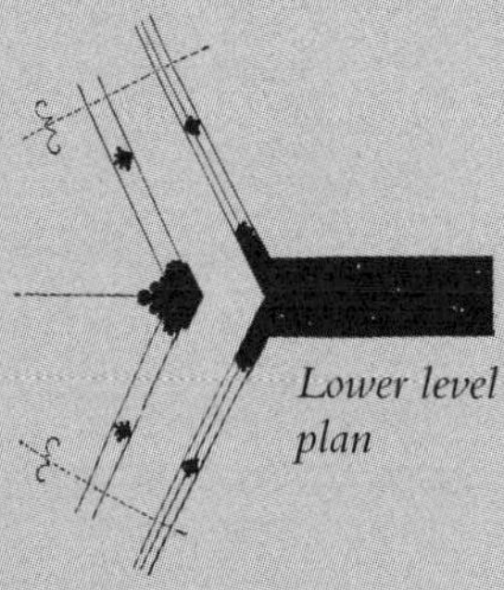

Lower level plan

BUTTRESS DRAINAGE SYSTEM
At Burgos Cathedral, of 1222–60, in northern Spain, as at some other cathedrals, the roof-drainage system incorporated the upper flyer. Water percolated from the roof of the central vessel through the bottom of the figure-sculptured finials and into a channel in the top of the upper flyer. It then discharged onto the aisle roof via a gargoyle.

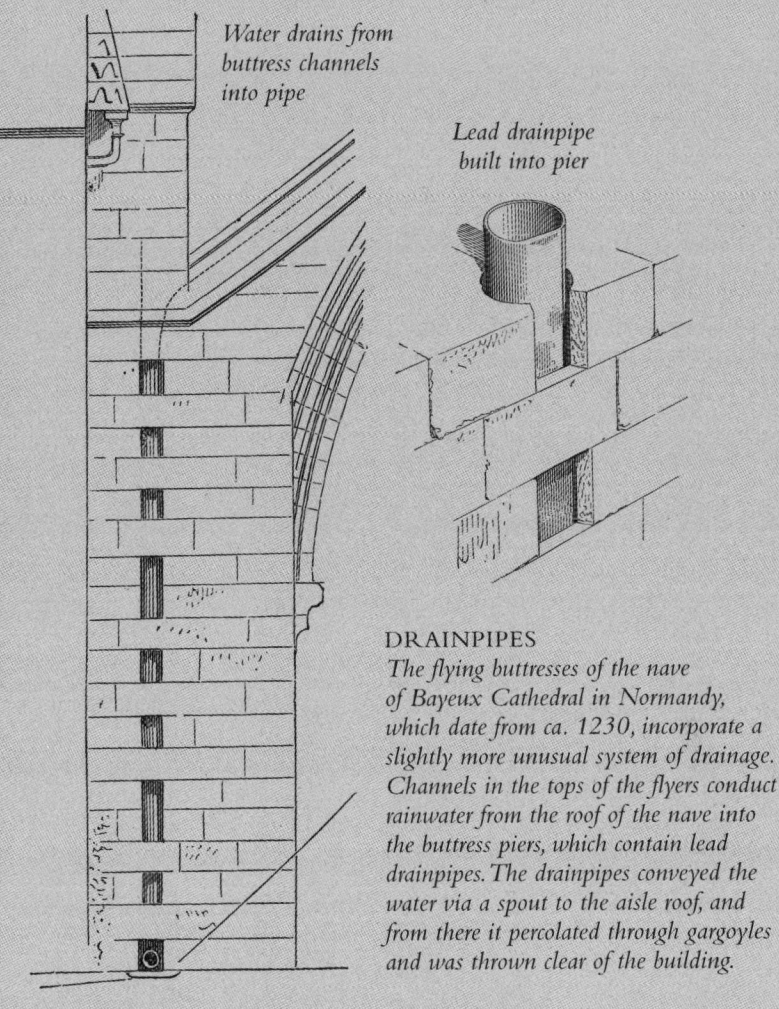

Water drains from buttress channels into pipe

Lead drainpipe built into pier

DRAINPIPES
The flying buttresses of the nave of Bayeux Cathedral in Normandy, which date from ca. 1230, incorporate a slightly more unusual system of drainage. Channels in the tops of the flyers conduct rainwater from the roof of the nave into the buttress piers, which contain lead drainpipes. The drainpipes conveyed the water via a spout to the aisle roof, and from there it percolated through gargoyles and was thrown clear of the building.

Plumbers

Medieval plumbers, whose name derives from the Latin word for lead (*plumbum*), were craftsmen specializing in the use of this metal. Although the scope of the craft was not entirely dependent on the building trade, plumbers were a necessary part of the construction team of a cathedral. Plumbers were both manufacturers, in that they resmelted and cast the metal, and fitters. Their work extended to roof coverings, guttering, piping, ventilation panels, and window cames (the lead in the latticed windows). In their role as builders, they were largely concerned with measures to protect the structure from water penetration. However, their biggest tasks involved the laying of lead roof coverings, a practice that sometimes involved the soldering of joints, which, in turn, meant that some means of heating the soldering iron was required. It is perhaps not entirely surprising, therefore, that accidents might occur. Thus it was that the fire of 1465 that gutted the Abbey Church of Bury St. Edmunds in Suffolk and brought the central tower down, was blamed on the carelessness of the plumbers working on the roof.

BUILDING SALISBURY CATHEDRAL

Constructing the Roof

By the year 1252, the stonework of the cathedral is to a great extent complete. The screen front at the west end has yet to receive its sculpture, the turrets their spirelets, and the flyers over the nave aisles are still in the process of being constructed, but the rest is finished. The most pressing job now is to complete the raising of the roofs over the nave and aisles. To this end, the carpenters are working high above the nave on platforms supported by the great tie beams made from timber donated by the king. The precut, marked timbers are being raised, one by one from the floor of the nave using a winch, and the roof trusses are being assembled on the tie beams. Within a very short time the entire cathedral will be ready for use.

Remaining flyers over the aisles in the process of construction with centering in place

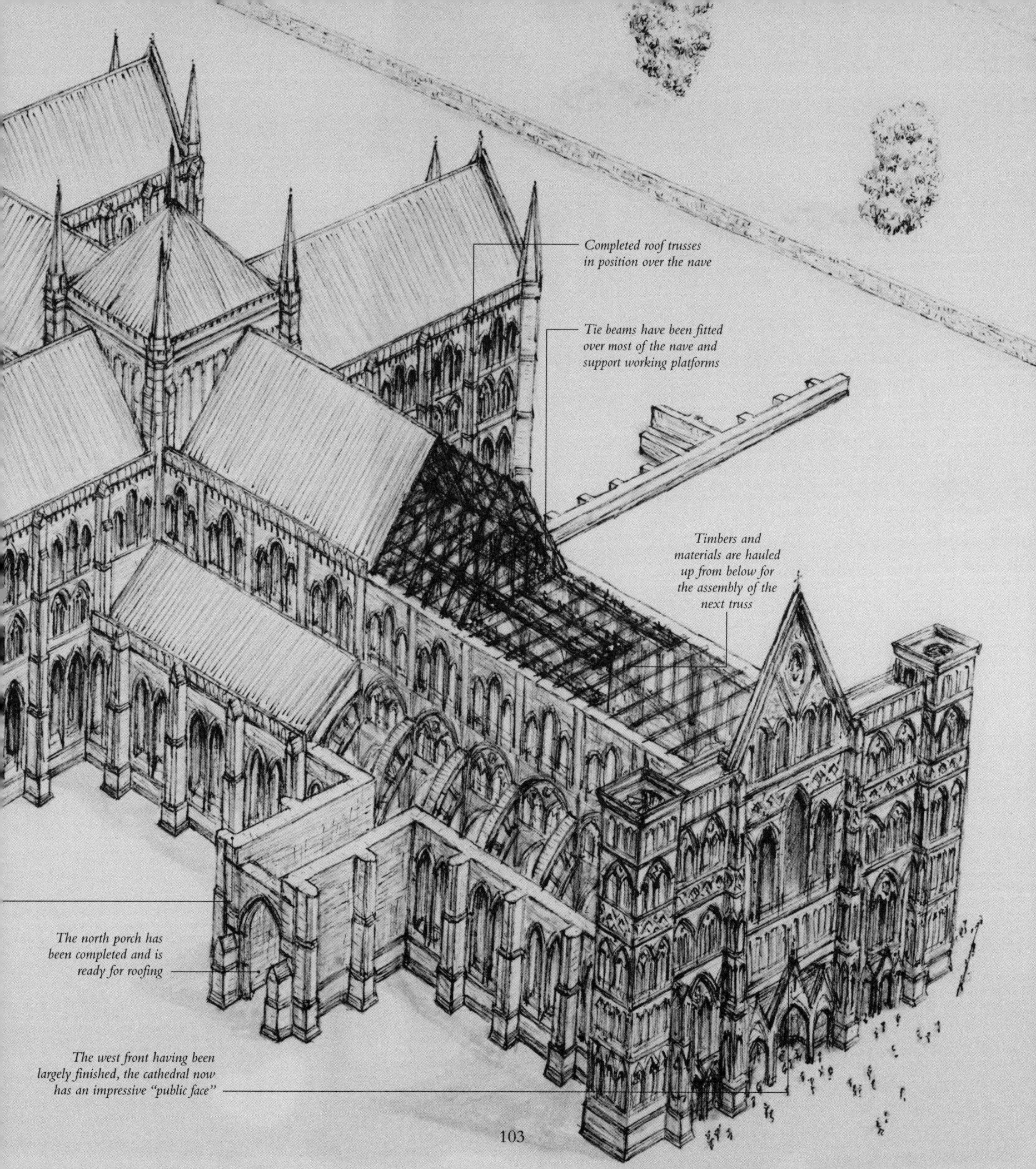

Completed roof trusses in position over the nave

Tie beams have been fitted over most of the nave and support working platforms

Timbers and materials are hauled up from below for the assembly of the next truss

The north porch has been completed and is ready for roofing

The west front having been largely finished, the cathedral now has an impressive "public face"

eaching
to Heaven

REACHING TO HEAVEN

Introduction

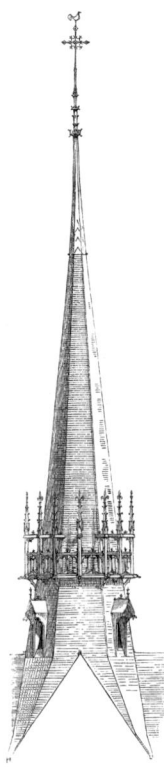

TOWERS HAVE PLAYED AN IMPORTANT ROLE in church architecture since antiquity. They were used to house the bells that summoned the faithful to worship, they served as lanterns to illuminate the building, and sometimes they were also intended to play a defensive role in times of danger. All these functions were in place by the fifth century when the Abbey Church of St. Martin at Tours, France, was built and from then onward appeared in various combinations throughout the medieval period. Although there is some variation, the favored positions for towers were at the west end and over the crossing.

Early towers were capped with low pyramidal roofs, but the coming of the Gothic style was accompanied by the universal adoption of the spire as the tower's standard accompaniment. It was an economical method for vastly increasing the height of a building and was the logical conclusion of an upward-reaching style of architecture. While the symbolism of spires may not have been articulated, there is no doubt that they enhanced the religiosity of a church and accentuated the heavenward theme. Architecturally, too, towers and spires were desirable attributes for a great church, adding substance and grandeur and making sure that the building was visible from a considerable distance away.

However, their construction involved substantial investments of time and money, and towers were not always given prominence in a design. Salisbury Cathedral, for example, was provided with only a short central lantern, and, instead of being flanked by a pair of conspicuous towers like many other great churches, the west front was framed by a pair of spindly turrets. It is worth noting, however, that the arrangement at Salisbury was later deemed to be inadequate, and so the central tower was raised by 80 feet (24.4 m), and a spire built on top of it (see pages 126–127). This, at 404 feet (123 m) high, is the tallest in England and is considered to be the tallest medieval structure in Europe.

Even where towers and spires were planned from the outset, they were to some extent an expendable luxury that could be abandoned if sources of funding began to fail. At Strasbourg Cathedral, for instance, although it was intended that the west front should have a pair of towers, only one was ever built, giving the facade a lopsided appearance that was never part of the design. There are also several known instances of spires being planned but never completed. One example is at Reims, where the stumps of the abandoned spires remain perched on the tops of the western towers.

Introduction

Although the tower and spire enhanced the architectural character of a great church, they were vulnerable parts of the fabric. In the absence of conductor systems, for instance, they were particularly prone to lightning strikes. The central tower of Durham Cathedral was struck by lightning in 1429 and again in 1459, incidents that eventually led to its replacement. The lantern on top of the dome of Florence Cathedral was struck in 1492 and severely damaged. In 1527, a lightning strike destroyed the central spire of Amiens Cathedral, and in 1561 the central spire of Old St. Paul's Cathedral, London, was brought down in a similar manner. The force of the wind was also a source of concern for the stability of exposed edifices such as spires, especially when they were made of timber. In 1362, gales brought down the central timber spire of Norwich Cathedral, and in 1584 that of Lincoln Cathedral.

Nor did natural forces pose the only danger. Towers—crossing towers in particular—had a tendency to fail. In the late tenth century, the tower of Ramsey Abbey came crashing down, a disaster that was blamed on inadequate foundations. At Gloucester, ca. 1170, one of the west towers of the abbey church collapsed, and in 1321 the central tower of Ely Cathedral fell. In 1407, just as the rebuilding of York Minster was drawing to its close, the thirteenth-century crossing tower collapsed. The central tower of Beauvais Cathedral, which rose to a height of just over 500 feet (152 m), and which was completed in 1569, came down only four years later in 1573.

In spite of these dangers, the medieval builders were not deterred. The structural inadequacies of the old Norman crossings were dealt with, and towers were built to greater heights. While towers were rebuilt, so that in one sense there has been no loss, this was not the case for spires. Cathedral spires were once much more common, on both western and central towers. The overall effect of medieval cathedral architecture that we see today is not as originally intended. It is worth considering the extent to which spires dominated the great churches of the Middle Ages. We know that in England spires formerly existed at the cathedrals of Canterbury (northwestern), Carlisle (central), Durham (western), Ely (western), Exeter (transeptal), Hereford (central), Lincoln (central and western), Old St. Paul's, London (central), Peterborough (northwestern), Ripon (central and western), St. Albans (central), and Worcester (central). None of these has been replaced, with the result that among English cathedrals comparatively few stone spires survive, and only one—Lichfield—retains both its western and central spires (see page 57).

REACHING TO HEAVEN

Western Towers

The convention of twin towers contributing to an imposing facade at the west end of a great church existed by the fifth century in Syria and became firmly established in western Europe by the time that the Abbey Church at Corvey, in western Germany, came to be built between 873 and 885. It remained a commonly employed motif throughout the Middle Ages. Indeed, a west front with twin towers became medieval pictorial shorthand for a great church, and a twin-tower motif came to be used decoratively on artistic pieces, including floor tiles and seals.

One of the western towers usually housed the bells. At such sites as Salisbury and Worcester, however, where no western towers were built, there was a freestanding bell tower instead. At Chartres, the twelfth-century northwest tower was originally built as a freestanding bell tower, but it was later incorporated into a new west front for the cathedral as one of two flanking towers. Twin towers, therefore, were partly functional, but to a large extent they were architectural, serving to create a striking effect.

The usual position for a pair of western towers was over the western bays of the aisles. In French cathedrals in particular, this arrangement played an important role in the articulation of the west front as a reflection of the underlying plan of the church, so that the central block represented the nave and the flanking towers the aisles. In England, where this relationship between exterior and interior was not so highly regarded, an alternative, albeit less prevalent, plan developed, in which the western towers were built outside the aisles. A number of twelfth-century great churches used this layout in England, notably the cathedrals of Old St. Paul's in London and Wells in Somerset. It also occurs at Rouen in Normandy and in a number of Spanish cathedrals, including León, Sigüenza, and Toledo.

Single western towers, although a common element of the plan in smaller churches, were less frequently a planned aspect of great church architecture. The exception was the Holy Roman Empire, where single towers centered at the west end were built at Freiburg Minster (1275–1301) under a master builder called Gerhardt, and at Ulm (1392–1492), which was designed and begun by Ulrich von Ensingen. A plan for the west front of Strasbourg Cathedral, drawn up by the master mason Michael Parler in the fourteenth century, also shows a single central tower. In the event, however, this plan was never executed and a twin-towered design substituted, although, ironically, only one of the pair was ever built, and the west front of Strasbourg is notable for its asymmetrical appearance.

Paris Western Towers

(Left) The western towers of Notre-Dame de Paris were built between ca. 1225 and ca. 1250 and were, thus, the final part of the structure to be completed. The low pyramidal roofs of the towers are hidden behind the parapets so that the towers have a flat-topped appearance that is in stark contrast to the narrow paired lancet windows. If, as seems probable, the towers were originally intended to be capped with spires, then the composition would have been transformed from its present rectangular character to one of much greater verticality.

York Western Towers

(Right) The west front of York Minster was unusual among English cathedral facades, having more in common with French practice in that it very much reflects the internal arrangement of central nave and flanking aisles. The western towers, which form part of this design, stand directly above the western bays of the aisles. Although the main body of the west front was finished by 1360, the towers themselves were left in abeyance until the reconstruction of the eastern arm had been completed and the church was fully functioning. They were largely built between 1432 and 1445.

REACHING TO HEAVEN

Crossing Towers

Crossing towers (the tower above the intersection of the nave, chancel, and transepts) have a similarly long pedigree to those at the west end, being derived from the low lantern towers that had been a feature of European church architecture since the Carolingian period. Two such lanterns, for example, were incorporated into the design of the Abbey Church of St. Riquier (789–98) in northern France, and the principle continued into the Gothic period (see pages 112–113). The need for lighting at the crossing was to some degree obviated from the thirteenth century onward by the general increase in the expanse of fenestration, and not all central towers retained the function of a lantern. However, there were good external architectural reasons for retaining a tower at this position. It marked the position of the crossing; it broke up the horizontal ridgeline of the roofs and so bolstered the vertical character of the building; and it might also act as a counterpoise to the western towers.

In churches where the body of the church was already very high, notably in France, the central tower was not a very prominent feature, and the builders were often content with raising a slim timber structure to mark the position of the crossing. Such was the case at Notre-Dame de Paris, Amiens, Cologne, and numerous other cathedrals. This fashion was probably more a matter of proportion than fear of any structural implications, and indeed, in England, where cathedrals were generally much lower, the central tower tended to be more prominent. Although at first many central towers in England were comparatively low structures, there was a tendency toward greater height in the later medieval period, and several existing towers were raised in height, including those at Lincoln (1307–11), Salisbury (ca. 1310), Wells (1315–22), and Durham (1483–90). Often they would be provided with a spire as well.

This was despite the crossing tower being a known weak point to the structure. In more than one instance the raising of a crossing tower proved too much for the existing supports. At Fountains Abbey in Yorkshire, where the late twelfth-century central tower was not planned from the outset, the piers and one of the crossing arches began to fail in the thirteenth century, necessitating remedial action at that stage, then again in the fourteenth and sixteenth centuries. It was probably due to this history of structural problems that when, in the sixteenth century, the decision was made to build a new bell tower, no attempt was made to raise the existing structure over the crossing. Instead, the new tower was placed in a very unusual position, at the north end of the north transept.

Wells Central Tower

(Above) The rebuilding of Wells Cathedral, in southwest England (here seen from the southeast), was carried out between ca. 1175 and 1260. The central tower was originally much lower but was raised between 1315 and 1322 to give it a more commanding appearance, and it was capped by a timber lead-covered spire.

Strainer Arches

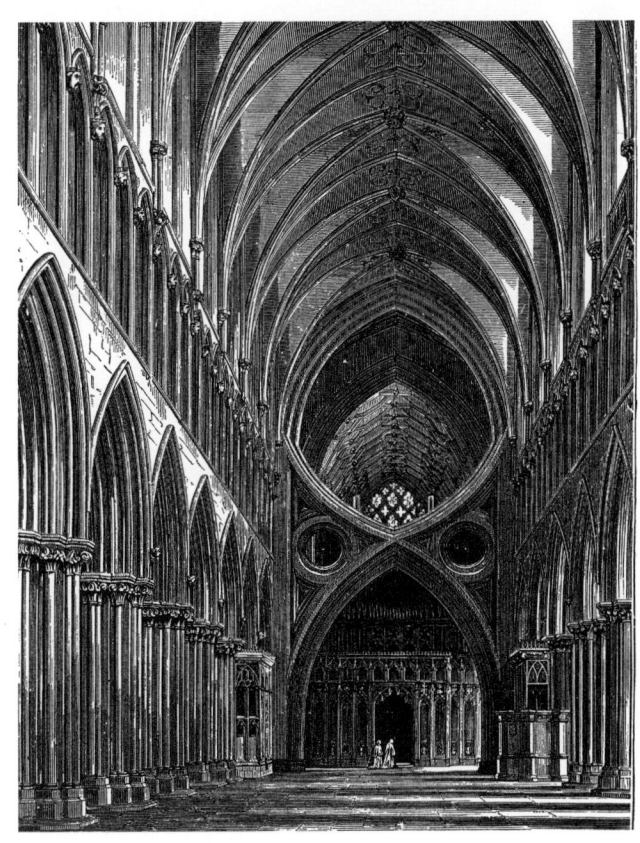

(Right) By 1338, it had become apparent that the new tower at Wells was putting too great a strain on the existing substructure and foundations and that the tower was becoming unstable. The problem was addressed by the cathedral's master mason, William Joy, who, in an attempt to shore up the crossing piers, was responsible a series of massive double strainer arches or scissor braces to be inserted between them. In this system, part of the force exerted by the tower on the crossing arches and piers is transferred to the scissor braces. This measure seems to have arrested the problem.

REACHING TO HEAVEN
Lanterns

While not all crossing towers were also lanterns, there is no doubt that this was the primary function of many crossing structures throughout the medieval period. In older churches that predated the great expansion of clerestory lighting of the thirteenth century, and in sunny countries, such as Spain, where clerestory windows had a tendency to be comparatively small, there was perhaps a greater need for illumination at the crossing.

LAON CENTRAL LANTERN
Laon Cathedral, rebuilt ca. 1160–90, is one of the earliest cathedrals in France to be built in the Gothic style. This west-facing section through the north transept and crossing shows the central lantern tower. Ribs rise from wall shafts at the corners and in the center of the four sides of the structure to carry the eight-side vault. The lantern is square and rises only one story above the roof, each side being lit by a pair of simple lancet windows.

TARRAGONA OCTAGONAL LANTERN
The thirteenth-century lantern over the crossing of Tarragona Cathedral is a comparatively low structure rising no more than ca. 25 feet (7.5 m) above the surrounding roofs. Octagonal in form, it is partly supported on a series of segmental, pointed squinch arches (see page 118) carried across the corners of the crossing. An eight-cell domed rib vault covers the interior, and the sides of the dome are pierced alternately by windows of three and four lancet lights.

ELY OCTAGONAL LANTERN
In 1322, the eleventh-century central tower of Ely Cathedral collapsed into the choir. Instead of simply rebuilding the tower, the opportunity was seized to create something altogether more original, possibly to illuminate a rather gloomy church, by opening out the crossing and raising an octagonal lantern, the lower stage in stone and the superstructure in timber. The identity of the architect of the Ely lantern is not known for certain. It is possible that the concept belonged to the sacrist Alan de Walsingham, but "a certain person from London" advised the chapter in the early stages of the design, and the king's master carpenter, William Hurley, was responsible for the design of the timberwork.

VALENCIA CIMBORIO

The cimborio of Valencia Cathedral on the west coast of Spain, which probably dates from the mid- to late fourteenth century, is a two-tier octagon with large windows containing tracery of late Geometric form. Instead of being glazed, these windows are filled with sheets of alabaster. The architect is unknown, although the master builder Martí Llobet carried out work on the lantern in 1430.

ST. OUEN, ROUEN

(Above) The late medieval lantern tower over the crossing of the Abbey Church of St. Ouen in Rouen, Normandy, is square at the bottom, rising through two stories, and surmounted by a two-tier octagon with openwork parapet and spiky finials suggesting a crown. The upper story of the tower and the lower story of the octagon form the lantern, the four cardinal sides being pierced by large gabled windows. The four corner buttresses of the tower rise above the parapet, and delicately crafted flying buttresses extend from them to the diagonal sides of the octagon.

REACHING TO HEAVEN

Timber Spires

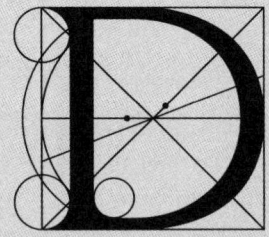espite stone being longer lasting and more resistant to the destructive forces of nature, the vast majority of spires were constructed of timber. The construction of a stone spire was a serious undertaking, often extending over a considerable length of time. The spire of the Church of St. James in Louth, Lincolnshire (see page 119), for example, which rises to a height of approximately 140 feet (43 m) above the top of the tower, took fourteen years to build, which represents a rate of approximately 10 feet (3 m) per year. In contrast, the erection of a timber-frame spire was not such a protracted affair. The preparatory work could all be undertaken in the carpenter's yard prior to any on-site construction. Here, the individual timbers would be cut to size and shape before being transported to the site for assembly. Putting the frame together on top of the tower was a comparatively speedy process, and the nature of the structure tended to eliminate the need for scaffolding.

Timber spires developed from the low pyramidal roofs that were raised over early towers. Modifications to the pattern of principal rafters rising from the four corners of the tower meant that instead of rising to an apex, they might support a continuous collar that acted as a base for a spire of octagonal section. An essential element in many timber spires in both England and France was a central mast that extended from the base to the apex, around which the rest of the timber framing was based. Once the frame had been assembled, it was fitted with boards and covered with lead. Other coverings, such as tiles and shingles, might be used in lesser churches, but for high-status buildings, such as cathedrals, lead was the favored option.

In France, due to the great height of many cathedrals, the timber spire (or flèche) was often used as an alternative rather than as an accompaniment to the central tower. While sharing many of the characteristics of conventional spires that rise from the tops of towers, the flèche, which rises directly from the crossing—as would the stone base of a tower—is a specialty architectural type in which a large part of the structure is concealed below roof level and which has a structural relationship with the adjoining roof trusses of the main building. The superstructures of these flèches were often treated in a highly decorative manner with ornamental woodwork and leadwork, which showed off the high level of artistic accomplishment attained by many medieval carpenters and plumbers.

Amiens Central Spire

In 1527, the central spire of Amiens Cathedral was struck by lightning and destroyed. The commission for a new timber spire was given to a carpenter called Louis Cordon who came from Cottenchy, a village approximately 5 miles (8 km) to the south of Amiens. He was assisted by Simon Taneau, and the spire was covered with lead by the chapter plumber, Jean Pingard. The work was completed in 1533.

The substructure was carried on a heavy timber platform that spanned the crossing above the vault. A long king post (A in the illustration below) rose from the center of the platform to the apex of the spire and formed the spine of the entire timber-frame structure. The ridge of one of the adjacent roofs (H, at the right-hand side of the illustration), indicates the extent of the timber frame beneath the roofline. The only visible part of the structure is above this level.

The spire itself, as seen from the exterior, comprises an ornately carved openwork timber screen, rising to a traceried and pinnacled crown from which emerges the lead-covered upper spire. Statues surmount the pedestals that surround the second tier of the timber screen; they include representations of Christ, the Virgin Mary, and numerous saints. The spire rises to a height of 422 feet (129 m).

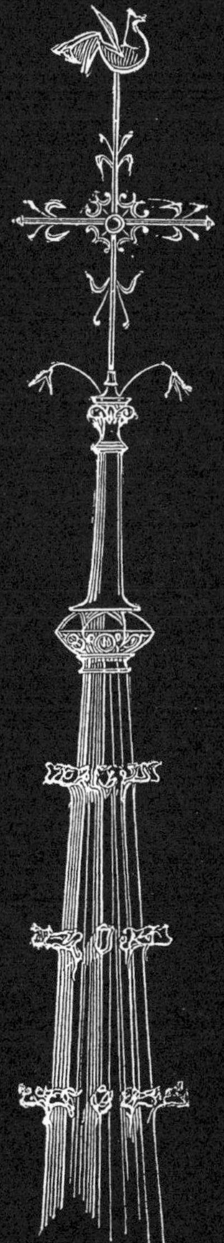

REACHING TO HEAVEN
The Flèche of Notre-Dame de Paris

Perhaps one of the best-known timber spires is the flèche over the crossing of Notre-Dame de Paris. It is, therefore, something of an irony that the present structure dates from 1858–60 and represents a reconstruction of the thirteenth-century spire by the architect Eugène Viollet le Duc. Its inclusion here is on the basis of Viollet le Duc's extensive knowledge of medieval carpentry, his knowledge of the prerestoration flèche in particular, his determination to emulate the methods of the medieval builders, and the insights this gives us into their approach to construction.

THE RUDIMENTS OF THE PLAN
(Right) This diagrammatic sketch explains the essentials of the structure, showing both the principles of the base below the roofline as well as the octagonal superstructure that rose above the roof. At the four corners (AB, AB) are the stone angles of the crossing. Two diagonal frames (A–A and B–B) each extended from one corner of the crossing to the other. At their juncture in the center was a king post (G), which formed the main vertical around which the superstructure was based. In addition, four lateral frames (A–K, B–K), which represent the end trusses of the roofs over the nave, choir, and transepts, were inclined at a 45-degree angle. These end trusses carry the ridge pieces (C–D) of those roofs, which support the octagonal base of the superstructure.

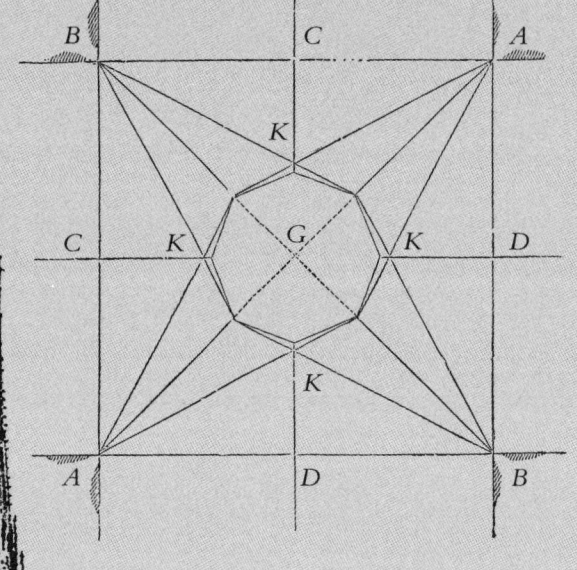

THE BASE PLAN
(Below) The accuracy of Viollet le Duc's reconstruction was to a large extent based on the in situ survival of the thirteenth-century base beneath the roofline, which was recorded before the reconstruction was carried out. This timber base is of interest in being an early example of a central spire constructed entirely in timber instead of on a stone base.

GENERAL VIEW OF THE FLÈCHE
(Left) Notre-Dame from the southeast showing the flèche in position. It rose above the roofline approximately 105 feet (32 m). The thirteenth-century flèche, which was badly damaged during the French Revolution, was taken down in the early nineteenth century.

THE DIAGONAL FRAMES

(Right) In this diagonal frame, which forms part of the base, a pair of short horizontal beams extend from the wall head and are supported by a post and arch brace (rising from A). This substructure carries the tie beam. A pair of valley rafters (C–D), which extend from the ends of the main beam to a central king post, indicate the junction of the roofs that meet at the crossing. Below them is a pair of cranked timbers (E–F), which are also fitted to the king post. These timbers are strengthened by paired braces (A–G), which clamp both sides of the timbers.

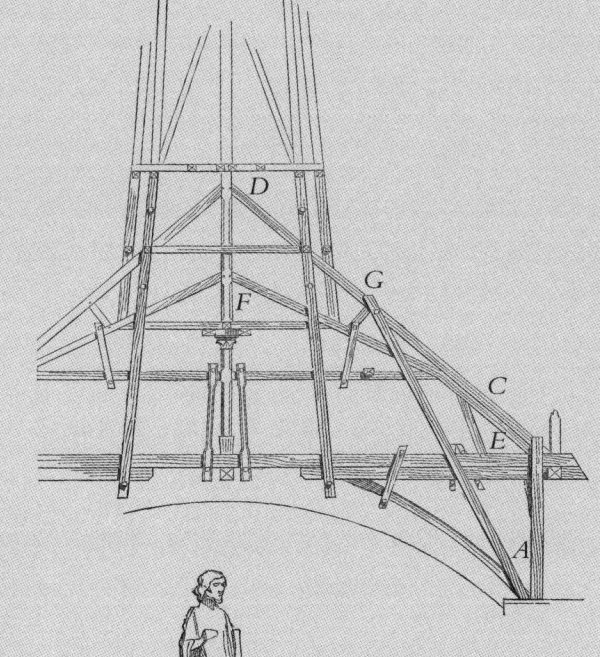

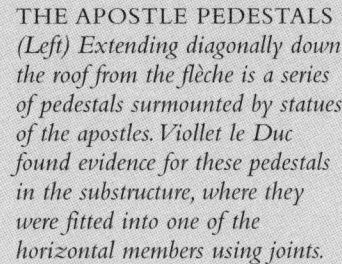

Apostle statue on a pedestal

THE APOSTLE PEDESTALS

(Left) Extending diagonally down the roof from the flèche is a series of pedestals surmounted by statues of the apostles. Viollet le Duc found evidence for these pedestals in the substructure, where they were fitted into one of the horizontal members using joints.

THE SUPERSTRUCTURE

(Right) The essentials of the superstructure above the roofline are the central king post, which rises through the flèche like a mast, and the inclined frame surrounding it that tapers toward the apex. The details of the outer panels are Viollet le Duc's, but there is nothing improbable about them. He has created a two-story structure complete with crocketed (adorned with curving foliage) spire and pinnacles. The detail serves to remind us of the skill of the medieval carpenter.

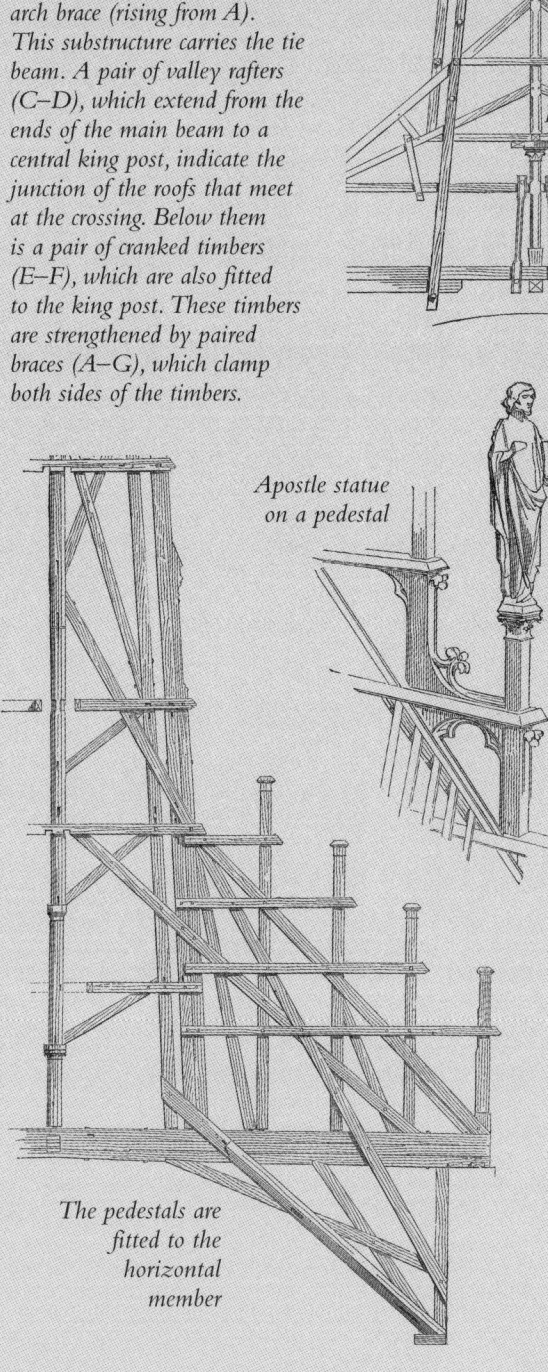

The pedestals are fitted to the horizontal member

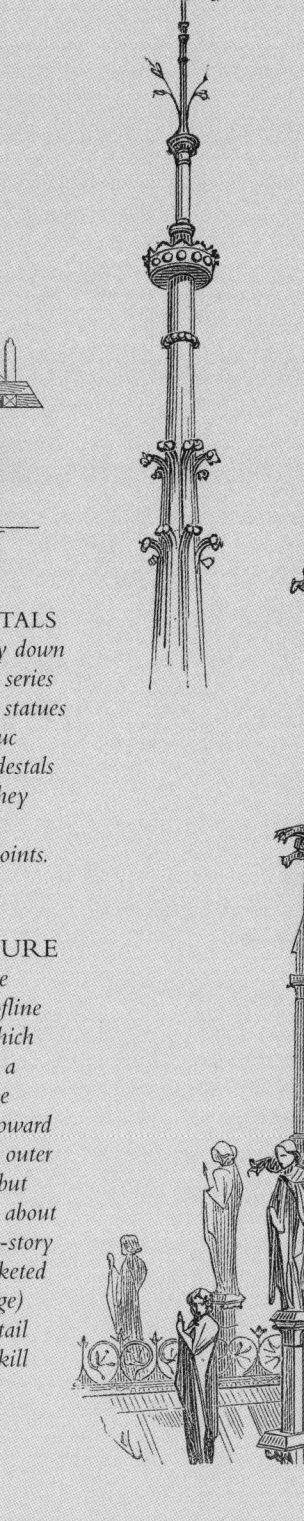

117

REACHING TO HEAVEN
Stone Spires

Because spires were usually octagonal in plan, the main structural problem faced by the medieval master mason was that of how to reconcile the polygonal form of the spire with the square top of the tower. The solution was to build four sides of the spire on the four walls of the towers, and the other four (diagonal) sides on squinch arches that spanned the internal angles between the corners of the tower (see opposite). Various precautions were taken against the undue thrust that might be exerted by the weight of a spire on the tower. At St. Michael's Cathedral, Coventry (see page 123), for instance, buttressing was felt to be prudent. Efforts to reduce the weight of the spire centered on the tapering of the wall thickness, so that a wide base was reduced to a narrow top. At Salisbury Cathedral, where the spire wall was 2 feet (610 mm) thick at the bottom, the inner face of the spire wall rises vertically while the outer face slopes inward until the thickness is no more than 8 inches (203 mm). Some other spires were even thinner in their upper parts, narrowing down to no more than 5 inches (127 mm). The inclined planes and the diminishing section of the spire meant that in order to ensure the accuracy of the assembly, both the drawing of the design and the preparation of the individual stones had to be carried out with a high degree of precision; this was all the more important when there was a high degree of surface ornamentation.

The construction of stone spires required serious attention to the provision of scaffolding, and there is evidence for both external and internal systems. Medieval illustrations sometimes depict the external scaffolding that encased a stone spire during its construction (see page 136) but tell us nothing about any internal arrangements. One building that does give insights into the process of building from the inside is the spire of Salisbury Cathedral. Extending from the uppermost story of the central tower to the top of the spire is a timber-frame structure replicating the shape of the spire. This seems to be a builders' scaffold, although tree-ring dating of the timbers suggests that the existing structural configuration is associated with repairs, not the construction of the spire. Nevertheless, there does not seem to be much doubt that the structure was largely erected from the inside. Of course, once the builders started to get close to the top, such a system would become too restrictive, and the final sections must have been completed from an external scaffold erected at the top of the spire.

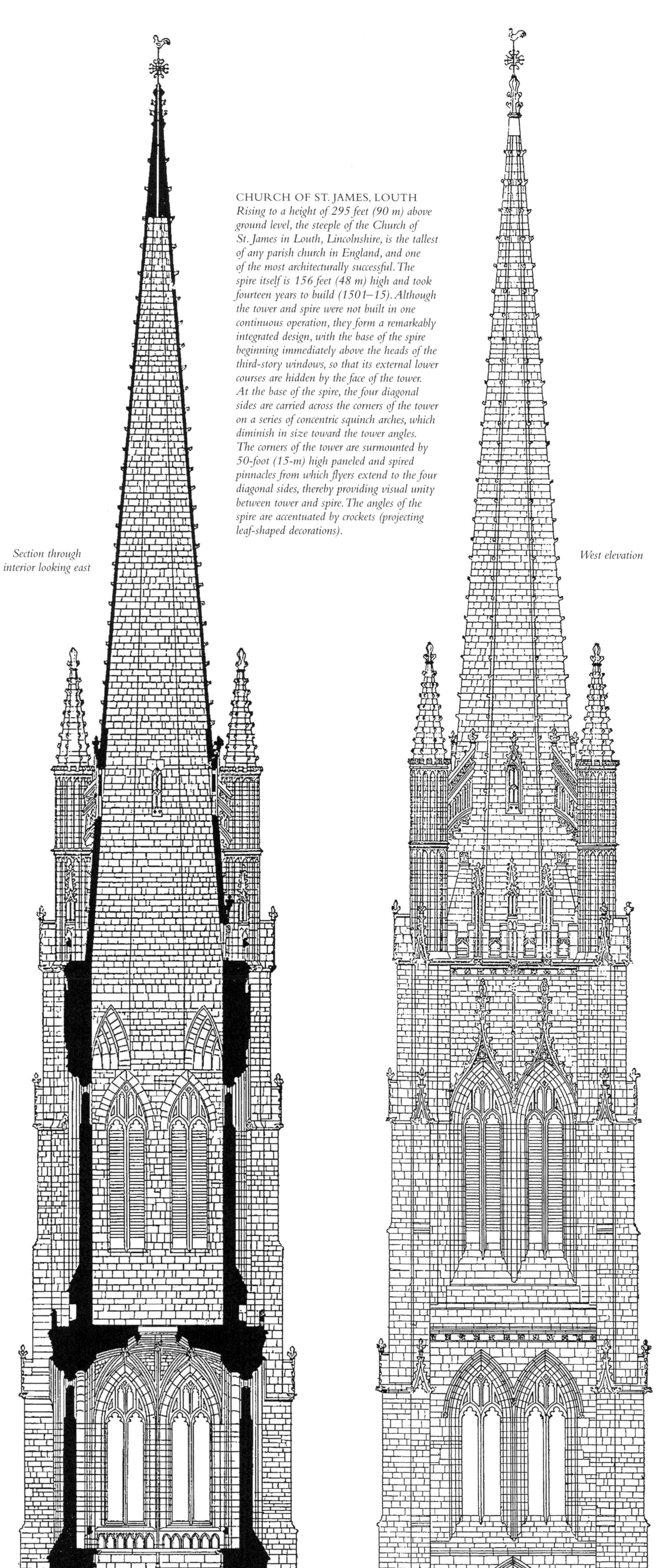

Section through interior looking east

CHURCH OF ST. JAMES, LOUTH
Rising to a height of 295 feet (90 m) above ground level, the steeple of the Church of St. James in Louth, Lincolnshire, is the tallest of any parish church in England, and one of the most architecturally successful. The spire itself is 156 feet (48 m) high and took fourteen years to build (1501–15). Although the tower and spire were not built in one continuous operation, they form a remarkably integrated design, with the base of the spire beginning immediately above the heads of the third-story windows, so that its external lower courses are hidden by the face of the tower. At the base of the spire, the four diagonal sides are carried across the corners of the tower on a series of concentric squinch arches, which diminish in size toward the tower angles. The corners of the tower are surmounted by 50-foot (15-m) high paneled and spired pinnacles from which flyers extend to the four diagonal sides, thereby providing visual unity between tower and spire. The angles of the spire are accentuated by crockets (projecting leaf-shaped decorations).

West elevation

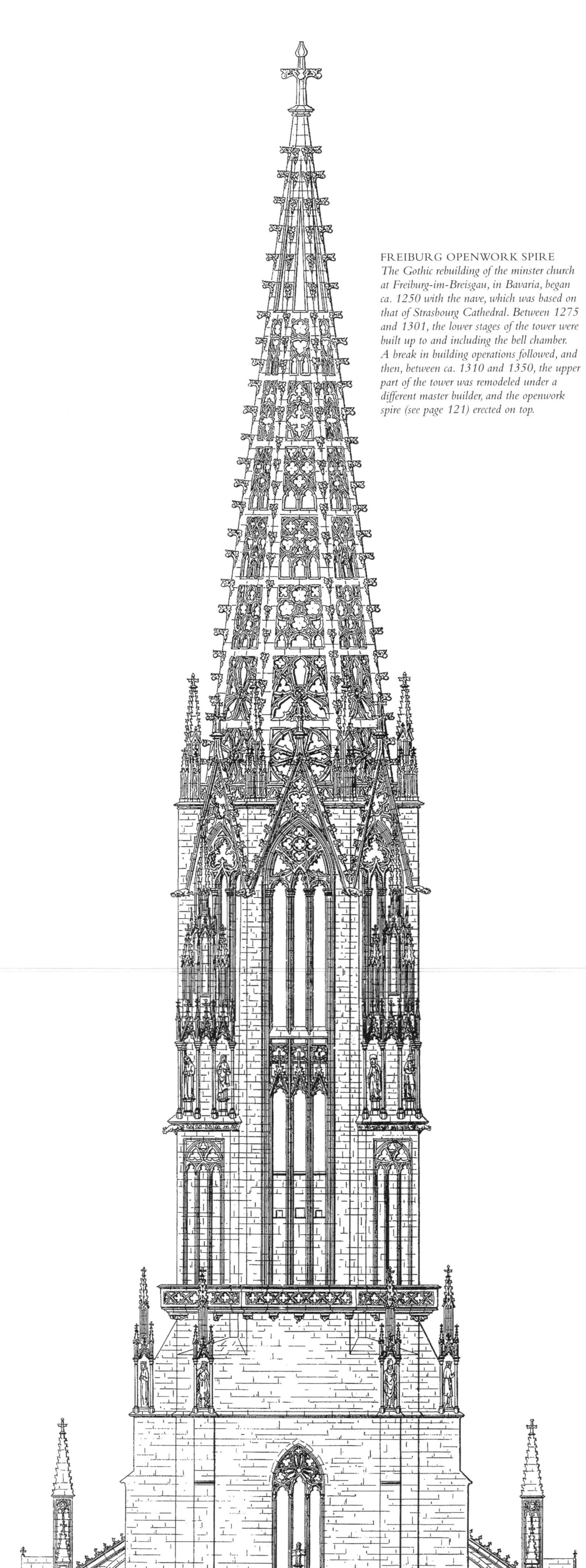

FREIBURG OPENWORK SPIRE
The Gothic rebuilding of the minster church at Freiburg-im-Breisgau, in Bavaria, began ca. 1250 with the nave, which was based on that of Strasbourg Cathedral. Between 1275 and 1301, the lower stages of the tower were built up to and including the bell chamber. A break in building operations followed, and then, between ca. 1310 and 1350, the upper part of the tower was remodeled under a different master builder, and the openwork spire (see page 121) erected on top.

REACHING TO HEAVEN

Openwork Spires

The two principal contributions of German architects to late medieval church architecture were the *Hallenkirche* (see pages 26–27) and the openwork spire. The latter seems to have been conceived in the early years of the fourteenth century at either Cologne or Freiburg. Perforated steeples had been erected at, for example, Séez in Normandy in the thirteenth century, but the principle was taken much further in Germany. Early fourteenth-century designs survive for the openwork steeples of Cologne Cathedral (not actually constructed until the nineteenth century), but the first in the sequence to be built was that of the west tower of Freiburg in the first half of the fourteenth century. An openwork steeple was designed for Ulm Minster in the late fifteenth century, but that too had to wait until the nineteenth century before it was built.

The Parler Family

The most famous name among the architects of medieval Germany is that of Parler, a family of high-ranking masons who worked in ancient Swabia and Bohemia (what is now southwestern Germany, Switzerland, and the Czech Republic) throughout the fourteenth century. Heinrich Parler I, who had worked at Cologne Cathedral, settled in Swäbisch-Gmünd in southern Germany ca. 1330, where he built the nave of the church. His eldest son, Johann, was appointed master mason at Freiburg Minster in 1359. The best-known scion of the dynasty is his second son, Peter Parler, who became master mason of Prague Cathedral in 1356, where he completed the choir and other works and where his portrait is carved into the fabric. He was also the designer of the Charles Bridge over the Vltava River and of other buildings in Prague. Johann's son, Michael, became master mason at Strasbourg Cathedral; another son, Heinrich II, acted as consultant to Milan Cathedral in 1392. Peter's sons Wenzel and Johann both followed him into the profession.

BURGOS SPIRES
Burgos, in northern Spain, was the capital of the old county of Castille, which became a kingdom in its own right in 1037. A cathedral had been established here in the last quarter of the eleventh century, but, from 1221, it was completely rebuilt in a Gothic style, the bulk of the work having been accomplished by 1260, although there are important later additions. Among these are the upper parts of the west towers and their spires, which were built between 1442 and 1458. The architect was a German master mason, Juan de Colonia (Johann von Köln), who was recruited by Bishop Alfonso de Cartagena when on his travels. This explains why there is a quintessentially German concept in a Spanish setting. This German master's name infers that he came from Cologne and may have worked on the cathedral, a building that had been in the making since 1248. The openwork spires of Cologne Cathedral were not yet in existence, but they were evidently planned, because the early fourteenth-century drawings survive. Either Juan de Colonia knew these drawings or he was aware of similar constructions elsewhere in Germany. Encircling each spire close to its summit is an openwork gallery. This is also a feature of the Cologne drawings, although not of Freiburg, and it also appears in the openwork spire of Strasbourg Cathedral, which was completed in 1439 by Johan Hültz of Cologne.

Managing the Effect

In essence, spires were built in order to create an architectural effect, and a number of devices were employed to manage that effect. Given that towers were usually rectangular and spires octagonal, the primary architectural challenge was to effect a discreet transition between the two elements, a task that was achieved in a number of different ways. One example is the southwest tower of Chartres Cathedral, begun in 1142. Here, the three lower stories of the tower are built to a square plan, but the upper story, which rises above the parapet level of the main building, is octagonal and, therefore, provides a convenient base for the stone spire. The transition from one form to the other is accomplished by the deployment of projecting gabled pinnacles at the diagonals of the octagon and even taller gables at the main sides. The gables all rise above the base of the spire and thereby mask the change.

At Oxford Cathedral, where the upper tower and spire date from the second quarter of the thirteenth century, there are four pinnacles at the corners of the tower screening the diagonals of the spire and then four large gabled windows breaking forward from the main sides. The whole ensemble serves to distract from the obvious disparity between the two components of tower and spire. In England, a distinct type of stone spire known as a broach spire was invented, perhaps inspired by timber prototypes. In this kind of construction, pyramidal features known as broaches rise from the corners of the tower and are tapered into the diagonal faces of the spire.

In respect of the spire itself, a number of methods were used to enhance and embellish its appearance. Because the long straight lines of a spire give rise to an optical illusion in which they appear concave, some medieval builders adopted the principle of entasis in which, instead of the sides of the spires being straight, they were constructed with a slightly convex curve to correct the illusion. Occasionally this was overdone, so that the opposite effect was created, as in the Abbey Church of St. Germain in Auxerre, where the lines of the spire appear overtly convex. Emphasis was given to the angles of the spire by embellishing them with either moldings or crockets. Stringcourses might be employed to break up the sides into a series of horizontal divisions. Traceried panels could give interest to the faces of the spire, as at Lichfield (see page 57) and Coventry (see opposite). Enhancement of otherwise plain surfaces might also be effected by the strategic deployment of windows or other openings, such as lucarnes.

Octagonal Crown

The tower of St. Michael in Coventry (now the cathedral) was built in the late fourteenth century; the spire followed in the 1430s. At Coventry, the tower was given an octagonal crown on which to set the spire. Pinnacles on the tops of the tower buttresses receive flyers extending from the angles of the octagon. The spire itself is divided by stringcourses into three horizontal divisions, which increase in height from bottom to top. The two lower ones are paneled, the upper one plain. The whole composition is exceedingly well proportioned and executed.

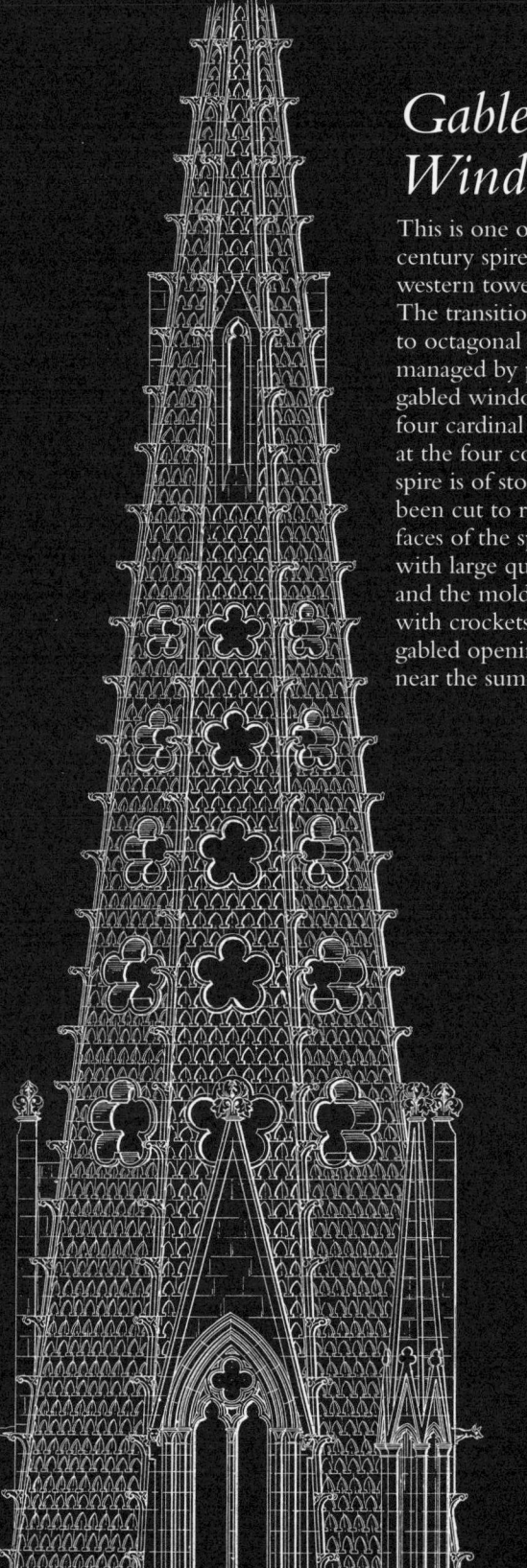

Gabled Windows

This is one of the two thirteenth-century spires that surmount the western towers of Séez Cathedral. The transition from square tower to octagonal spire has been managed by placing a large gabled window at each of the four cardinal faces and pinnacles at the four corners. Although the spire is of stone, the masonry has been cut to resemble tiles. The faces of the spire are perforated with large quatrefoil openings and the molded angles decorated with crockets. There are small gabled openings, or lucarnes, near the summit.

REACHING TO HEAVEN

The Dome of Florence Cathedral

One of the great achievements of the later Middle Ages was the raising of the dome over the crossing of Florence Cathedral, the most ambitious project of its kind to be attempted since the construction of the Pantheon in Rome in the second century. The dome spans a width of 143 feet 6 inches (43.7 m) and rises from a height of 170 feet (52 m) at its base to 295 feet (90 m) at its apex. It has a pointed profile and is built on an octagonal plan on a series of ribs. In the fourteenth century, when it was designed, the conventional way of raising a structure such as this would be to erect it on centering, but the most remarkable aspect of its construction was that it was built entirely without centering, following a proposal by Filippo Brunelleschi. The process by which Brunelleschi's plan was devised and carried out between 1418 and 1436 is well documented and provides us with insights into the process of design, construction, and patronage in the medieval world.

CONSTRUCTION OF THE CATHEDRAL
Work on the construction of Florence Cathedral was initiated in 1296, the initial plan being designed by the master mason and sculptor Arnalfo di Cambio. After a hiatus in the early fourteenth century, the project was revived in the 1350s and a revised design agreed by 1368. It was planned that the crossing should be roofed with a dome, a model for which was built by the master mason Neri di Fioravanti. By 1418, work on the dome had yet to begin, but the process was put into motion with an open invitation for the submission of plans to raise the vault. After the acceptance of Brunelleschi's plan, building commenced in 1420 and by 1436 the dome had been completed up to the base of the lantern.

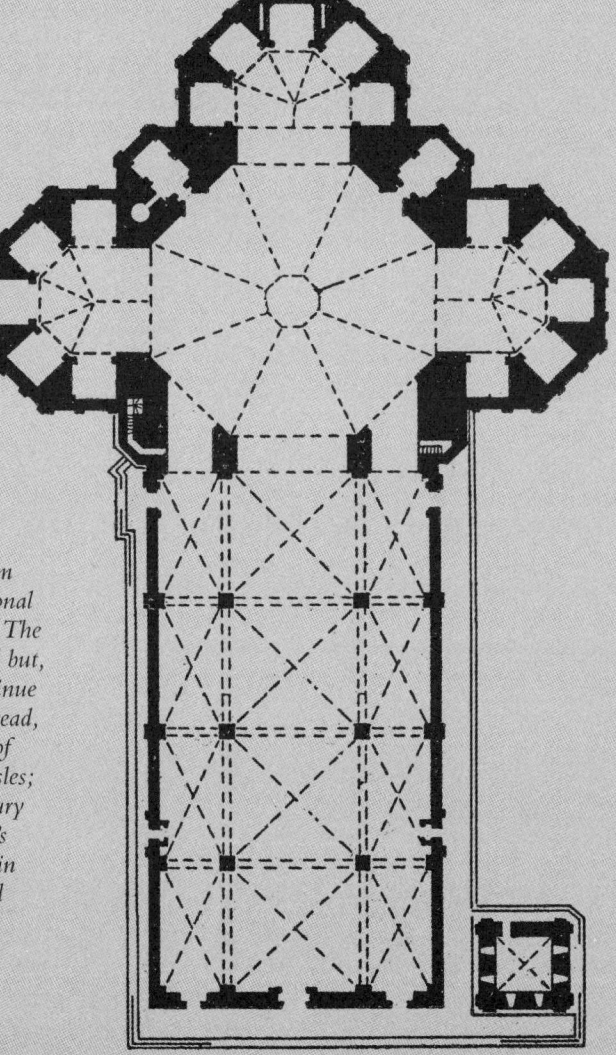

THE PLAN OF THE CATHEDRAL
The cathedral is cruciform in plan with semi-octagonal transepts and presbytery. The crossing is also octagonal but, unusually, does not continue the line of the nave. Instead, it is equal to the width of both the nave and its aisles; this is a fourteenth-century modification to Cambio's design and has resulted in a much larger ceremonial space than normal.

Brunelleschi

Filippo Brunelleschi (1377–1446) was born in Florence, the son of a notary, and at the age of fifteen he was apprenticed to a goldsmith. An interest in machines and mechanics led him to clock making, but he first came to general notice in 1401 when he took part in a competition to make a set of bronze doors for the baptistery of San Giovanni in Florence. He spent several years working in Rome and studying the ancient buildings of that city, during which time he also made a study of perspective. Brunelleschi returned to Florence in time to take part in the competition for raising the cathedral dome. It was at this juncture that he made his first ventures into architecture, receiving four separate commissions in 1419. Appointed with Lorenzo Ghiberti as joint *capomaestro* to the cathedral in 1420 to oversee the construction of the dome, he soon overshadowed his fellow master and established his control over the project. He invented lifting machines for hoisting the stone blocks up to the dome and for assisting in the construction of the lantern that now surmounts it. Although he was also responsible for the design of the lantern, he did not live to see it built.

LANTERN
The design of the lantern was chosen by means of a separate competition, and the commission was awarded to Brunelleschi in 1436. Brunelleschi designed a new hoist for raising the stone from the ground to the top of the dome, but the construction work on the building itself had only just begun when Brunelleschi died in 1446. The lantern is octagonal, rises to a height of approximately 75 feet (23 m), and is capped by a hollow bronze ball and cross. The interior of the ball is accessible by steps rising through the lantern.

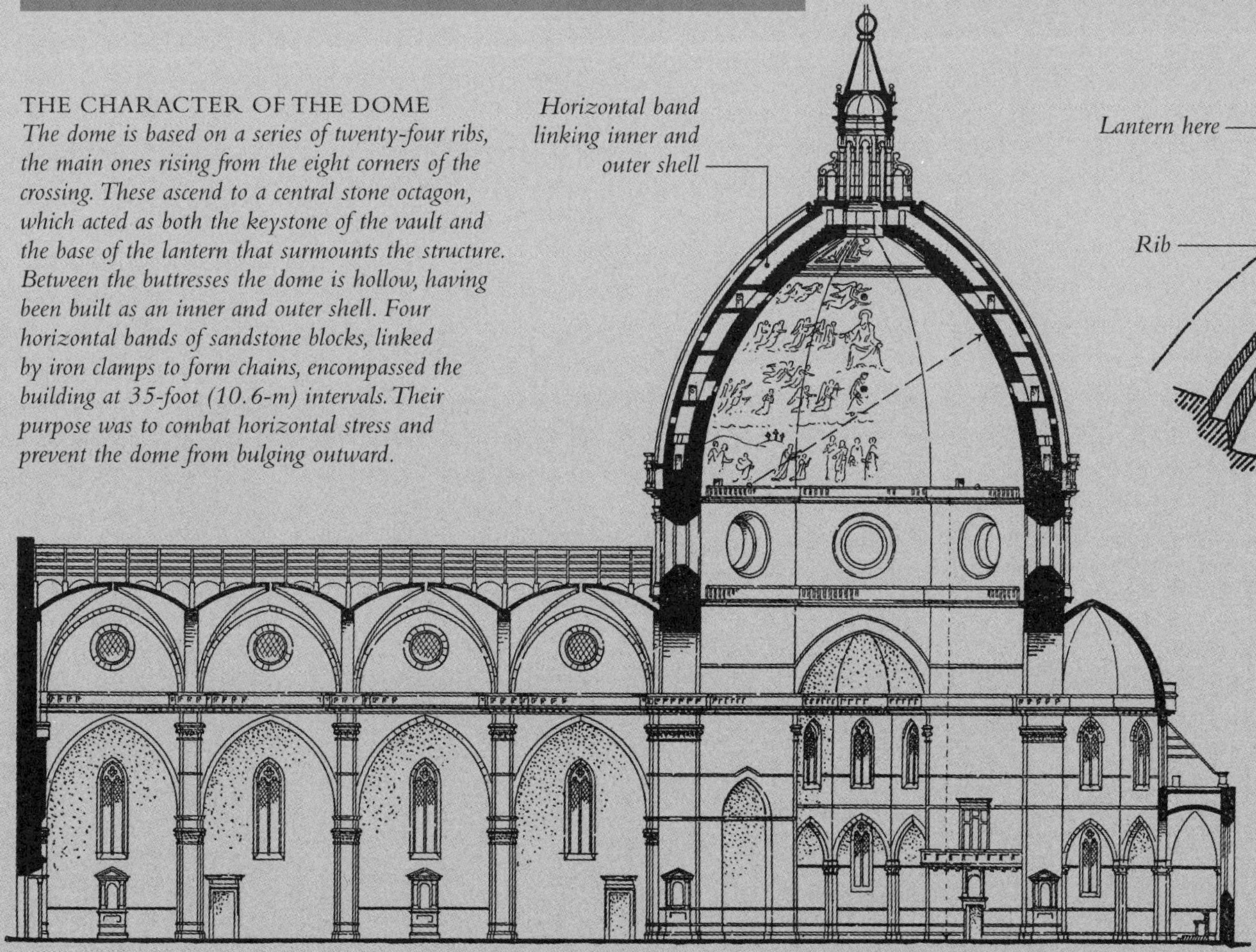

THE CHARACTER OF THE DOME
The dome is based on a series of twenty-four ribs, the main ones rising from the eight corners of the crossing. These ascend to a central stone octagon, which acted as both the keystone of the vault and the base of the lantern that surmounts the structure. Between the buttresses the dome is hollow, having been built as an inner and outer shell. Four horizontal bands of sandstone blocks, linked by iron clamps to form chains, encompassed the building at 35-foot (10.6-m) intervals. Their purpose was to combat horizontal stress and prevent the dome from bulging outward.

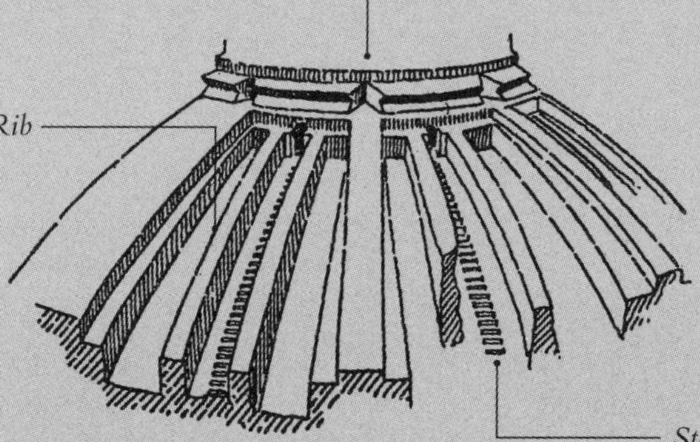

SECTIONAL CHARACTER
(Above) This cutaway drawing of a section of the dome near the summit shows the ribs, the spaces between them (designed to lessen the weight of the structure and to aid maintenance), and the inner shell of the vault with the flights of steps built into their surface.

BUILDING SALISBURY CATHEDRAL
Raising the Spire

By ca. 1265, the cathedral, including the cloisters and chapter house, had been completed, but another 45 years or so were to elapse before work began on what is the most spectacular feature of Salisbury: the great central tower and spire, the tallest structure of its kind in England. Here, it is shown in the later stages of its construction ca. 1330. Having been reinforced by iron ties, the thirteenth-century tower has been raised by two stories, and the first stage of the stone spire has also been built. The importance of the carpenters in facilitating masonry construction is illustrated by the internal timber-frame scaffold, around which the spire is being erected. This scaffold, which rises 180 feet (55 m) from the bottom of the tower, extends above the completed stonework to the proposed apex of the building; it is a substantial construction itself, and provides a secure base from which to work. Materials are hauled up by machine from the crossing and the masons are able to ascend to the bottom of the tower by staircase.

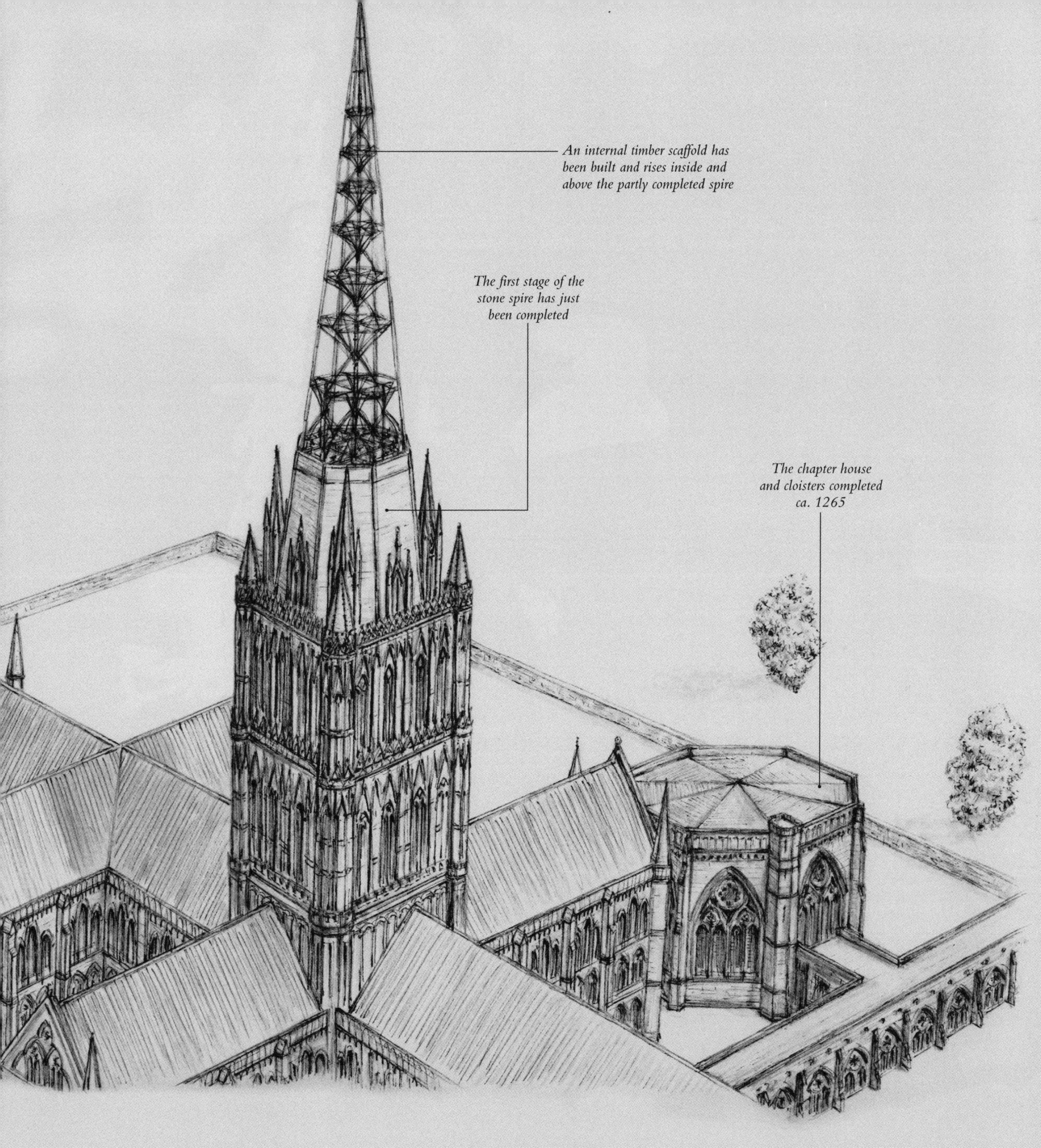

An internal timber scaffold has been built and rises inside and above the partly completed spire

The first stage of the stone spire has just been completed

The chapter house and cloisters completed ca. 1265

The Cathedral in Color

Nowadays, cathedrals are not usually thought of as colorful structures, but the architectural impact of a newly built cathedral would have been enhanced by the adornment of the fabric with a good deal of color. Statuary was painted in chromatic schemes to bring it to life, windows were filled with richly hued stained glass to create kaleidoscopic effects, and ceramic tile pavements were laid down in multicolored patterns. These, together with other decorative features and materials, would have contributed to a building of rich polychromatic quality very different from the subdued tones of today. The examples in this section give a flavor of how a newly completed cathedral may have looked at the time. Another aspect of this section comprises beautifully colored illustrations from contemporary manuscripts, an invaluable resource that provides us with precious information about medieval builders' tools and construction techniques, and the manner in which a medieval building site was organized, as well as giving us glimpses of the individual workers who contributed to cathedral building in the Middle Ages.

THE ARCHITECT OF THE UNIVERSE

This and other depictions of God the Father, creator of heaven and earth, using a pair of compasses in planning the universe, is an indication of the prestige and respect the architects of the great cathedrals had attracted by the thirteenth century. While compasses were not the exclusive preserve of master masons, they were one of their essential tools, almost a badge of office, symbolizing the mason's mastery of geometry and proportion and his ability to create buildings of gravity-defying appearance. This image uses this fact to draw a comparison between the wondrous works of God and the often awe-inspiring creations of the medieval master builder.

THE CATHEDRAL IN COLOR

BUILDING IN THE THIRTEENTH CENTURY

(Left) Various craftsmen are shown here. Two freemasons appear at ground level in the bottom right-hand corner of the picture, both wearing gloves. One knocks a stone into shape with a mallet and chisel; the other uses his wooden square to check the accuracy of the block. Interestingly, this instrument also appears to have molding profiles at each end, so it has presumably been made for this specific job. To the left and center, three laborers mount a ladder. One bears a bowl of mortar perched on his shoulder on which he wears a pad; the other two carry a number of stone blocks on a bier, which is partially supported on their shoulders by straps extending from handle to handle. On the working platform at the top of the building are two masons, one holding a pointing trowel, who must be laying the stones in position, and the other a mason's ax for trimming the stones to size as necessary; both wear gloves. There is a bowl of mortar between them, and they are receiving a load of stones from a hoist powered by a treadmill-and-pulley system.

THE USE OF HURDLES IN THE FOURTEENTH CENTURY

(Right) The special interest of this building scene is the evidence it provides for the use of hurdles made from withies (willow branches), not only for scaffolding platforms but also for inclined walkways or ladders. The latter appear to have been fitted with triangular-section steps. The two leading laborers making their way up the lower ladder carry hods on their shoulders; bringing up the rear are two more men bearing a load of tiles. A fifth laborer with a hod descends the upper ladder. Other workers depicted include two mortarmen at the foot of the building and a laborer with a bowl ready to receive mortar. At the top of the tower are a number of masons. One, holding a pointing trowel, stands on a working platform carried on cantilevered beams, while the others work on the parapet. The mason in the center checks the accuracy of the stone course with a lead-weighted level.

THE CATHEDRAL IN COLOR

THE PATRON VISITS THE SITE
(Left) The patron inspects the building works, attended by his army. In the bottom left-hand corner of the picture, a freemason, or cutter, works a block of stone with a mason's ax, his wooden square resting on top of the stone. On other stones are a pair of compasses and another square. The figure above the masons is a carpenter working on a plank of wood with an adze. The workplace of the two craftsmen is scattered with chippings of these materials. Coming around the corner of the building are two laborers carrying building materials, one with a wicker pannier and the other a two-handled hod. A third figure, who has just entered the portal, also carries a pannier. These workmen on the ground are supplying those within the building, where a number of roughmasons, or layers, are raising the walls. There is a crane and a ladder in the background.

CARPENTERS AT WORK IN THE FIFTEENTH CENTURY
The story of the construction of Noah's Ark has given the artist the opportunity to depict the carpentry trade in action. The workmen in front of the Ark undertake a variety of tasks: one operates a jack plane, another uses an auger to drill a hole in a beam, a third an ax, and a fourth uses a curved saw to cut through a beam. Shavings and chippings are scattered over the ground, as are a number of tools: chisels, axes, mallets, a brace, and an auger. The Ark itself looks very much like a timber-frame house, although, rather unusually, the sides are being made from vertical boards. More familiar to the cathedral builder would be the practice of roofing the building with boards. These are being nailed to the roof trusses and purlins with hammer and nails, a box of which hangs from the ridge. In a cathedral, of course, these boards would have been covered with lead. At the far right-hand side of the roof one man is engaged in hammering a wooden peg into a joint with a mallet.

THE CATHEDRAL IN COLOR

RAISING THE WALLS IN THE FIFTEENTH CENTURY

At the foot of the tower, amid a clutter of dressed stone blocks, one freemason cuts with a mason's ax, while another is engaged with a pair of compasses and a square. Several of the stones appear to have been inscribed as a guide to the cutters. To the right of the tower, a man, perhaps a quarry worker, unloads stone from a camel. Just below him, in the bottom right-hand corner, a group of three men are involved in raising a block of stone with a windlass and pulley system. Another hoist is being employed for raising stone on the other side of the tower and one farther up the building for hauling up a bucket. Smaller stone blocks are being supplied to the layers by men bearing them on their shoulders. To the left of the tower is an open-front timber workshop, in front of which are two mortarmen, one mixing and the other carrying a box of mortar on his shoulder. At the top of the tower are two working platforms carried on beams cantilevered out from the sides of the building.

SCAFFOLDING AND CENTERING IN THE LATE MIDDLE AGES

The main interest of this picture is the evidence it provides for the use of timber in medieval building. The doorway at the foot of the tower contains the wooden centering on which the arch has been constructed, and the building seems to have been entirely encased in timber scaffolding. Two scaffolders are engaged in extending the scaffold above the level of the masons working at the top of the tower, in anticipation of the edifice rising higher, and a third man on the lower-level working platform is using a saw to cut a timber to size. Runged wooden ladders are in use, and the large crane being operated from within the tower is entirely of timber. This machine is being controlled by a hand-operated wheel, and it is interesting it depicts the built-in steps on both the main post and the boom. Cranes were of various types and designed for the particular circumstances in which they were to be used. This one uses iron pincers to grip the stones.

135

THE CATHEDRAL IN COLOR

CHURCH BUILDING IN THE FIFTEENTH CENTURY (Left) On the right is a mortarman with a bucket of water at his feet, busily engaged in mixing mortar in an area bounded by wooden boards. To his left are two freemasons, each comfortably seated on a stool, and each working on a molded stone block. Both wield masons' axes and both have a form of square or straight edge, with which one is assessing the accuracy of his stone. Three laborers carry buckets of mortar to the layers employed in building the walls of the nearest church. Another man in the background manhandles a stone. The picture also shows a tower and two spires encased in scaffolding.

STONEMASONS AT WORK IN THE FIFTEENTH CENTURY (Right) In the foreground, numerous building workers are busily engaged in their trades. Several freemasons work stone blocks. In the front row (from left to right): an ax is wielded to roughly hew a stone to shape; a sculptor completes a statue with a rasp; an ax is used on the bedding face of a molded block; and a hammer and chisel are employed to cut a slot in the bedding plane of one of the stones, probably to facilitate lifting by a lewis. In the bottom right-hand corner, two mortarmen are at work, one mixing and the other adding water; walking away from them is a laborer carrying two buckets, presumably taking the mortar to the roughmasons. Behind them, two men are transporting one of the finished stone blocks on a stretcherlike bier. The building itself is an imaginative rendition borrowing freely from the sculptured facades of French Gothic cathedrals. The upper part is in a different color, suggesting it is newly built, as if there had been a break in building. On the top of the structure, a huge crane powered by a treadmill is being used to hoist the dressed stone and place it in position.

THE TILE PAVEMENT OF SALISBURY CATHEDRAL CHAPTER HOUSE
The chapter house of Salisbury Cathedral was under construction from 1258 and had been completed by 1266. Both the chapter house proper and the vestibule that led into it from the east cloister walk were floored with pavements of encaustic tiles. Unfortunately, these were taken up in the 1850s during the restoration of the building, although ex situ tiles survive in the Chapel of St. Peter. Fortunately, the pavements were recorded and published before they were dispersed. The pattern is an interesting one: symmetrical in that it is based on a series of L-shape bands radiating from the central octagonal column and based on four equal quadrants; and also asymmetrical in that the widths of the bands and the patterns of the tiles within them are not laid out in a regular fashion. The main bodies of the tiles were red or black with yellow inlaid patterns, mostly of foliate or animal designs, and provided a spectacular effect in this original arrangement specially designed to reflect the plan of the chapter house.

THE GREAT PAVEMENT OF WESTMINSTER ABBEY
(Right) The remarkable pavement that still covers the floor of the presbytery in Westminster Abbey was laid down in 1268. It is an example of *opus sectile* (ornamental paving made from marble) work and was made by Italian workers of the Cosmati school of craftsmanship, brought over to Westminster specifically for the job. The pavement is made of pieces of Purbeck marble, which frame patterns made up of colored stones, including alabaster, lapis lazulis, limestones, marbles, porphyry, and serpentine as well as colored glass. Some of these materials were procured locally, but some would have been brought from Italy and possibly pilfered from Roman buildings. The pavement had been commissioned by Abbot Richard de Ware, who was appointed in 1259 and had traveled to Italy in that year to receive the Pope's confirmation of his appointment. It was probably at this time that he became aware of the work of the Cosmati, but it was on a second trip to Italy in 1267–68 that he would have brought the mosaic workers back with him. The name of the master craftsman in charge was Petrus Ordoricus of Rome, who is also believed to have designed the tomb of Pope Clement IV, dating from ca. 1270.

THE CATHEDRAL IN COLOR

THE WESTERN PORTALS OF AMIENS CATHEDRAL Amiens Cathedral, which was destroyed in a fire of 1218, was rebuilt from ca. 1220, starting with the nave. By 1236, the nave had been completed, including the portals of the west front, which, like many French cathedrals, incorporate a substantial design of sculptural decoration. Sculptured displays such as this were intended to be painted in color, and although such decoration is no longer evident, this reconstruction gives an impression of how the Amiens portals might have appeared. To generations brought up to see cathedrals as bastions of visual sobriety, this comes as something of a culture shock, but to the Christians of the Middle Ages, such brightly colored spectacles were a major part of the attraction of a great church. These colored portals were the gateways to a spiritual world that was in sharp contrast to the hardships of everyday life.

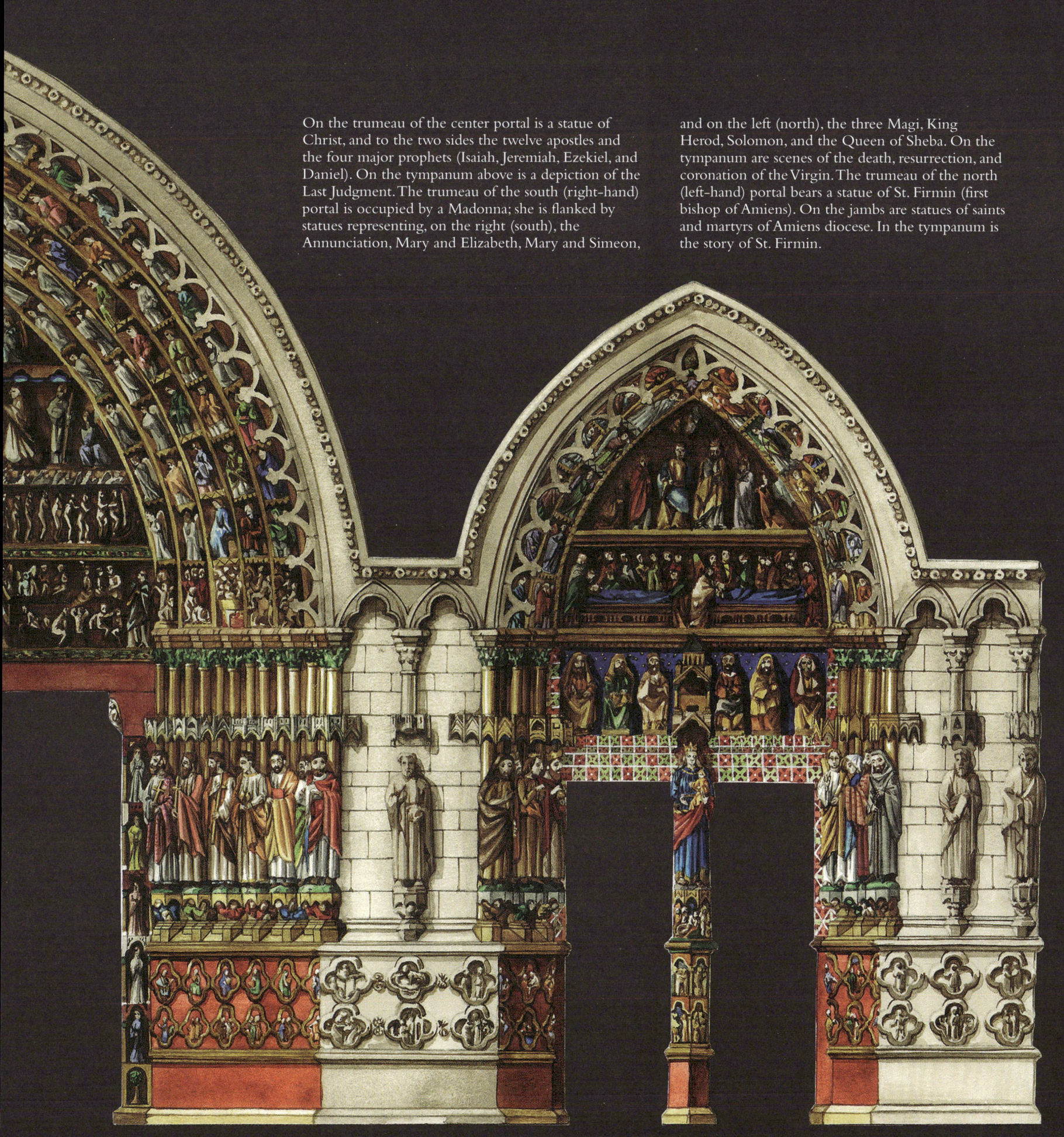

On the trumeau of the center portal is a statue of Christ, and to the two sides the twelve apostles and the four major prophets (Isaiah, Jeremiah, Ezekiel, and Daniel). On the tympanum above is a depiction of the Last Judgment. The trumeau of the south (right-hand) portal is occupied by a Madonna; she is flanked by statues representing, on the right (south), the Annunciation, Mary and Elizabeth, Mary and Simeon, and on the left (north), the three Magi, King Herod, Solomon, and the Queen of Sheba. On the tympanum are scenes of the death, resurrection, and coronation of the Virgin. The trumeau of the north (left-hand) portal bears a statue of St. Firmin (first bishop of Amiens). On the jambs are statues of saints and martyrs of Amiens diocese. In the tympanum is the story of St. Firmin.

A STAINED-GLASS WINDOW IN CHARTRES CATHEDRAL (Left and right) This drawing shows the upper part of an early thirteenth-century stained-glass window in Chartres Cathedral. It lights the south bay of the north transept's western aisle and portrays Christ's parable of the Prodigal Son (Luke 15, 11–32). The parable itself is more succinct than the window, and it is evident that the designer has used his imagination to elaborate on some of the incidents in order to correlate the number of scenes with his design. Thus, the scant information from the parable that the prodigal son "wasted his substance with riotous living" is given no fewer than seven medallions, showing various aspects of riotous living, including (from left to right along the bottom line) lying in bed, being caressed by two courtesans, and playing a board game (gambling?). There is no doubt to the value of such devices as teaching aids. The illiterate could be led through the story, medallion by medallion, the vivid pictures providing a somewhat cinematic experience, and no doubt providing a considerable attraction for that reason.

THE CATHEDRAL IN COLOR

CHARTRES CATHEDRAL
SOUTH TRANSEPT WINDOW

One of the major stained-glass window designs lies above the portals of the south transept of Chartres Cathedral, where the wall is pierced by five lancets surmounted by a rose window. The design dates from ca. 1220–30 and was donated by Pierre Mauclerc, Duke of Brittany. In the central lancet, the Virgin Mary carries Christ the child; the other four lancets contain the four major prophets of the Old Testament, from left to right: Jeremiah, Isaiah, Ezekiel, and Daniel, each carrying on his shoulders one of the four evangelists, Luke, Matthew, John, and Mark respectively. In the centerpiece of the rose window is Christ in Glory, a seated figure with a hand raised in benediction. He is surrounded, within the inner ring of medallions, by the four symbols of the evangelists: man (Matthew), lion (Mark), ox (Luke), and eagle (John); these alternate with pairs of angels. Within the two outer rings of medallions are the twenty-four Elders of the Apocalypse.

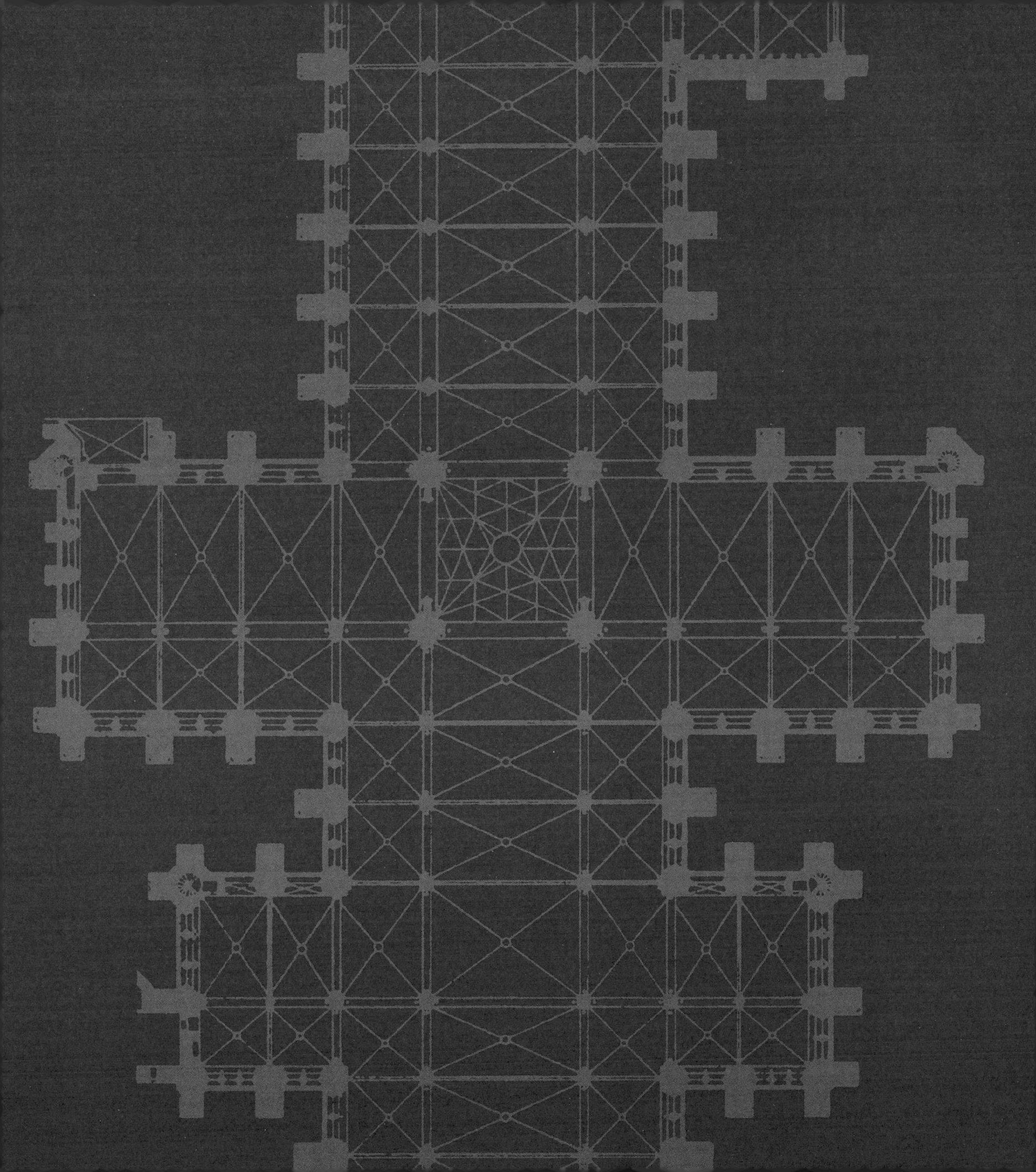

Seeking the Light

SEEKING THE LIGHT

Introduction

THE ILLUMINATION OF A CATHEDRAL was an issue of particular interest to the medieval builder. The aisled character of the structure meant that, although the nave did receive some daylight from the lateral windows of the side aisles, it was dissipated by the arcade. Gallery lighting was similarly diffused, and the triforium was generally blind because it corresponded with the position of the aisle roof and so could not be fenestrated. The only direct lighting, therefore, had to come from the west end and from above the level of the aisle roof, that is, the clerestory. The choir, which was screened off from the rest of the church, was even more reliant on the clerestory for its illumination, although it received additional light from the east window.

Also, in an age in which a great deal of attention was devoted to the high vault, either through its great height (particularly in France) or through the design of increasingly intricate rib patterns (as in England), good lighting was indispensable if these great works were to be appreciated fully. The clerestory, therefore, was the area that provided the greatest opportunity for improving the general lighting conditions within the central aisle and one that was to receive a great deal of attention during the thirteenth century.

It was, perhaps, appropriate, that in a building intended to bring to mind the Heavenly Jerusalem of the Book of Revelation, the main source of illumination should come from above. The mystical quality of light was indeed very much in the thoughts of medieval church builders, and there is no doubt that since Abbot Suger's rebuilding of St. Denis (see page 25), the ethereal nature of light diffracted through stained glass had been a major consideration in evoking an appropriate atmosphere of spirituality in cathedrals and other great churches.

The restricted lighting of many Romanesque great churches produced gloomy interiors, and it is significant that, when an opportunity arose to improve the situation, as at Ely Cathedral after the collapse of the central tower in 1321 (see page 112), it was seized upon with alacrity. The desire for greater expanses of glass was already evident by the end of the twelfth century. At Notre-Dame de Paris, the late twelfth-century twin lancet windows of the clerestory, which had been thought adequate at the time, were already considered unsatisfactory by the early thirteenth century, when measures were taken to improve the lighting by a complete remodeling of the fenestration at this level, which resulted in enlarged clerestory windows.

Introduction

The evolution of the window is indeed a striking facet of cathedral design in the Gothic era, and there is no doubt that the area of fenestration expanded as architects took advantage of the reduced structural significance of the walls to substitute glass for stone. At the same time, individual windows developed from predominantly plain functional openings of limited extent to major architectural features of enormous size and significance.

The increase in the size of individual windows went hand in hand with the development of tracery, in which a stone framework of glazing bars and transoms subdivided the window opening. The practical function of tracery was partly to break down the size of the opening and so restrict the size of the glass panels, but also to bolster the strength of the frame, thereby reducing the risk of damage from wind pressure. As with most Gothic structural measures, it also became an important decorative element, introducing extra interest to what had been a comparatively austere part of the fabric. Tracery went from simple perforations independent of the window itself to an integrated part of the window structure, and from simple geometric designs to more complicated configurations.

The main areas of fenestration were the aisles and the clerestory. In most continental great churches, the clerestory was carried around the apsidal east end, and the aisles continued as an ambulatory with projecting chevet (see pages 24–25) chapels being lit independently and often generously. In England, where most churches had square east ends, the cathedral builder had the opportunity to create a munificently proportioned window, and seldom did he fail to rise to the challenge. The English east end was one of a number of cathedral facades in which great windows might be employed to provide a spectacular effect; others were the gable ends of the transepts and the west front.

In France, the rose window was highly favored as the centerpiece of a great-church facade. Most cathedrals, including Laon, Chartres, Paris, Reims, Amiens, and Strasbourg, accommodate at least one—often several—significant examples. Bourges is an exception, but even here the great west window incorporates a rose that acts as the focus of the design. The rose did not play such an important role in English architecture, but giant windows of conventional form became a common feature in the later medieval period. One of the greatest is at York Minster, where the size of the late fourteenth-century east window is sometimes compared with that of a tennis court—the glazed area measures approximately 76 feet 6 inches (23.6 m) by 31 feet 6 inches (9.6 m).

SEEKING THE LIGHT

Lancets

The lancet window (narrow window with a pointed arch) was one of the characteristic elements of the early Gothic style, replacing the semicircular arched openings of the Romanesque and making a major contribution to the pointed character of early Gothic architecture. Some of the earliest examples are at the Abbey of St. Denis. On the west front of 1135–40, they appear in concert with semicircular arches, and in the eastern chapels of ca. 1140, they were arranged in pairs. These are quite wide with modestly pointed arches, a type used in other twelfth-century French great churches. It is this type that was deployed in William of Sens' reconstruction of the eastern arm of Canterbury Cathedral from 1174; these are some of the earliest systematically deployed lancet windows in England.

The Canterbury lancets were arranged both singly and, like those of St. Denis, in pairs. While single lancets have limited artistic possibilities, grouping has considerably more potential, and it is in this area that the medieval architect concentrated his efforts. In England, the lancet was a highly significant part of the cathedral builder's vocabulary from the late twelfth century to the middle of the thirteenth century. At Wells, lancets, both glazed and blind, play an important role in the articulation of the west front, even though they are to some degree subsumed within the sculptural decoration that constitutes the principal feature. At Ripon Minster, in Yorkshire, it is the lancets themselves that are the main decorative element; the west front is almost entirely covered by groups of lancets, with two tiers of five lights illuminating the nave.

Contrasting plans were used in the two transepts of York Minster, which were constructed between 1225 and 1250. The south transept, which was the first to be completed, has a highly ornate gable end in which lancets play a major role in a variety of sizes and groupings, although without, perhaps, a unifying style. The gable of the north transept is a quite different composition. The Five Sisters window comprises five very tall lancet windows, narrow in proportion to their height, which rise from the plinth to the middle of the clerestory level. Above them, beginning above clerestory level, and, therefore, entirely contained by the vaulting ribs, are another five smaller lancets, graded in height to reflect the profile of the vault internally and the gable externally. It is a simple but very effective design. The Five Sisters was one of the last of the great lancet window designs of the thirteenth century; the future of window design was in the development of tracery.

Lincoln Choir Lancets

The rebuilding of the Norman Cathedral of Lincoln began in 1192, and dendrochronological analysis of the roof timbers over St. Hugh's choir, which stood at the east end of the building, suggests a felling date of 1202–1203, indicating that the walls of this part of the building had probably been completed by that time. The three-story external elevation shown here is entirely fenestrated with lancet windows, but in an engaging variety of size and combination that emphasizes the inventive possibilities of the form. Each bay has a pair of lancets at aisle level, an arrangement that is imitated in miniature in the gallery above. In the clerestory, however, the windows are tripartite, the main central light being flanked by two narrower openings, and the whole ensemble framed by two blind arches of the same width as the central light. The windows are ornamented with banded colonettes (narrow, decorative columns) and hood molds (projecting moldings).

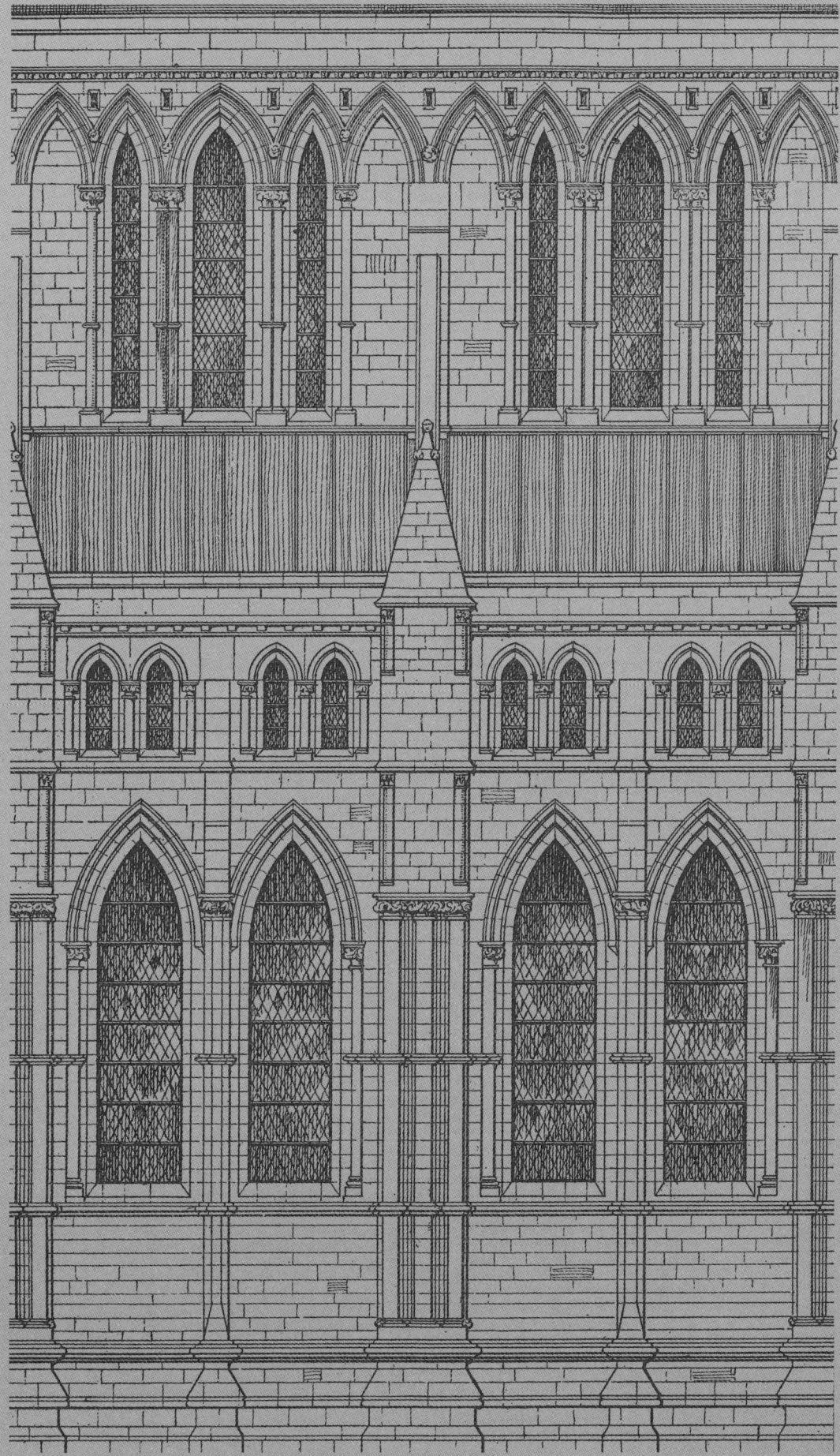

SEEKING THE LIGHT

Plate Tracery

Where two or more lancet windows were positioned side by side and situated beneath a common arched hood mold, the result was a blank area of stonework between the lancets and the hood. In these circumstances, there was often a desire to provide some kind of decorative feature, often an oculus of a simple geometric shape. Simple circular openings had been occasional features of church design from an early date, having been built into gables or lanterns, so the oculus was simply an adaptation of an existing form. However, the combination with arched lights formed the basis of a type of decorative detail known as plate tracery, a name that denotes the perforation of an area of solid walling.

Medieval oculi comprise a number of shaped ashlar blocks, each forming a segment of the figure. Because the lower segments of the oculus were in close proximity to the heads of the lancets, one block could often be used to form parts of both openings. In this way, the ensemble became an integrated structural system instead of a series of separate apertures. More interesting tracery designs could be created by introducing additional geometrically shaped perforations, either to vary the shape of the oculus or to provide it with satellite openings.

The development of plate tracery owes much to the evolution of the rose window (see pages 156–157), which also stemmed from the plain oculus. Large rose windows containing stonework patterns were being built from the early twelfth century in Italy (as at San Zeno Maggiore, Verona, of ca. 1123). In France, plate-traceried rose windows of considerable size and complexity were being built by the third quarter of the twelfth century. One such example is in the north transept facade of Laon Cathedral of ca. 1160–70. This feature, which has a diameter of some 27 feet (8.2 m), incorporates tracery based on a repeated circle-base pattern of eight-foiled figures, with smaller circular perforations in the intervening areas. Some twenty to thirty years later, an even larger rose—more than 39 feet (12 m) in diameter—was built into the west front of Chartres; it used some of the same plate-tracery motifs as Laon. An interesting aspect of the design of Chartres is that smaller plate-traceried rose windows, the design of which were based on elements of the west window, were also combined with the paired lancets of the clerestory (see opposite). This also happened at Bourges Cathedral, which was begun around the same time as Chartres, although the clerestory oculi are not so pronounced. Such combinations as these provided the basic patterns from which later tracery developed.

Soissons Plate Tracery

(Below) The choir of Soissons Cathedral dates from ca. 1200 and was strongly influenced by Chartres. The clerestory windows are no exception, although the modifications made to the design by the architect of Soissons have given the combination of lancets and rose a greater coherence. The lancets have been elongated and the rose has diminished in size and significance. Instead of a semicircular arch, the window lights are now set beneath a pointed arch, and the whole arrangement is framed by colonettes, which continue around the arch as a molding.

The Nave of Chartres

(Above) The rebuilding of the nave of Chartres Cathedral was undertaken between 1194 and ca. 1220. While the lower lights of the clerestory windows are simple paired lancets, they are subordinate to the large plate-traceried rose window that surmounts them and to which all attention is directed. The rose and the lancets are quite separate structural entities but are nevertheless intended to form a composition. This relationship is accentuated by the fact that the rose is set beneath a semicircular arched hood mold, which gives greater unity to the bay. The rose is recessed from the wall face, which gives it greater definition but which also lightens the weight of the carved segments that make up the window.

SEEKING THE LIGHT

Bar Tracery

The combination of a pair of lancets and a plate-traceried oculus under a common hood mold left blank spaces of walling between the three openings (see page 153). In the next stage in the development of tracery, these too were pierced to create a more delicate arrangement in which the area of stonework was diminished and that of the openings increased. Whereas plate tracery was made from stone blocks, or plates, integrated with the surrounding walling, it became evident that the tracery element could, in fact, be made of a framework of ribs, or bars, of molded section. This was a more economical method of construction, the individual components of the ensemble were less unwieldy, and a finer aesthetic effect was achieved. This type of construction is known as bar tracery.

Some of the earliest bar tracery is in the choir of Reims Cathedral of 1211 onward (see opposite). An interesting aspect of the design is its employment of the plate-traceried pattern used at Soissons, so establishing continuity between the two types, although its execution in the new idiom gives a radically different result. After its introduction at Reims, bar tracery became the norm, appearing in all the subsequent great churches of France. The transition between the two types can be seen at Bourges Cathedral, built between ca. 1195 and ca. 1266. Here, the clerestory windows of the choir, which was built between ca. 1195 and ca. 1214, were given plate tracery, whereas those of the nave, which was raised later, have bar tracery. The pattern, however, is the same.

The introduction of bar tracery into England came somewhat later than in France. The earliest is possibly that in the great west window of Binham Priory Church in Norfolk, which was completed before 1244. While the date of the Binham window is controversial, there is less doubt about the use of bar tracery in Henry III's rebuilding of Westminster Abbey from 1245, a building that borrowed freely from French models, notably Amiens, Reims, and the Ste.-Chapelle in Paris. The Westminster chapter house windows, which are among the earliest of the traceried windows at Westminster Abbey, are copied from those at the Ste.-Chapelle.

Early bar tracery is dubbed geometric due to its reliance on overt geometrical forms. The employment of geometric patterns became increasingly intricate, and a greater variety of geometric figures was introduced. In the fourteenth century, there was an increasing tendency to move away from the blatant geometric basis of tracery patterns by blurring the edges of the separate components to create more integrated designs.

Early Bar Tracery

(Left) The cathedral of Reims was rebuilt after a fire of 1210, beginning at the east end under the master mason Jean d'Orbais. This drawing depicts one of the eastern chapel windows, although the pattern was used throughout the cathedral. The design was based on that of Soissons (see page 153), but here its treatment as a single opening is unequivocal, the use of bar tracery allowing a degree of integration that far surpasses that of the Soissons windows. Structural as well as visual unity is achieved because, instead of being separate openings within the wall, the lancets and the surmounting oculus (derived from the rose) are both composed of voussoirs and, therefore, form elements of a single tracery.

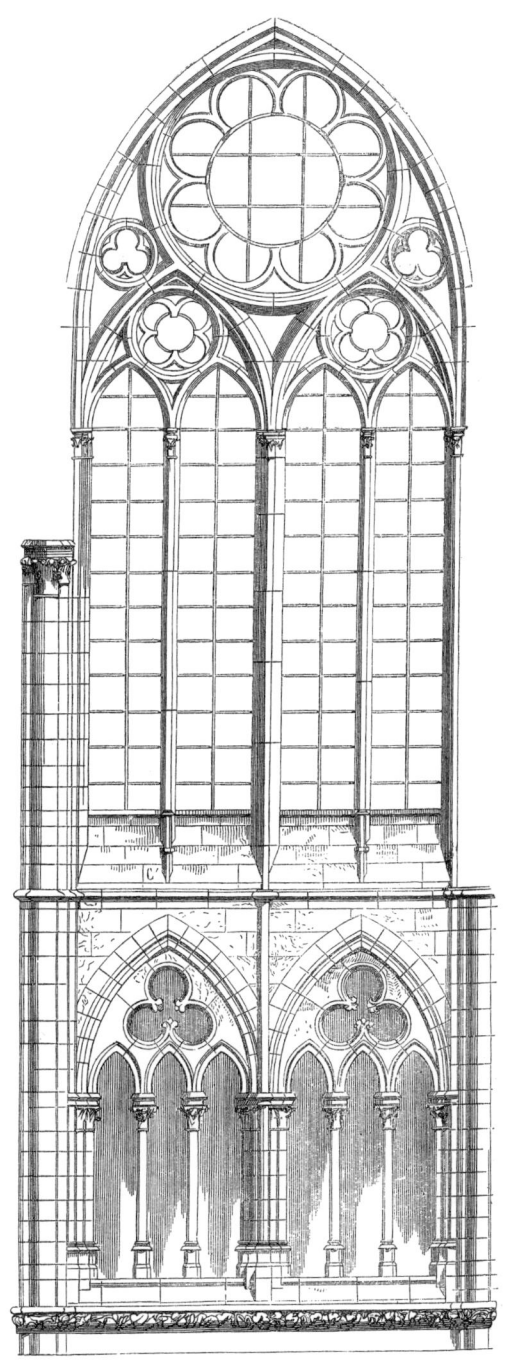

Bar Tracery Refinements

(Right) Amiens Cathedral was rebuilt from 1220 to the designs of the master mason Robert de Luzarches. In the ten years since the design of the Reims windows, ideas about window tracery had developed and were given full rein here. The nave clerestory window shown here elaborates Jean d'Orbais' pattern for Reims. The motif of paired lancets and surmounting oculus has been retained but developed into a larger design in which it is repeated at two different levels.

SEEKING THE LIGHT

Rose Windows

Normally situated in a gable and used as the centerpiece of a facade, the rose window found particular favor in France. At the Abbey of St. Denis, Abbot Suger's west front of ca. 1135–40 contains a rose window, although the original tracery pattern has been replaced. Thereafter it was a standard component of the facade in France, with major examples appearing at the cathedrals of Laon, Paris, Chartres, Reims, and Amiens. This popularity was not replicated in England where, although a number of great churches employed the rose window in the gable ends of transepts (for example, Lincoln and York), none used it as a feature of the west front.

PARIS RAYONNANT STYLE
Between 1250 and 1270, the two transepts of Notre-Dame de Paris were lengthened and each provided with a rose window more than 40 feet (12.5 m) in diameter. It is the radiating glazing-bar patterns of rose windows such as this from which the name given to the French Gothic style of the thirteenth century—rayonnant—is derived. As the illustration shows, the design was based on dividing the circle into segments and then adding a common geometrical design to each segment.

LINCOLN DEAN'S EYE
In existence by 1220, the window known as the Dean's Eye is situated in the gable of the northwest transept north wall of Lincoln Cathedral. It is a plate-tracery composition in which the geometry of the design is clearly evident. The pattern is based on the division of the main circle into sixteen segments, and the use of subsidiary circles centered on the dividing lines.

LINCOLN BISHOP'S EYE
Although the Dean's Eye would at the time have been matched by one of similar date in the south gable of the southwest transept, the original window was replaced in the fourteenth century, probably ca. 1330, by the present one, which is known as the Bishop's Eye. This is a quite different construction, with elaborately patterned tracery in the prevailing flowing style (see page 162). The design is based on two large leaf shapes, each containing a central stem from which a number of cusped veins extend to form a heart-shaped motif.

REIMS FACADE
(Above and right) The north transept of Reims Cathedral dates from between 1211 and 1241. Like many other French facades, at the heart of this elevation is a rose window, here situated at clerestory level. It forms, with the main portal and the gable, one of a horizontal sequence of three prominent architectural features. Unlike the plate-traceried roses that contribute to the clerestory windows of Chartres (see page 153), it is set beneath a pointed arch, which echoes that of the portal. The window has a spoked design, with twelve shafts radiating from a central oculus and dividing the window into segments.

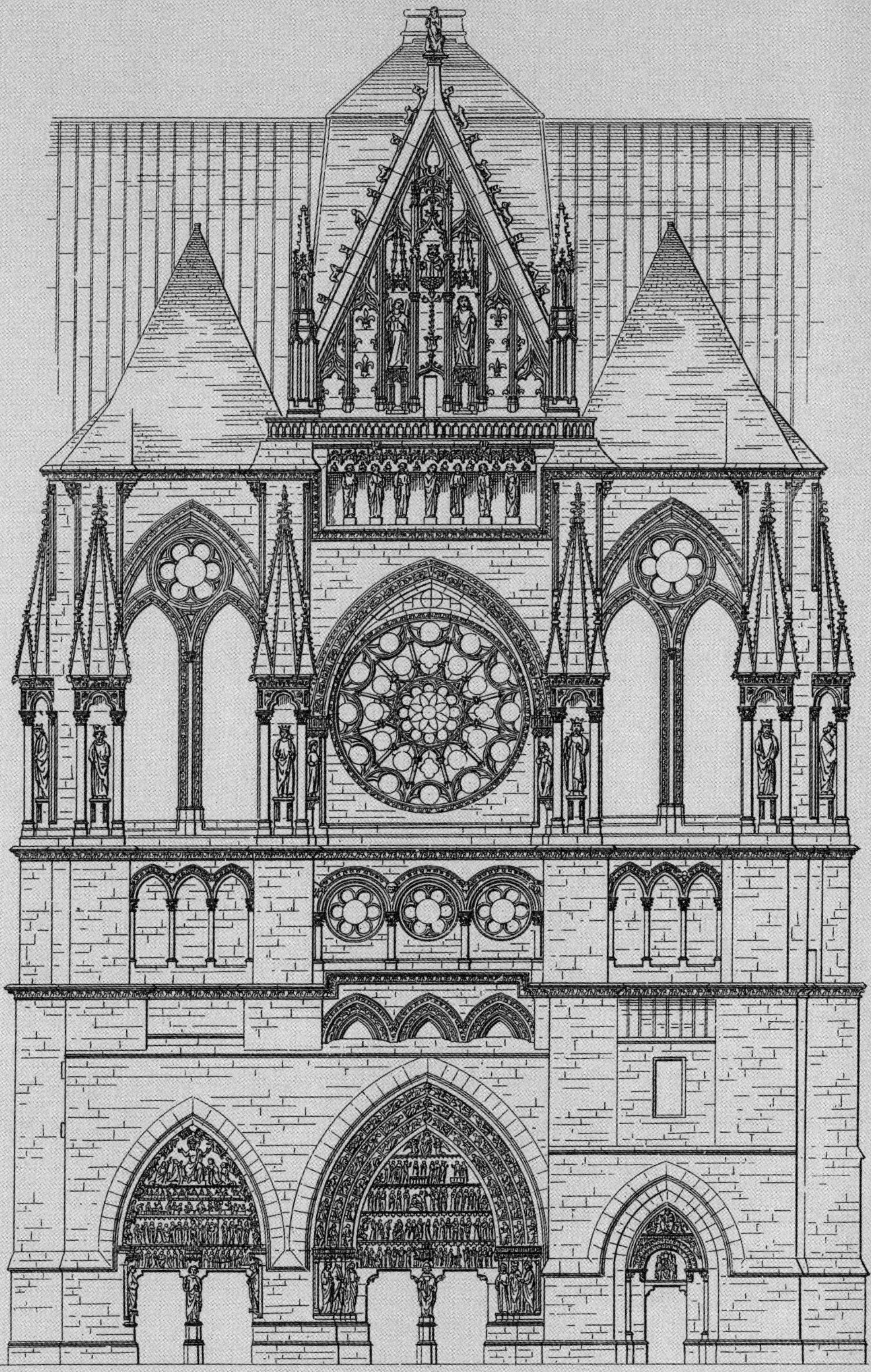

DESIGN FOR A WINDOW AT LAUSANNE
One of the drawings in Villard de Honnecourt's portfolio is a design for "a round window of the church of Lausanne." Lausanne Cathedral does have a plate-traceried rose window in the south transept dating from ca. 1220, but, although there are some superficial similarities between the two, Villard's sketch is a radically altered version of the design. The reasons for this are unclear, but it may be that Villard wished to "improve" a pattern that he considered uninspired or old fashioned.

SEEKING THE LIGHT

Rear Frames

Generally, windows were constructed flush with the outer face of a wall. In the thin-walled clerestories of many French great churches, the window occupied the whole of the wall thickness, and its interior surface was flush with the main internal elevation. However, in a comparatively thick-walled church, between the window and the internal elevation there was an arched space, or embrasure, within the thickness of the wall. This embrasure had to be designed to reconcile the recessed window with the interior. One method was to construct an internal openwork frame flush with the interior elevation.

LINCOLN ANGEL CHOIR
The Angel Choir of Lincoln Cathedral was built between 1256 and 1280. It is a three-story structure with arcade, false gallery (so called because, unlike a true gallery, it is not glazed but opens to the aisle roof space), and clerestory. Following Westminster Abbey, the upper two stories both have bar tracery. The clerestory also has a traceried rear frame, and a wall passage passes between the two elements. The tracery mirrors that of the glazed exterior frame, but here, on the inside, the frame is carried on shafts with foliated capitals.

DURHAM NORTH WINDOW
The north window of ca. 1280 in the Chapel of the Nine Altars in Durham Cathedral is a large-scale six-light composition with Geometric tracery. Here, too, there is a wall passage contained between inner and outer window frames. In contrast to Lincoln, however, where the tracery patterns are the same, the inner frame at Durham only replicates the main transoms and glazing bars, so that the glass is not obscured. In this instance, the main purpose of the rear frame is to impart strength to the window frame. This picture shows the long stone ties that link the two frames to give greater stability to the structure, and the iron rods that tie the mullions to the window jambs.

External elevation

Internal elevation

External tracery pattern

Internal tracery pattern

ST. URBAIN DE TROYES

The Collegiate Church of St. Urbain de Troyes, in Champagne, was founded by Pope Urban IV, who was born in Troyes. Consequently, although it is a comparatively modest building in comparison with the great churches of France, it was well funded and employed an innovative master mason. Unusually, the late thirteenth-century nave aisle windows are square-headed and incorporate glazing bars that break through the head to suggest gablets (decorative motifs in the form of a small gable). The internal tracery, which is of extreme delicacy and which only occupies the head of the arch, employs a completely different pattern; this design is repeated in the blind arcading of the internal walls and within interior openings.

SEEKING THE LIGHT

Crystal Palaces

The use of flying-buttress systems transferred the weight of the vault away from the walls, so that they no longer needed to have pronounced load-bearing qualities. As a result, the medieval builder was able to reduce the thickness of the walls and increase the size of the windows. One result of this subordination of the walls was that, for many great church builders, expanding the area of fenestration became an important architectural objective, and was to remain so right to the end of the Middle Ages.

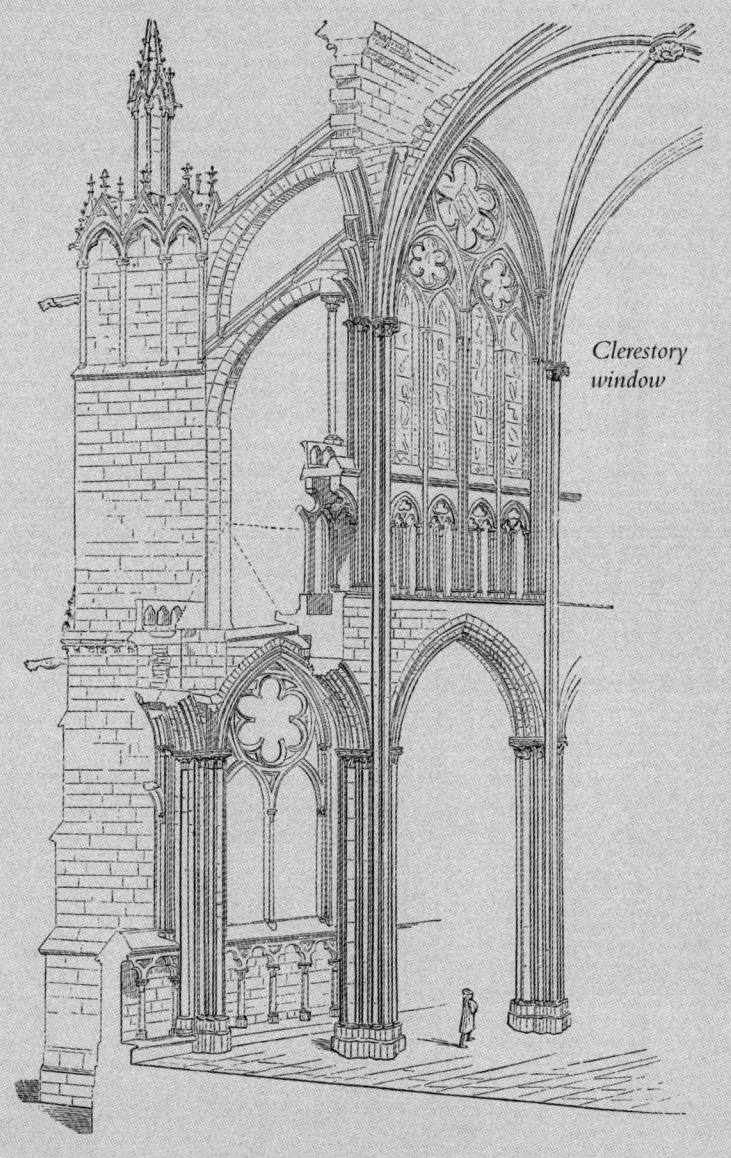

Clerestory window

Clerestory window

ST. DENIS
The Abbey Church of St. Denis, near Paris, had been partially rebuilt by Abbot Suger between ca. 1135 and ca. 1150. Suger completed the west front and choir, but the replacement of the old nave and transepts did not begin until 1231, by which time the architect of St. Denis was able to draw on the work at Amiens and also Paris, where the clerestory windows were enlarged ca. 1220. At St. Denis, the illumination of the central vessel by means of maximizing the area of fenestration was taken even further. At Amiens, the nave triforium is blind, but at St. Denis, the outer wall behind the triforium is glazed, so that it becomes a downward extension of the clerestory, and the whole of the wall area above the arcade is fenestrated.

GLOUCESTER EAST WINDOW
The old Norman choir of Gloucester Abbey (now the cathedral) was remodeled between ca. 1337 and ca. 1360. While much of the older fabric was retained, it was radically transformed from a massive, gloomy space into a thoroughly modern, diverting, and light-filled area. The clerestory windows were opened out into large expanses of glass, but the highlight of the new choir was the great east window, which gives the impression that the entire wall is made of glass. Such enormous glazed areas were characteristic of the late medieval period and were made possible by the prolific use of mullions and transoms.

YORK CHAPTER HOUSE
The chapter house of York Minster was built between ca. 1280 and ca. 1290. Apart from the stone plinth, which accommodates the chapter seating, the walls appear to be entirely of glass, the windows sitting directly beneath the vaulting. Externally, where the buttresses and window spandrels account for a greater expanse of stonework, and the windows lack an illuminated background, the effect is not so accentuated, but the interior provides quite a different experience. The chapter seating—which is ranged around the interior of the building—and the stunning timber vault, both highly significant items in their own right, form a framework for housing the windows.

Mason Setters

As we have seen (page 39), the main division in the masonic workforce was between those who cut the stones (freemasons) and those who placed them in position (roughmasons). Both were skilled jobs; the roughmasons were much more highly remunerated than the laborers, but the freemasons were considered to be more skillful, and consequently received higher pay than the roughmasons. Freemasons could command higher wages still when they were employed as setters. This was obviously a highly skilled operation, and the term probably relates to the construction of the complex structural and decorative plans that were particularly prevalent in the later Middle Ages. These included tracery, vaulting, and wall treatments, in which the intricate patterns and large numbers of components meant that a high degree of precision was required in cutting and assembly or the entire design would be compromised (see, for example, pages 90–91 and 163).

SEEKING THE LIGHT

Late Medieval Window Design

In the later Middle Ages the well-defined geometric tracery patterns of the thirteenth century began to give way to less rigidly delineated designs. The medieval architect was assisted in this development by the introduction of the ogee arch, a form with Asian origins, comprising a double arch of both concave and convex curves. Its inclusion in geometrical-base patterns allowed sinuous transitions between one figure and another, resulting in a flowing appearance and a more integrated configuration of lines. In England, these ogee-base designs are known as flowing or curvilinear tracery. The ogee arch came to England in the 1290s and made its debut in window tracery at St. Stephen's Chapel, Westminster Palace. It made a strong impact on window designs of the first half of the fourteenth century, mostly through a form of flowing tracery known as reticulated. Reticulated tracery is a repetitive geometric design in which the window head is filled with regimented tiers of composite geometrical figures. The introduction of the ogee softened the character of such patterns and allowed the separate elements to flow into one another. Following its inception ca. 1300, it became a standard and highly popular form of window tracery for more than fifty years. More innovative and interesting forms followed, mostly in the north and the East Midlands, reaching the height of their development in the 1330s in the great west window of York Minster and the south transept rose window of Lincoln Cathedral (see page 156).

The elements of this ogee-based flowing style spread from England to France by the late fourteenth century (the west screen of Rouen Cathedral is one of its early manifestations), where it developed still further as the flamboyant style, so called for its supposed flamelike appearance. The flamboyant became the characteristic French style of the fifteenth and sixteenth centuries. In England, however, the progress of flowing tracery came to an abrupt halt around the middle of the fourteenth century, and its place was taken by a radically different style, dubbed perpendicular from the manner in which some of the glazing bars take an uncompromising vertical path through the tracery. Interestingly, it too had its genesis at St. Stephen's Chapel, although Gloucester Cathedral, where rebuilding began ca. 1331, was the first major church in the perpendicular style. The form of the great south window of ca. 1335—and, therefore, a contemporary of the west window of York Minster—suggests the influence of the royal masons. It was this style, rather than that of the northern school, that prevailed and became the national style of England for the next 200 years.

Carlisle East Window

The east window of Carlisle Cathedral probably dates from between ca. 1320 and ca. 1330 and is one a small group of related fourteenth-century, large-scale windows in northern England in the flowing style. Other examples are at Selby Abbey (east window), York Minster (west window), and Beverley Minster (west window), all in Yorkshire. Each of these windows has a geometrical basis to its design, although to some extent this has been obscured by the intricacy of the patterns and the flowing nature of the tracery. The basis of the Carlisle plan can be more clearly appreciated here in the reconstruction (below) of the manner in which the window has been set out. A diagram of this kind must have been prepared by the master mason prior to the preparation of the stones. This window was a substantial undertaking; it is more than 50 feet (15 m) high and 30 feet (9 m) wide, and the tracery alone comprises eighty-six molded stones of individual design (right).

Plan of molded stone pieces

Master mason's initial geometric plan for the tracery design

SEEKING THE LIGHT

Construction Techniques

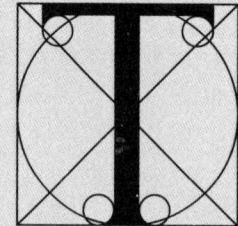The process for a traceried window began by drawing out the design, first on parchment, and then, once the final form had been agreed with the patron, at full size. The full-size drawing was constructed geometrically on a tracing floor, a flat plaster-covered surface. Few tracing floors have survived; the best preserved, complete with incised window tracery designs, is the plaster floor of the room over the chapter house vestibule at York Minster, a space that seems to have been reserved for the masons; another is over the north porch of Wells Cathedral. These floors have survived because they were laid in discrete areas within their respective cathedrals, but many would have been temporary and would have been destroyed once they had served their immediate purpose.

The design would have been drawn out at full scale with a pair of compasses and a straightedge. Once the design had been completed, it could be used as a model from which to fashion the templates. Each stone within the pattern would have had its own template made from wooden boarding, indicating the shape of the profile. These were then issued to the mason cutters. In addition to the template for the frontal profile, which might itself be quite a complex shape, there would be a template for the molded sectional profile as well. The cutting work demanded a very high level of skill and precision because, in such a tight-fitting ensemble, there was very little room for error.

When all the stonework had been completed, it would probably be laid out on the ground or on some prepared surface to make sure that the whole assembly fitted together before the mason setters began construction in situ. In a complex design, a marking system would have been necessary in order to denote the position of each stone within the tracery pattern. Such positioning marks have sometimes been found, hidden from view, on the bedding faces of tracery members. Construction began with the arched lower lights. These could be of considerable height: those of the clerestory windows at Amiens Cathedral are 24 feet (7.3 m) from sill to the apex of the arch; those of the west window of York Minster 31 feet (9.5 m). This piling up of the mullions to such heights seems slightly precarious, but scaffolding would have been in place, and centering would probably have been used. It was also the practice to secure such narrow vertical structures with lead-joined iron dowels.

Rose Window Construction

(Below) This detail of a small late twelfth-century rose window in the Church of Montreal in Burgundy gives an impression of the character of plate tracery and the manner in which a window of this nature might be assembled. In this example, the window consists of three concentric rings of traceried blocks with simple arched perforations with intervening cusps. The soffits of the arches are grooved in order to accommodate the iron frames of stained glass panels. The cups of the inner circle are also grooved to take the iron ring that would have held the central glass panel. The three stone rings would have been built up to midheight, then the central ring completed with centering (possibly utilizing the iron ring itself). Subsequent rings could then be completed without centering.

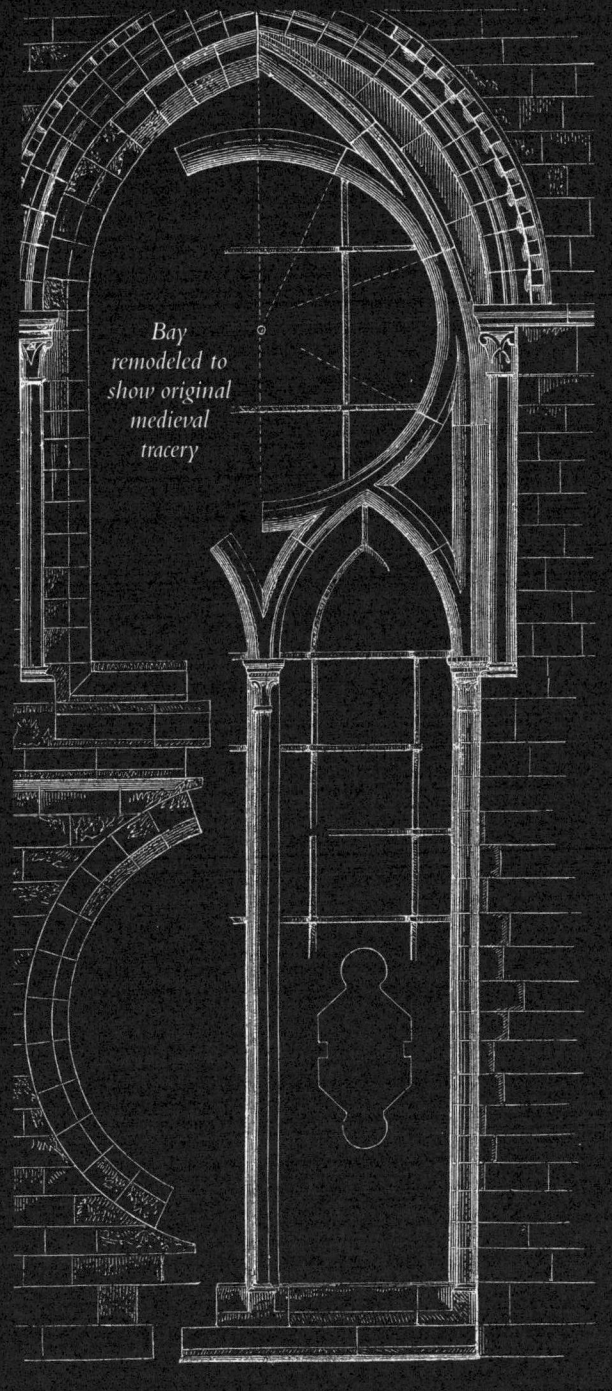

Bay remodeled to show original medieval tracery

Iron dowel in tracery block

Inner block with groove for iron ring

Traceried block with groove for glass panel

Notre-Dame Tracery

(Above) The rebuilding of the Cathedral of Notre-Dame de Paris, which began ca. 1160, resulted in a four-story elevation (see page 54). Around 1220, the upper walls were remodeled and the clerestory windows enlarged. In the nineteenth century, Viollet le Duc restored one of the bays to its original appearance, which enabled him to examine the construction techniques employed by the thirteenth-century builders. He found that some of the tracery members were fitted with iron dowels to secure the assembly.

BUILDING SALISBURY CATHEDRAL

Constructing the Chapter House Windows

The date is 1260, and the chapter house is in the process of being constructed. The design of this structure, which is a largely independent building, is inspired by that of its counterpart at Westminster Abbey, completed in 1253 as part of Henry III's rebuilding program. The Westminster chapter house was one of the first buildings in England to incorporate bar tracery in the windows; that tracery pattern is to a great extent replicated at Salisbury. Here, the transoms and tracery of the very large windows form an integral part of the structure and they are being raised in concert with the walls. The mason setters are making sure that the constituent members fit together tightly, while the remaining tracery components are laid out in order on the ground ready for use.

Tracery being placed in position

Tracery members laid out ready for use

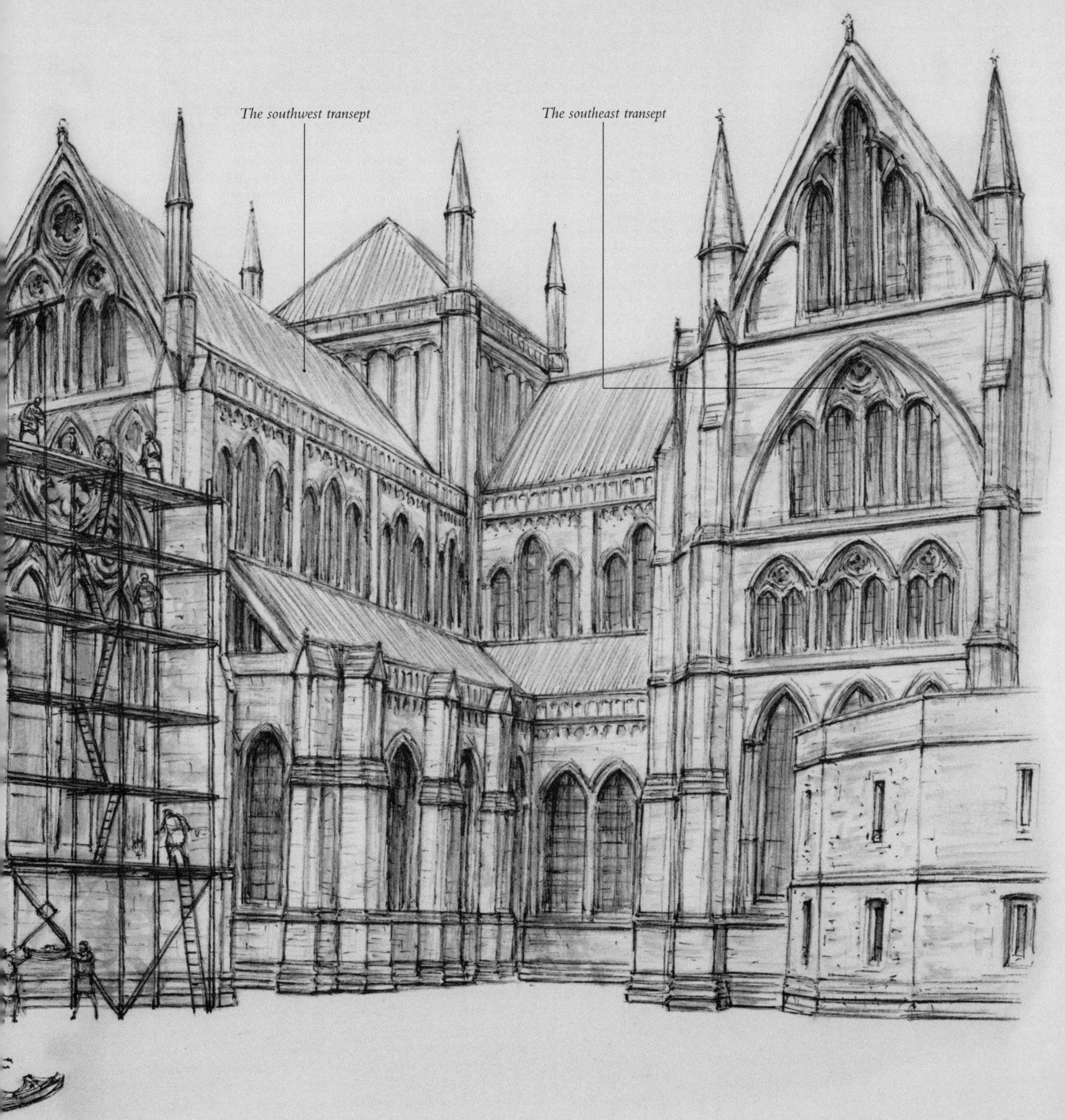

haping
the Stone

SHAPING THE STONE

Introduction

IN CONTRAST to that of his modern counterpart, the medieval sculptor's work was overwhelmingly related to architecture or architectural monument, and it cannot be understood fully in isolation, for there is no doubt that the functional components of a building often determined the form, or at least established the parameters, of the carver's design. Medieval buildings had a number of structural punctuation marks that attracted sculptural decoration and that were, from an early date, an object of the sculptor's attention. Capitals, corbels, arches, and tympani (between the lintel of a doorway and the arch above it) were among the features routinely carved into decorative forms by the Romanesque sculptor, either with geometrical designs or pictorial representations. The forms and confines of these components undoubtedly affected the artist's style and choice of subject.

While the arrival of the Gothic style created a new aesthetic in architecture and sculpture, medieval buildings continued to demonstrate the relationship between the two. The pointed arch created an accentuated spandrel, which became a favored place in which to locate sculpture. Like the tympanum, it framed a confined area that presented challenges to the sculptors and that influenced the character of their work. The development of the Gothic vault, with its increasingly complex networks of ribs, was accompanied, from the mid-thirteenth century, by the evolution of the vault boss, as medieval builders in England used the many rib intersections for sculptural embellishment. The most prolific collections of sculptured vaulting bosses date from the fourteenth and fifteenth centuries, when the use of the highly decorative lierne vault was at its height. The steeply pitched roofs necessary to accommodate the high vaults of the thirteenth century gave rise to an efficient drainage system in which the potentially damaging water was thrown clear of the building. The appearance of long drainage spouts, or gargoyles, to serve this purpose provided new features that lent themselves to sculptural enhancement.

Although sculpture certainly developed in accordance with the architectural framework, there was also a tendency for architecture to be affected by the desire to incorporate sculpture into the design, so that in many cases carved work came to form an important and integral part of a building's fabric. The deep portals of Continental cathedral facades were necessary to house the large collections of columnar figure sculpture that lined their flanks. In England, the west front developed as a screen for the display of sculptural designs. One early example of an English screen front was that of Wells Cathedral in Somerset, which dates from around 1220–50. Others followed at Lincoln, Salisbury, and Lichfield.

Introduction

A consideration of the subject matter of medieval sculpture will tell us something of the process of design and the degree of control that the sculptor exercised over it. Most ecclesiastical sculpture had a religious or moralistic subject. The overriding theme of Gothic religious sculpture was that of the Fall of Man through sin, as represented by the story of Adam and Eve, and his Redemption (deliverance from sin and death) through Atonement (reconciliation of Man with God). Redemption was attained through Christ's sacrifice, and episodes from Christ's story, from the Immaculate Conception onward, dominate the sculptural repertoire. Old Testament scenes were important not only as illustrations of the consequences that might arise from disobeying God's will but also for providing prophetic parallels with the life of Christ. The sacrifice of Isaac corresponds with that of Christ's Crucifixion, while Jonah's regurgitation from the belly of the whale is a metaphor for Christ's Resurrection. These biblical subjects were intended as teaching aids for educating the illiterate, and there is no doubt whatsoever that they, and the wider designs that they contributed to, would have been dictated by the patron, perhaps with some input from the sculptor regarding both the layout and how it might be accommodated in the architectural framework. The manner of execution, however, would have been largely a matter for the sculptor.

While Christianity may have provided the principal source of inspiration for the sculptor, some undoubtedly non-Christian subjects also figure. Some of these have a bearing on Christian theology and teaching, but other fantastic or grotesque creatures may simply be products of the imagination, which some found profane. Certainly, to Bernard, Abbot of Clairvaux (1090–1153), much pre-Gothic decorative sculpture had no relevance to, or compatibility with, Christianity. St. Bernard's influence was deeply felt in the architecture of the Cistercian movement, the austerity of which was in sharp contrast to the work of less exacting orders. With the onset of the Gothic style, in which the heaviness of the Romanesque was replaced by greater elegance and verticality, many of the dubious subjects of late Norman sculpture were swept away. Nevertheless, this characteristic mixture of nonsense and the grotesque remained an undercurrent of the medieval sculptural tradition, becoming increasingly popular again during the later thirteenth and fourteenth centuries. In the short term, in some of the early Gothic work at Wells Cathedral, for example, there appeared a more studied attempt at humor and caricature in sculpture of a secular character, an element of light relief contrasting with the more serious religious and stately sculpture.

SHAPING THE STONE

The Medieval Sculptor

Like other medieval artists, the stone sculptor was an apprentice-trained craftsman who had undergone a thorough grounding in the techniques of his trade. In the early medieval period, when the art of sculpture was in its infancy, it is unlikely that the sculptor was recognized as a distinct category of mason. However, as the standard of sculptural craftsmanship improved in tandem with the evolution of the Gothic style, so the sculptor came to be regarded as a specialist. Recognition of that status is reflected in the descriptions in contemporary documents of such workmen as Adam the Carver, who was engaged in the choir of Norwich Cathedral in 1314–15. Within the ranks of the sculptors themselves there may have been different areas of expertise. Names, such as Walter the Imager, suggest that figure work or image making may itself have been considered a distinct occupation.

What set the sculptor apart from other workers in high-quality stone may be explained by contrasting moldings and sculpture. Moldings, which all freemasons might be expected to produce, were cut to the form of a template, designed and supplied by the master mason; their execution was a mechanical exercise by a skilled stonecutter. The greater dimensional qualities of sculpture, however, not only made more taxing technical demands on the craftsman, but they also provided scope for interpretation, and those who rose to the challenge are to be regarded as artists. Indeed, the artistic nature of much carved work must have guaranteed the sculptor a sufficiently high degree of independence, enabling him to imbue his work with his own particular style. For this reason, it is the study of sculpture that will bring us closest to the largely anonymous architectural craftsmen of the Middle Ages.

Most of our attributions to named artists are based on written evidence, building accounts being the principal source. One of the earliest of these references is from the accounts for Westminster Abbey to a certain William Ixeworth, who, in 1253, was paid 53 shillings and 4 pence (roughly the equivalent of £1,500, or $2,300, in today's money) for two ymaginibus (images or statues). It has been suggested that these pieces are the figures of Gabriel and Mary from the Annunciation scene that occupy the niches on each side of the chapter house doorway. Conversely, it has been suggested that the differences in style make it unlikely that the two pieces are by the same hand. This is a point of view that is open to argument, but, more than anything else perhaps, the controversy highlights the sometimes inadequate nature of the documentary evidence and the difficulties in tying particular pieces of works to individuals.

West Front, Exeter

(Below) Dating from the 1340s and later, the west front of Exeter Cathedral is in the English tradition of facade design. Instead of the emphasis being on the portals, here they are simple openings within a screen. The screen incorporates two tiers of niches containing statues, the lower ones on pedestals carved with angels. The significance of the lower tier of statues, most of which represent high-ranking seated figures, is uncertain. They have been interpreted variously as kings (of Judah and England) and as the twenty-four elders of the Apocalypse; the upper tier appears to consist of prophets and apostles.

Chartres Facade

(Above) The south transept of Chartres Cathedral exemplifies the French approach to facade design. Here, there are three deeply recessed portals, all lined with figure sculpture, and with themed sculptured tympani and archivolts (architrave moldings). A statue of Christ stands against the central column (trumeau) of the central portal with the twelve apostles ranged along the two jambs. Above, on the lintel, the Last Judgment, and on the tympanum, Christ in judgment flanked by Mary and John and surrounded by angels. The left-hand (west) portal is dedicated to the martyrs, and the right-hand (east) portal to the confessors, and each is provided with appropriate scenes. In addition to the portal plans, there is a boldly projecting tripartite gabled porch. Each of the four supporting piers and the three archivolts are decorated with themed groups of figures.

Sometimes the evidence is less ambiguous. We know, for example, that several different craftsmen were involved in the design and sculpture of the series of monumental crosses raised toward the end of the thirteenth century by Edward I of England in memory of his late wife, Queen Eleanor. The Waltham Cross statues, in Hertfordshire, were made by the court sculptor, Alexander of Abingdon, and the Hardingstone Cross in Northamptonshire was by William of Ireland. The two sets of images display striking differences in style. Furthermore, although we do not know the name of the man who carved the sculptures for a third Eleanor Cross, at Geddington, Northamptonshire, it is evident from a comparison of the form that we are dealing with another, distinct sculptor.

This case is unusual in linking named craftsmen to distinctive artistic styles, but such instances are few, and generally we must rely on comparative analysis in attempting to determine the main lines of stylistic development and distinguish the hands of individual craftsmen. Where comparative evidence exists, differences in style can be discerned between contemporary pieces. Sometimes no more can be said of these distinctions than that they result from the craft traditions that evolved in the conditions peculiar to different parts of the world. In other instances, however, where there is an unusually large amount of surviving work, it seems apparent that a particular style is the result of a dominant individual. Such an interpretation has been put on the rich and distinctive forms of carving that appeared in Herefordshire during the second quarter of the twelfth century and at Beverley Minster, East Yorkshire, during the second quarter of the fourteenth century.

In some single plans of sculpture, it may be possible to discern the works of more than one craftsman. The architectural historian Nikolaus Pevsner believed that at least three different craftsmen were involved in carving the late thirteenth-century foliage sculpture in the chapter house of Southwell Minster, Nottinghamshire. His theory was based on the premise that differences in the treatment of the foliage at Southwell were the result of a typological development, which he interpreted as a result of the diverse aesthetics of different generations of sculptors. This, however, is unlikely to be an adequate explanation for the variations in style among the figure sculpture of the Angel Choir, Lincoln Cathedral, which dates from ca. 1270–80, and which has been classified as the work of at least four, possibly six, different workmen. Differences in physical type, bodily attitude, treatment of hair and drapery, hands and feet, all play their parts in the classification of the sculptures as the works of different craftsmen.

Shaft Corbel, Exeter

(Below) This corbel from the eastern arm of Exeter Cathedral is situated immediately above an arcade pier at the point where two arches meet. Its triangular shape follows the curving of the flanking arches, and its purpose is to carry the wall shafts that extend up to the vault and to decorate and disguise the junction between the shafts and the piers. The corbel dates from the late thirteenth century, a period during which the naturalistic rendition of foliage was at the height of its popularity. In this example, the sculptor has depicted mulberry leaves and berries.

Exeter Boss

(Right) In the later medieval period, a prolific tradition of both wood and stone boss carving evolved in England in concert with the development of the lierne vault. This example from the fourteenth-century nave of Exeter Cathedral shows the martyrdom, in 1170, of Thomas Becket, Archbishop of Canterbury, a popular saint and martyr and the object of pilgrimage. The size of the boss has determined the crowded quality of the sculpture, although the result is highly charged with drama and action.

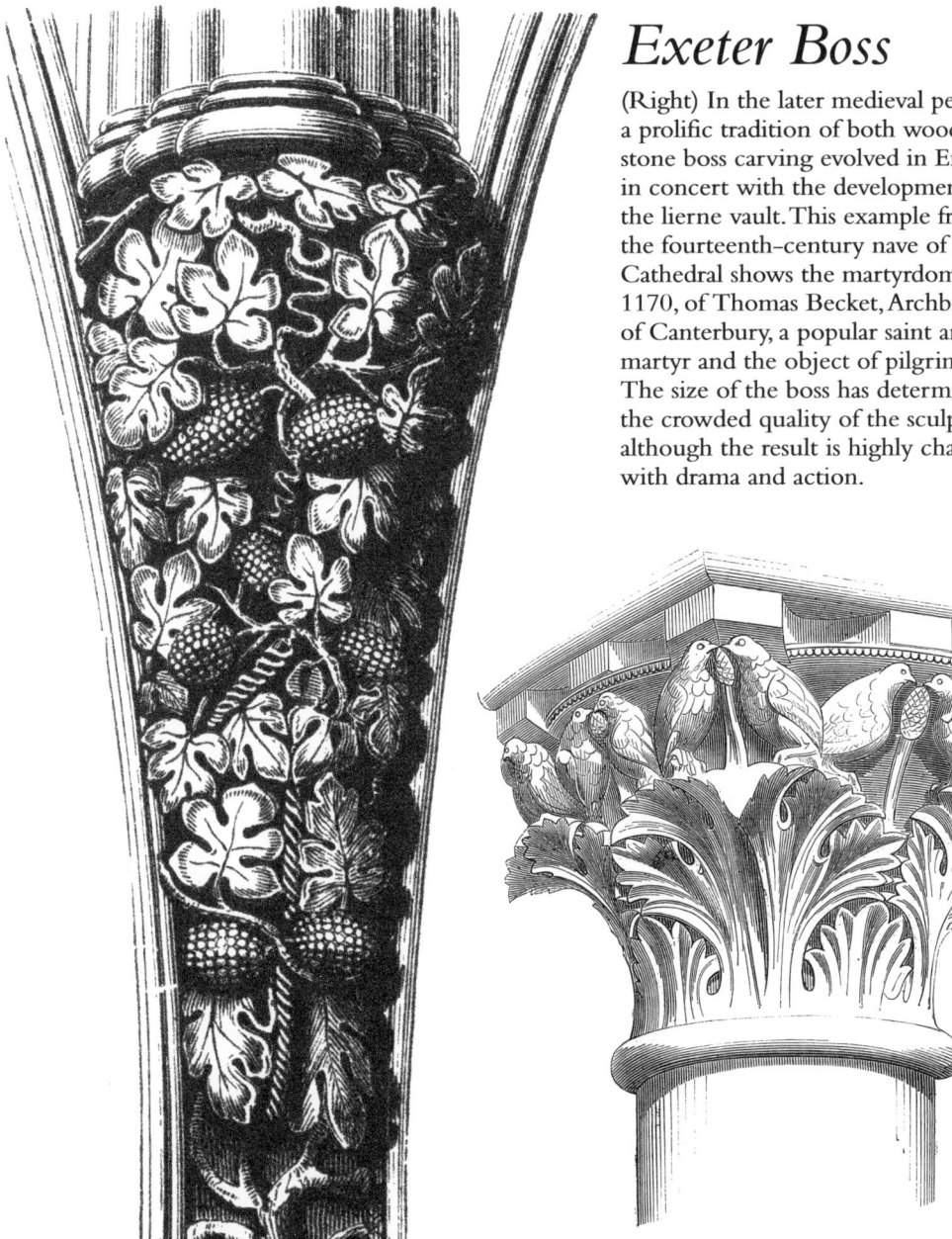

Bird Capital, Sens

(Left) Capitals, which formed the junction between a column and an arch, were natural areas for sculptors to exploit, with antecedents extending back into the mists of antiquity. The foliage that surrounds this capital of the 1140s in the choir of Sens Cathedral is derived from classical acanthus-leaf motifs, but it also includes closer studies of nature in the form of the birds that encircle the top. The capital has been skillfully designed to effect the transition from the circular section of the shaft to the square abacus that forms the top of the capital.

SHAPING THE STONE
Allegory

Allegorical representations were often used as illustrations in undertaking moral instruction. Some of these embodiments of enlightenment and ignorance, or good and evil, are strikingly effective in conveying their messages. Enlightenment is noble, ignorance contemptible; good is attractive, evil repellent. While certain conventions were observed, they were not always the same conventions, and the themes, while limited, gave the sculptor a good deal of artistic licence.

Synagogue   *Church*

CHURCH AND SYNAGOGUE
These two statues of ca. 1230, which used to flank the north portal of Bamberg Cathedral in Bavaria, Germany, are examples of an important and popular allegorical theme. They are Synagogue (left), who personifies the Old (pre-Christian) Law, and Church (right), who represents the New (Christian) Law. Church is always a regal authoritative personage with a confident bearing. Here, she is crowned, her left hand holds a model of a church; in her right hand is a staff surmounted by a cross. In contrast, Synagogue is always a drooping blindfolded figure with a louche or defeated air. The Bamberg Synagogue holds a broken reed in her right hand and is just managing to hang onto the Tables of the Law in her left. The intended symbolism is clearly evident. The shaft below Synagogue is decorated with two carved figures—a devil with winged legs and a Jew wearing a pointed cap. Below Church a mutilated seated figure holding a scroll in the left hand, his right hand seemingly raised in benediction, may represent Christ. Above him in two tiers are the symbols of the four Evangelists: the lion (Mark), the bull (Luke), the eagle (John), and man (Matthew).

THE LIBERAL ARTS
(Below) The Seven Liberal Arts (Grammar, Rhetoric, Logic [or Dialectic], Arithmetic, Geometry, Astronomy, and Music) were the cornerstones of education in the Middle Ages. The fact that the great churches were also seats of learning explains why they sometimes incorporate personifications of the Arts in figure sculpture. The example given here is from the porch of the late thirteenth-century tower of Freiburg Minster in Bavaria. Here, Geometry (second from the left) is shown holding a square, while Music (second from the right) is holding a bell.

VIRTUES AND VICES
(Above) Such contrasting pairs of sculptures are also to be found in the representations of the Virtues and Vices. This late twelfth-century pair, which compare Largesse and Avarice, are to be found (now much decayed) at Sens Cathedral within the north portal of the west front. Largesse (top) appears as a crowned seated female figure with an open countenance; with each hand she throws open a chest of money, clearly displaying them as an offering. She is flanked by a pair of suspended lamps in the form of crowns, and she has a pair of vases containing flowers at her feet. Avarice, on the other hand, is a shifty individual in a contorted posture sitting on a chest, the lid of which is held down by the left hand. The right hand is in a distorted clawed attitude, and there is a bag of money hidden beneath her feet.

SHAPING THE STONE

Figure Sculpture

Perhaps the most challenging aspect of the sculptor's art, and the element to which other facets of his repertoire was subordinated, was the rendition of the human form. The twelfth-century revival of three-dimensional figure sculpture, after the long hiatus in the art that followed the demise of classical civilization, was fueled by the cathedral-building boom and the accompanying requirement for iconographical carving to instruct the faithful and assist the depiction of the heavenly Jerusalem. Figure sculpture added the human element to Christian theology. Many biblical stories already carried a strong emotional appeal, but figure sculpture brought them to life to an extent that cannot often be appreciated today, because most medieval statues have now been stripped of their painted decoration. In their heyday, however, they would, in many instances, have presented an idealized, but uncannily lifelike presence, particularly once the sculptor had mastered bodily attitudes and mannerisms and become more adept at portraying emotion.

Madonna

(Left) The Madonna and child is one of the most memorable images of medieval art, and a pose of which most sculptors would have had first-hand knowledge. This particular statue, the *Vierge Dorée* (Gilded Virgin), is from the mid-thirteenth-century south transept portal of Amiens Cathedral where it occupies the trumeau (pillar). This very human representation of a mother and child, in which there is an obvious sympathetic connection between the two figures, is indicative of the emotionalism that entered art during the second half of the thirteenth century.

Coronation of the Virgin

(Above) The final scene in the cycle of episodes from the life of the Virgin is her coronation as Queen of Heaven. This drawing is from the tympanum of the left-hand portal of the west front (the Portal of the Virgin), Notre-Dame de Paris, which dates from the early thirteenth century. Christ and the Virgin, who are both enthroned, are flanked by a pair of kneeling angels bearing candelabras, while a crown is being placed on the Virgin's head by the Holy Spirit.

Gallery of Kings

(Above) This section from the Gallery of Kings at Amiens Cathedral occupies the center of the west front, which dates from 1220–43. Kings are a frequently encountered theme in ecclesiastical sculpture, often depicting kings of Israel and Judah, who form part of the genealogy of Christ, or, in some cases, more recent monarchs. These kings, which represent ancestors of Jesus, are bigger than life-size and are in the pronounced vertical postures that characterized much early thirteenth-century figure sculpture.

Christ

This sculpture of Jesus Christ is the centerpiece of the sculptural scheme decorating the west front of Amiens Cathedral. It stands in front of the central trumeau within the central portal, being one of a series occupying comparable positions in French cathedrals. It is flanked by sculptures of the Twelve Apostles, which line the two sides of the portal. Christ's right hand is raised in benediction; his left hand clasps a book representing the New Testament.

The Visitation, Reims Cathedral

(Above) Shown here are two of the mid-thirteenth-century statues that line the central portal of Reims Cathedral, depicting a scene that commemorates the visitation of Mary to her cousin Elizabeth before the birth of Jesus. The figures are influenced by classical models and show considerable movement. Mary is in the attitude known as *déhanchement*, in which the weight is thrown onto one hip; the head is tilted to one side, resulting in an S-shape curve that became a characteristic of figure sculpture in the later thirteenth and fourteenth centuries.

SHAPING THE STONE

Development of Foliage Sculpture

igure sculpture was the focus of the sculptor's art, but a good deal of the peripheral decorative detail, and much of the sculptor's output, was in the form of foliage. Early medieval foliage is based on stylized classical models, but an early form of Gothic foliage was the crocket, an outward curling leaf, probably derived ultimately from Corinthian capitals. A form of crocket capital was introduced into England at Canterbury Cathedral by William of Sens between 1174 and 1179; in a modified form, it enjoyed a brief vogue during the late twelfth century and early thirteenth century, although in France it enjoyed much greater popularity.

Around 1200, a form of decoration known as stiff leaf emerged in England and became the standard form of foliate decoration there for much of the thirteenth century. Stiff leaf is stylized foliage of curling trefoiled leaves on the ends of long stems. Later in the century the leaves became more deeply undercut, and the high point of the genre coincided with the construction of the Judgment Porch of Lincoln Cathedral in the 1260s, where the treatment of stiff leaf demonstrates that an extremely high level of technical skill had been developed.

The development of such expertise was used with considerable effect in the next distinct phase of foliage decoration. Naturalistic foliage was introduced to England from France, where some of the earliest is in the Ste.-Chapelle in Paris, which dates from the early 1240s. In England, the earliest is probably that at Westminster Abbey, where it was used in conjunction with stiff leaf and crockets only shortly after it had been introduced at the Ste.-Chapelle. The high point of this naturalistic style is the lavishly decorated chapter house of Southwell Minster, Nottinghamshire, of ca. 1290. The chapter house of York Minster, a close contemporary of Southwell, was decorated in a similar, although more restrained, fashion. Other notable examples can be seen in the choir of Carlisle Cathedral and the east end of Exeter Cathedral.

The vogue for naturalistic foliage was shortlived and had run its course by ca. 1310, being succeeded at Exeter and elsewhere by stylized foliage in which the leaves have a flabby, lumpy or undulating appearance. This undulating (or bubble) foliage became the characteristic decorative detail of the period between ca. 1300 and ca. 1360. By the third quarter of the fourteenth century, these forms were giving way to neat, restrained conventional flowers and leaves of square design that comprise tightly knit bands around capitals or along screens or appear as a series of individual items often over hollow chamfers.

Boss at the Ste.-Chapelle

(Below) At the Ste.-Chapelle in Paris, the conventional foliage carving of the early thirteenth century, which had hitherto characterized the decoration of Gothic cathedrals in France, gave way to forms modeled on nature, as depicted in this vaulting boss of ca. 1240.

Notre-Dame Choir Capital

(Left) The choir of Notre-Dame de Paris was built between ca. 1160 and 1180. The decoration of this arcade capital is typical of the stylized and staid leaf forms of the twelfth century that were of classical inspiration.

Capital, Beverley Minster

(Above) The eastern arm of Beverley Minster was rebuilt up to the first bay of the nave between ca. 1220 and ca. 1260. Work resumed on the nave around 1311, and, although the broad character of the thirteenth-century design was adhered to, some of the detail is strikingly different. This capital from the nave is decorated with the undulating foliage that had just come into fashion and which is in stark contrast to the stiff leaf capitals of the choir.

Galilee Porch Capital, Ely

(Right) This capital of ca. 1250 in the Galilee Porch at Ely Cathedral is decorated with stiff-leaf foliage, a stylized form of leaf decoration that enjoyed great popularity in England between ca. 1200 and ca. 1280.

SHAPING THE STONE

Angels, Spirits & Demons

Biblical narrative and moral instruction involved a range of supernatural beings, both good and evil, and the medieval sculptor was called upon to give these form. On the side of good were the angels—the attendants and messengers of God—bringing news from on high. Usually they are shown winged, perhaps to emphasize their association with heaven, and often they play musical instruments. In the thirteenth century, they become particularly benign in appearance. In contrast to the benevolent and upright angels are the many carvings of demonic aspect: ugly, deformed, and mutant creatures that seem the very embodiments of evil. While many of these may appear to have nothing to do with Christianity, they are, in fact, reminders of the forces of evil that are ever present, waiting for the opportunity to cause strife and discord.

STE.-CHAPELLE ANGELS
(Above and right) Angels were used in the decoration the arcade spandrels of the Ste.-Chapelle in Paris of ca. 1240. The awkward shapes of the spandrels were turned to advantage by depicting the angels with outstretched wings. These examples served as a source for Westminster Abbey where the spandrels of the transept triforium arcades were also filled with angels in ca. 1250. Westminster may, in turn, have been the source for the more ambitious series to be found in the arcade spandrels of Lincoln Cathedral's Angel Choir of 1256–80.

REIMS ANGEL
(Left) Reims Cathedral has a particular association with angels, because not only do a number of life-size sculptures occupy prominent positions in the western portals, they also ornament the buttresses of the nave (as shown here) and chevet. It is an unusually abundant and conspicuous display and draws attention to the cathedral as a representation of heaven on earth.

STRASBOURG ANGEL
(Right) This statue of an angel sounding a trumpet ornaments the central pillar of ca. 1225–30 in the south transept of Strasbourg Cathedral. It depicts the Last Judgment. The pillar is a highly unusual conception, in which three tiers of brackets set between the main shafts accommodate a series of sculptures. The angels are on the second tier.

GARGOYLES

Gargoyles—the protruding drainage spouts that threw rainwater away from the building—were often carved in the form of beasts, sometimes of dragonlike or demonic form. The extended character and elevated position of the feature probably inspired the elongated and winged creatures with which they are sometimes adorned. One such beast from the Ste.-Chapelle is shown here (below, top) clasping the building with its talons, poised ready to swoop down and devour its prey. Another winged creature (bottom), which ornaments the Cathedral of Clermont-Ferrand, is in a semihuman guise and is in the process of carrying off a lost soul.

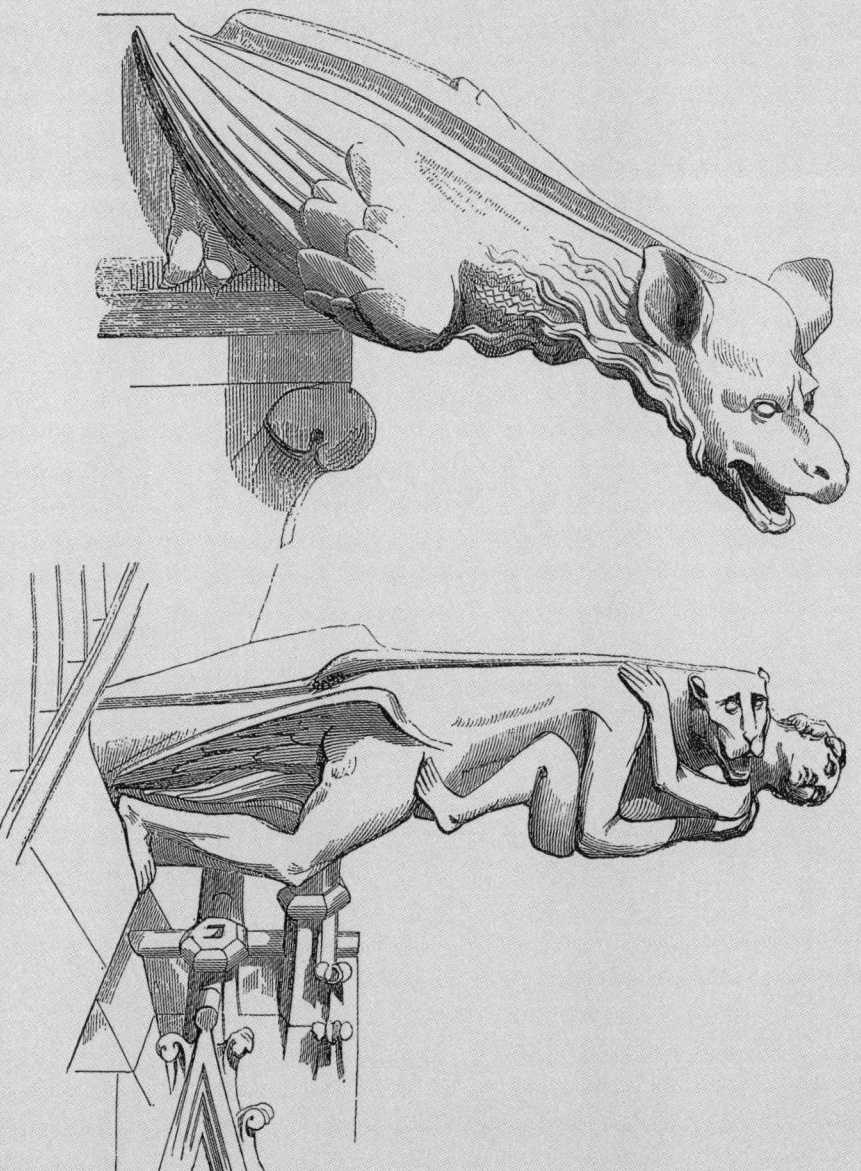

AUXERRE CAPITALS

(Above) The choir of Auxerre Cathedral, built between 1215 and ca. 1235, contains a significant collection of ornately sculptured capitals. Among them are a number of supernatural beings, some of which are shown above. On the left are two hideous demons, hinting at the torments awaiting in hell but nevertheless displaying a vulgar sense of humor. The mysterious face on the right, however, seems downright sinister. This is one of the many medieval representations of green men, faces obscured with foliage masks or disgorging foliage from their mouths and other facial orifices. This particular example, in which the leaves appear to grow out of the face, is reminiscent of images in Villard de Honnecourt's portfolio, which dates from the same period.

183

SHAPING THE STONE

Techniques

he medieval sculptor had a range of tools at his disposal, each with a particular suitability for a specific task. Once a suitably sized stone had been quarried, a mason's ax would be used to cut it roughly to size. Subsequently, the sculpture would be roughed out with a punch, or point, a narrow-bladed tool, the function of which was to reduce the stone by detaching large flakes of waste. Afterward, a claw chisel, an instrument with a toothed blade, might be used to smooth out irregularities and make a roughly level surface. Chisels of various widths were used to give the stone a smoother surface and to carve foliage and other types of intricate detail. Any remaining imperfections were removed with a rasp, or file, and, finally, with an abrasive with which the stone was given a smooth finish. This sequence was not invariable and not all these instruments were used in every circumstance. The character of the stone played its part in deciding the choice of tool, and the preferences of the sculptors in determining the modus operandi.

It is seldom possible to reconstruct the sequence of operations from a finished product. While many of these implements leave characteristic marks on the surface of the stone, in most cases they were removed by the finishing processes. However, unfinished pieces occasionally come to light in which clues to the methods used by the sculptor survive. One such work is an aborted statue recovered during excavations at the College of the Vicars Choral near York Minster. It survives in various stages of completion and retains a number of tooling marks from which it has been deduced that at least three different implements had been used. The first of these had a $5/32$-inch (4-mm)-wide blade, and was identified as a mason's point. The second, described as a small claw chisel, had a toothed blade $29/32$ inch (23 mm) wide. The third instrument for which there is evidence was some kind of abrasive, possibly a sandstone, that was used to produce the finished surface.

There is some evidence for sculpture being worked at the quarries. At Corfe, in Dorset, for example, archaeological excavation of a Purbeck marble quarry site has revealed numerous fragments of carved work amid large deposits of chippings. Purbeck, however, may be a special case, because carvers in this medium were specialty craftsmen and more likely than other sculptors to have been closely associated with the source of supply. In other cases, where it is suggested that sculpture was supplied directly from the quarry, the evidence is less compelling.

Sculptors at Work

A panel from a stained-glass window in the St. Chéron Chapel, Chartres Cathedral, depicts sculptors at work on a figure sculpture laid on an inclined bench. In the right-hand scene, the sculpture is being roughed out with chisel and mallet. In the left-hand scene, the figure has been largely completed and the sculptor is working with a rasp clutched in both hands to create a smooth finish within the statue's clothing folds. In both instances, the figure standing to the left holds a mason's ax.

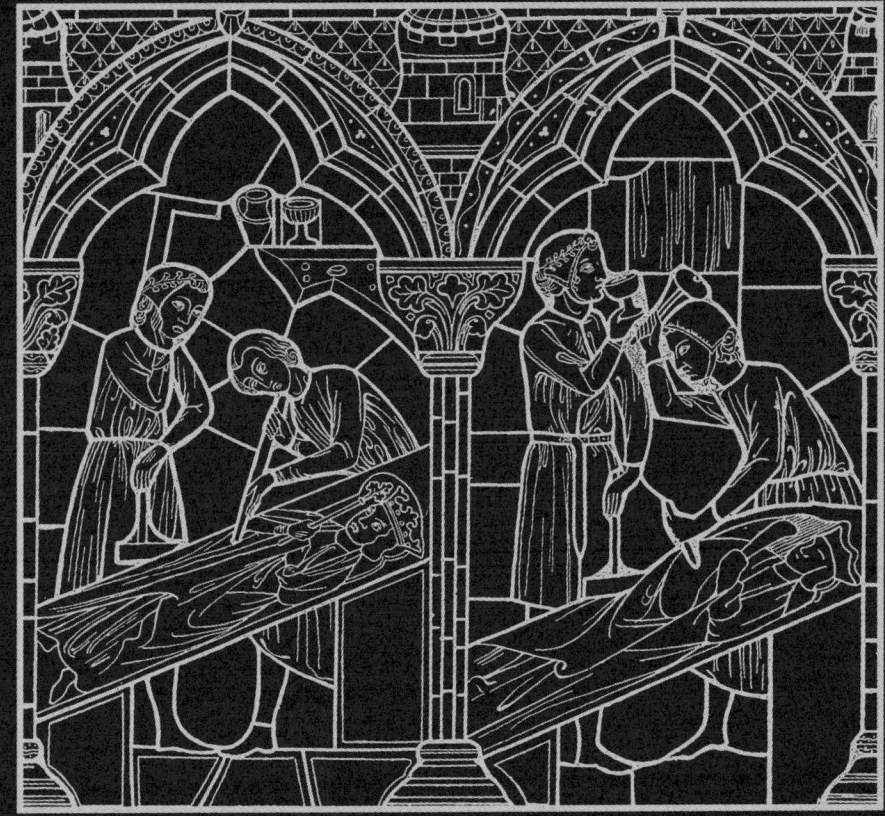

Finishing Touches

This detail from a fifteenth-century illustration of the construction of the Temple of Solomon shows the kneeling figure of a sculptor working on the nearly completed statue of a king. Using both hands to grasp a tool, apparently a file or rasp, the sculptor completes the piece by removing any remaining rough areas.

Such a theory has been mooted for the statuary of Wells Cathedral west front, on the grounds that the statues vary considerably in size: some are confined tightly within the niches, whereas others have fallen short and have consequently had to be raised on pedestals. However, given that the sculptors must have been instructed on the required dimensions of the images, the error might equally have occurred if the statues had been made on site. The Wells sculptures reflect the original sizes of the blocks from which they were carved; doubtless dimensions varied from block to block, and any shortfall in the height of the statues resulted from the limitations of the raw material rather than the location of the sculptors' workshops.

Some sculptures were made on a grand enough scale to render creation from a single block of stone impractical, in which case it was made in several portions and then pieced together when the work was erected in its intended position. One example is the statue of Gabriel from the Annunciation scene that formerly adorned the front of Westminster Abbey chapter house. The wings were evidently carved independently of the figure and attached to it with mortise and tenon joints. Many of the fifteenth-century statues from the upper tier of the west-front screen at Exeter Cathedral were each carved from two blocks of stone, and a resin-based adhesive applied to the joint. As in the case of the Gabriel statue, there was probably a practical reason for this, which was related to the difficulties of handling large and heavy blocks of stone.

The assembly of sculptures made from more than one block was not always so well coordinated. The spandrels of the triforium arcade in the Angel Choir of 1256–80 at Lincoln Cathedral, for instance, incorporate sculptured panels depicting angels. In two cases, the wings of the angels, which are stretched over two separate stones, fit together badly, and this illustrates that the two processes were undertaken separately. Similarly, at Exeter Cathedral, angel carvings in the spandrels of the central doorway of the west front have evidently been trimmed after completion to fit them into a restricted space.

While most sculpture was finished prior to being placed in position, there were occasions when carving must have been carried out in situ. One example is the composition of fourteenth-century figure sculpture that was carved between the orders of the twelfth-century chapter house entrance of Haughmond Abbey in Shropshire. However, such cases are rare and are confined to the remodeling of earlier works.

Voussoir Construction

While the sculptural highlights of a cathedral's great ceremonial portals were the large statues that lined their sides, little was left uncarved. The voussoirs making up the archivolts of the structure were often embellished with little figure sculptures. This was the case in the south portal of Amiens Cathedral (right), which dates from the first half of the thirteenth century. Until the fifteenth century, such sculptural designs were entirely integrated with the voussoirs so that it would have been necessary to employ a highly skilled artisan endowed with artistic talents to cut each and every stone. In the late Middle Ages, ways were found to make sculptural decoration available more cheaply. The fifteenth-century portals of the Collegiate Church of Notre-Dame at Semur-en-Auxois in Burgundy display an example of this economizing process. Here, a different technique is displayed, in which the sculptured voussoir is broken down into three different types of component, which exhibit different degrees of sculptural artistry. Plain molded voussoirs alternate with sculptured voussoirs, which act as bases/canopies for independently manufactured figure sculptures. These figures are set within the niches formed by the voussoirs, where they are secured by hooks. This system divided the work into a series of graded tasks and allowed an economical division of labor.

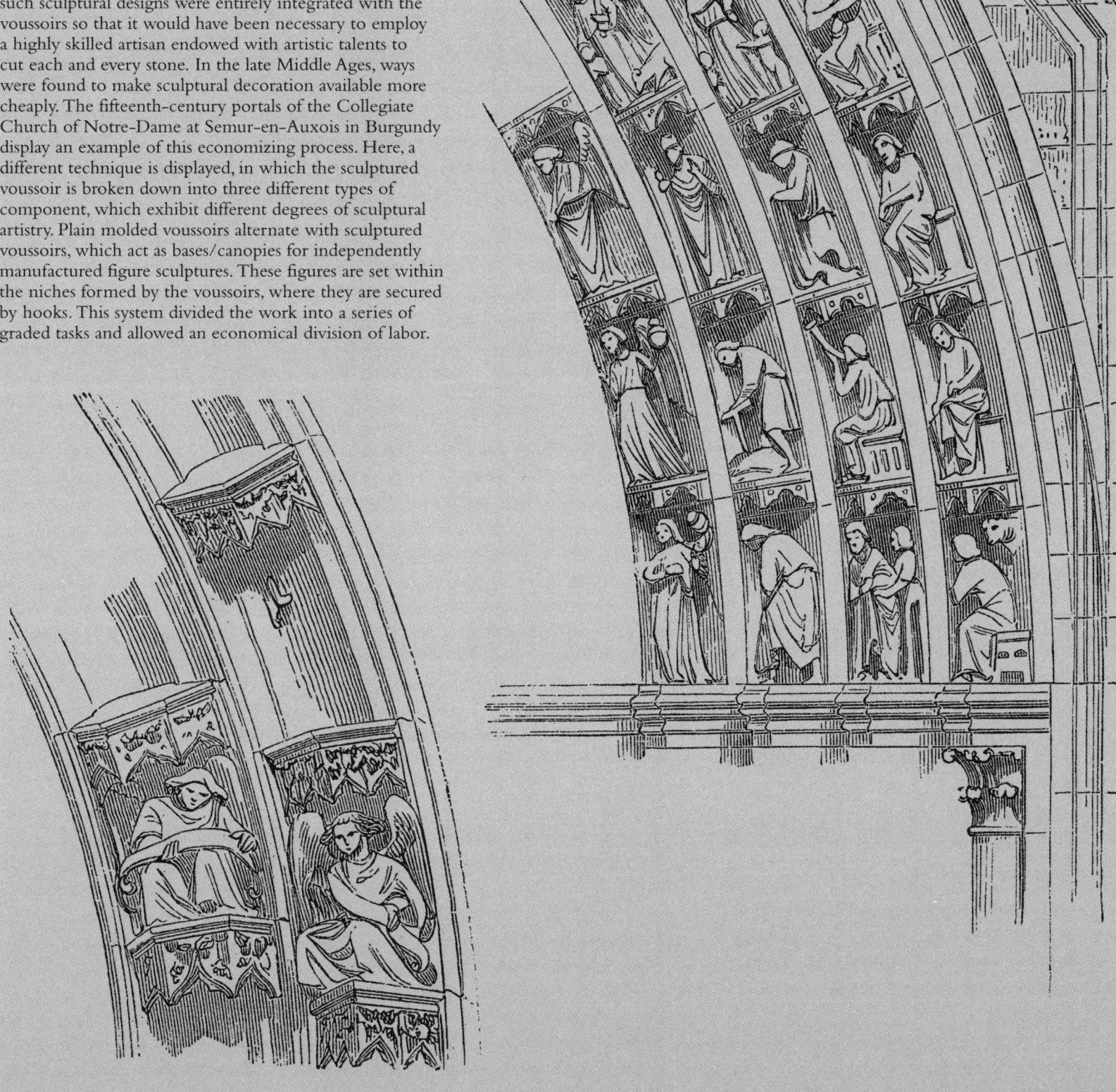

In addition to being made in two sections, the statues of the Exeter west front were also hollowed out at the back—not an uncommon practice for figures destined for niches, because they would have been visible only from the front. Hollowing reduced the weight of a piece and facilitated handling and lifting. Although machinery might be utilized in lifting the statuary into position, at Exeter and elsewhere the restrictions imposed by the niches would have necessitated some manual handling, so weight was a crucial issue.

As far as individual figure sculptures were concerned, positioning was not a complicated process, but if a work formed part of the structural fabric of a building or was of an architectural nature, and, therefore, made up of numerous components, complications might ensue. One way of ensuring that the individual pieces of a sculptural design were set in their correct places was to inscribe them and their corresponding positions on the building with a series of distinguishing marks. In their simplest form, such fitting or position marks comprised a sequence of numerals, suitable for denoting which statue was to occupy which niche. More involved designs, however, required more complex systems of identification.

An interesting program of marking was used by the masons who worked on the west front of Reims Cathedral, where the sculptured surrounds of the three doorways formed a single decorative design. Each stone was designated with a unique combination of marks to denote its allotted place in the design. Thus, the jamb stones of the central doorway were identified either by a crescent (left-hand side), or by an inverted T (right-hand side); in addition, the stones on each side were numbered to indicate their relative positions. These numbers are in the form of circles, each divided by a cross, which vary in quantity according to their position in the design. Like the jamb stones, the voussoirs are numbered to show their position in the design. Similar systems are used for the central- and right-hand doorways, although the marks are different.

Many, if not most, sculptures were painted. The surface of the stone was primed with gesso, a very fine plaster manufactured from ground gypsum, which provided a smooth surface on which to apply the paint. Medieval painted decoration seldom survives, although archaeological analysis at Exeter, Amiens, and other cathedrals has discovered traces of the medieval colors that have allowed for reconstructions to be made. Such restorations can give vivid impressions of the enhanced effect painting must have had.

Hollowed-Out Sculpture

(Below) This life-size statue of the Virgin and Christ of 1340–50 from the Île-de-France is made of limestone and stands to 5 feet 8 inches (1.73 m) in height. Because the statue was only intended to be seen from the front, no attempt has been made to finish the back. Indeed, the back of the figure has been hollowed out to reduce its weight and thereby facilitate the process of transport to its intended position. Such matters of economy and practicality had to be taken into consideration.

CRESCENT
This positioning mark of a crescent and four lines is situated behind the statue of Joseph on the left-hand (north) side of the central portal as indicated in the main drawing.

OTHER POSITIONING MARKS

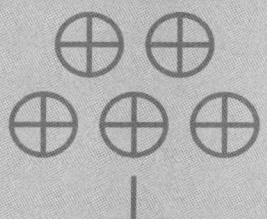

INVERTED T
The jamb stones of the central doorway of Reims Cathedral were marked with an inverted T on the right-hand (south) side. The crossed circles indicate the position number.

Positioning Marks

Illustrated above is part of the central portal of Reims Cathedral, which dates from the mid-thirteenth century, and which, like many other French cathedrals, incorporates a major design of sculpture, including a substantial collection of life-size figures. In a complicated arrangement such as this, in which each piece of sculpture had a specific place allotted to it, it was important to ensure that the assembly was carried out correctly. The system adopted here was to inscribe the masonry with a sequence of marks that indicated the positions of the different pieces.

ARROWHEAD
A positioning mark of an arrowhead and three lines appear behind the statue of the smiling angel on the right-hand (south) side of the central portal.

urnishing
the House
of God

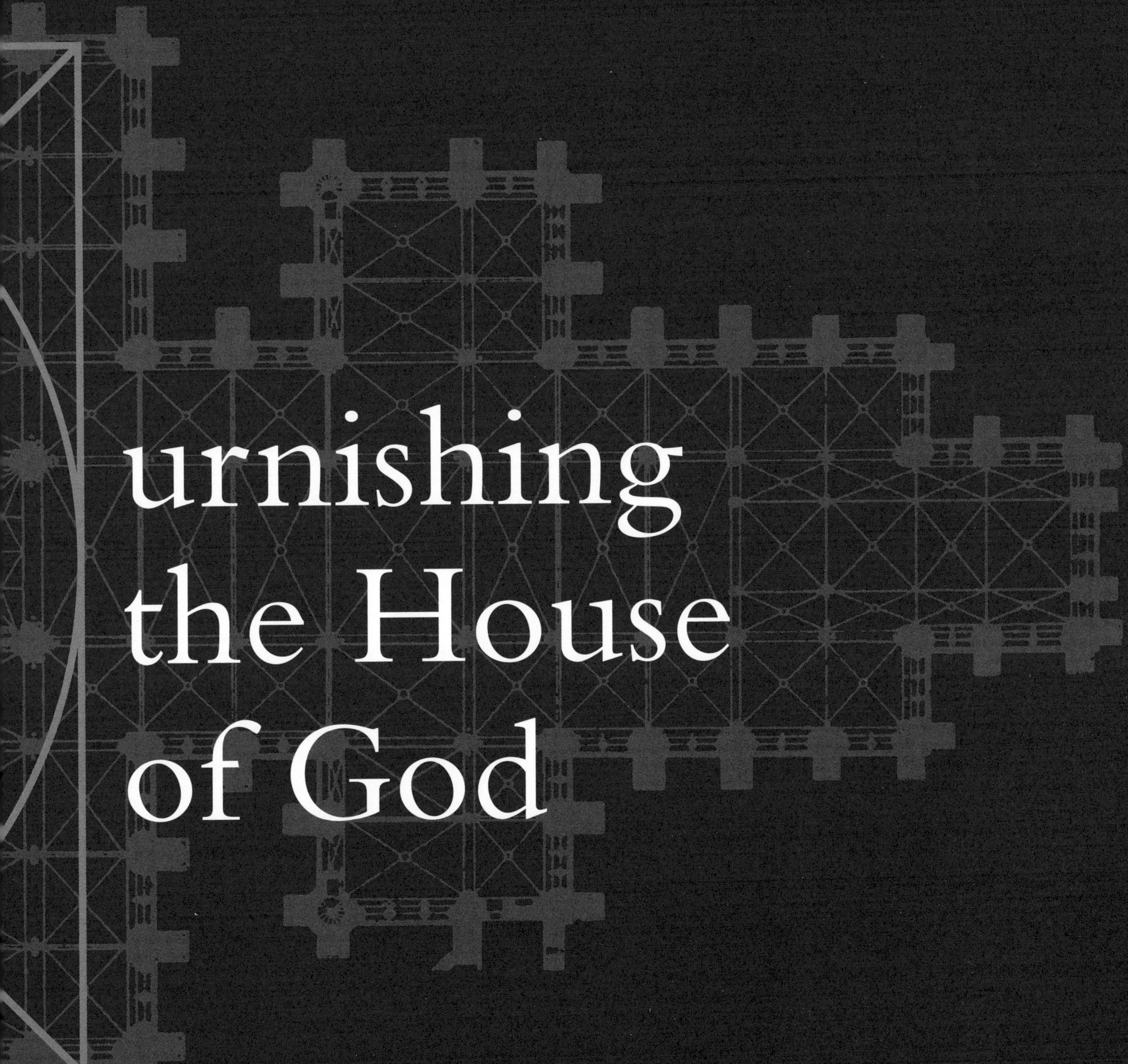

FURNISHING THE HOUSE OF GOD

Introduction

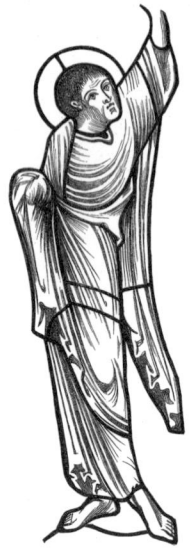

AS THE BUILDING NEARED COMPLETION, specialty craftsmen would be engaged to complete the fixtures and fittings, often setting up their workshops and manufactories in close proximity to the site. Tilers were required to design, manufacture, and lay the ceramic pavements that provided durable, safe, and decorative surfaces. Carpenters were needed to make the choir stalls and screens, glaziers to supply and fit the stained-glass panels for the windows, and smiths to forge decorative ironwork for gates and rails. Sculptors in both wood and stone were just as essential to the enrichment of a cathedral's interior as they were to the ornamentation of the exterior. Like the masons, the practitioners of these crafts combined functionality with decorative intent, and there is no doubt that the furbishment of a cathedral's interior added greatly to the aesthetic effect. The wear and tear of centuries mean that it is no longer possible to fully appreciate the extent to which the finishing processes affected the visual impact of the cathedral, but it is clear from Abbot Suger's writing that, for some churchmen, costly adornment was a highly desirable objective, enhancing the sense of awe and reverence and heightening the religious experience.

One of the most significant losses from most medieval churches is their use of color, because painted decoration was very widely used, and its disappearance over time has radically altered the internal appearance of the majority of cathedrals. Walls were universally painted, often with whitewash, which must have produced a very bright background, in contrast to the largely plain stone walls of today, and this would have acted as an effective screen onto which the colored rays of light emanating from the stained-glass windows might be projected. It was a common practice to augment such washes by painting red lines over them to imitate masonry blocks, an effect that can be seen at Salisbury Cathedral, where elements of the original pattern survive, in part restored. At Salisbury, both walls and vault were painted to suggest ashlar, but the design was augmented by foliage motifs, and the choir vaults by medallions containing figures of Christ, the evangelists, the apostles, and the prophets. As in other trades, a hierarchy of craftsmen was no doubt employed in the painting. They executed the contributory aspects of the design according to the degree of skill that they demanded. As we have seen (page 140), painted decoration might also be employed on sculpture to bring the iconography into vivid focus, but, equally, fixtures and fittings, including screens, might be painted with imagery that augmented the more three-dimensional displays.

Introduction

In furnishing their interiors, the great churches both drew on and stimulated the development of industry, seeking and providing unrivaled opportunities to showcase the best that the latest advances in industry and craftsmanship had to offer. Much of the innovation in the manufacture of artifacts associated with medieval buildings occurred in France, the powerhouse of Gothic cathedral building. The main centers for the production of colored glass, for example, were Normandy, Lorraine, and Burgundy, Normandy glass being considered superior to the others. England also had centers of glass production, most importantly in the southeast (the Weald) and the Midlands (Staffordshire), but in both centers only white glass was made, so that all colored glass had to be imported, and even Continental white glass was sometimes preferred to its English equivalent. For this reason, the best collection of twelfth-century stained glass in England, that at Canterbury Cathedral, is sometimes considered as part of the sequence of stained-glass designs that adorned the French sites of St. Denis, Notre-Dame de Paris, and Chartres.

The three major elements needed for the manufacture of glass were sand and plant ash (preferably beech), which were the principal ingredients, and fireclay, which was used for making the glass pots, or crucibles. The industry was carried out in wooded areas to maintain a supply of ash, but these had to be judiciously located to allow access to the other materials. Different colors of glass were obtained by adding particular metallic oxides, including cobalt (blue), copper (green), iron (red), and manganese (purple). The molten material was then blown and sheets of glass formed. Manufacture, then, was carried out away from the cathedral sites, and the different colored glass sheets would have been supplied to the glaziers. It was they who carried out the artistic processes required to convert the sheets into window panels, either in their permanent workshops or in temporary premises at the cathedral sites.

Ceramic floor tiles, on the other hand, could be made locally and prepared on site, always provided that suitable clay was available. Medieval tile kilns have been excavated at a number of sites, including the Royal Clarendon Palace in Wiltshire (thirteenth century) Repton Priory in Derbyshire (fourteenth century), and at Norton Priory in Cheshire (fourteenth century). All these examples had two furnace chambers, each provided with a stoke hole through which the kindling would have been fed. These chambers would have been arched over and firing chambers built on top. The tiles would have been stacked in the firing chamber and covered with a temporary roof.

FURNISHING THE HOUSE OF GOD

Tile Pavements

Tiles were formed on a flat, sanded work surface (probably a board) by cramming the clay into bottomless wooden molds, and then trimming the excess material from the top. Once the tiles had been shaped, the edges might be trimmed with a knife to produce a bevel, or chamfer, slanting inward from top to bottom. When the finished tiles finally came to be laid on a mortar bed to form a pavement, this bevel would produce a space between them, invisible from above, into which the mortar would seep, so giving the pavement greater adhesion. Having been formed, the tiles were allowed to dry, and, before being fired, were painted with a lead glaze. Different additives produced different color effects, but if a light color was required, the tile was painted with a white slip (a thin clay-and-water mix) before the application of the glaze. When dried, the tiles were stacked on edge in a wood-burning kiln and then covered with a temporary roof. The kilns were fired, and the temperature was raised gradually to ca. 1,830°F (1,000°C), a process that lasted nearly a week.

A popular type of floor tile originating in France and much used in early Gothic great churches was the mosaic tile, in which interlocking tiles of different geometric shapes were laid in alternate colors to produce a pattern. This type of pavement may have taken its inspiration from the works of the Italian makers of stone pavements in *opus sectile*, in which high-quality colored stones, such as marble and porphyry, were cut to shape to fit into a pattern. The leading example of this type of floor north of the Alps is the one laid down by Italian craftsmen in front of the high altar of Westminster Abbey in 1268 (see page 139). Instead of being formed in molds, mosaic tiles were cut from the wet clay using metal templates. The technique was brought to England in ca. 1200 by peripatetic French craftsmen, who moved from building site to building site, setting up temporary tileries on the spot. Vast floor areas were tiled in this manner in the Cistercian abbeys of Yorkshire (Byland, Fountains, Meaux, and Rievaulx) during the first half of the thirteenth century, when the mosaic floor was the predominant form of tile pavement. Although some large pavements with highly complex patterns were made from mosaic tiles, production was probably labor intensive and the room for error considerable, and this was no doubt reflected in the cost.

St. Denis Mosaic Tiling

The floor of the twelfth-century Chapel of St. Cucuphas, in the chevet of the Abbey of St. Denis, is covered with a mosaic tile pavement laid out in a number of parallel strips, aligned with the orientation of the chapel and separated by lines of plain tiles. Each of the strips contains a different pattern so that there is no particular coherence in the design, although it does showcase the different effects that could be achieved using this technique.

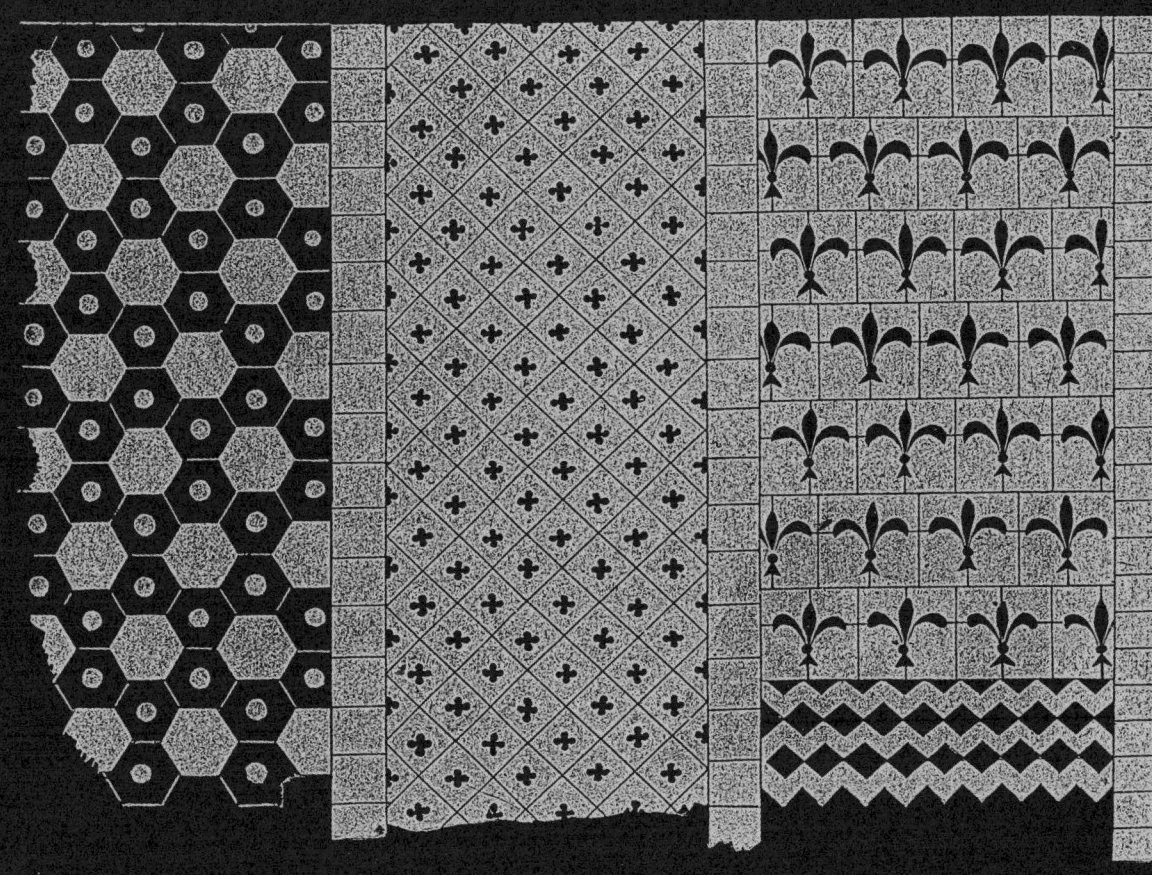

Tile Construction

This detail of the different types of the St. Cucuphas chapel floor tiles shows how the individual elements were shaped and how they fitted together. The structural character of the pavement resembles that of a regularly shaped jigsaw puzzle.

A quite different concept lay behind another type of decorative floor tile. This was the relief tile, the name describing the nature of the pattern, which was raised on the surface. Although relief tiles were more ancient in origin, having been in use by the eleventh century, they continued to be employed throughout the medieval period. A related type was the counter-relief tile, in which the pattern was sunken instead of raised, but the technique used in the manufacture of the two kinds was the same in that they were impressed with wooden stamps.

It was probably the counter-relief tile that provided the inspiration for another category of floor tile, known as the encaustic tile. This was developed in France in the late twelfth century, and, from the mid-thirteenth century, overtook mosaic tiling in popularity, becoming the most sought-after type. The first part of the manufacturing process followed that of the counter-relief tile. Thus, after the tile molds had been filled in the normal manner, a pattern was impressed on the upper surface with a wooden stamp, leaving an indentation. When the tiles had dried, these impressions were filled with white clay, which was also allowed to dry before glazing and firing.

Some encaustic tiles accommodated discrete patterns, while others formed part of a larger pattern. All, however, had a designated place within the overall floor plan. The manufacturing advantage of the encaustic tile over the mosaic tile was that the pattern was integral to the tile, and so there was no necessity for tiles of different shapes, unless they formed part of a circular design. Also, from an aesthetic viewpoint, designs could be more complicated and finely detailed, and, therefore, more interesting, than the geometric patterns to which mosaic-tile floors were confined.

It was in England that encaustic tiles reached the height of their development as an art form. Their progress was greatly assisted by Henry III, who had numerous such pavements made, both for his own residences and religious houses under his patronage. At Clarendon Palace, in Wiltshire, the pavement of the King's Chapel of 1240–44 had a circular pattern made up of tiles of various shapes and sizes. As might be expected, it is an exclusive custom-made design. The same is true of the chapter house pavement at Westminster Abbey, which was laid down in the 1250s and which is one of the best two-color tile floors to have survived. Here, however, despite the building being octagonal, the tiles are mostly square and are laid in long parallel strips.

Four-Tile Pattern

(Below) Although many encaustic tiles contained a complete motif or pattern, others were designed to make up part of a larger design. Four-tile patterns were common, like this thirteenth-century example from one of the chapels of Laon Cathedral. The practice permitted variations in the scale of subjects while adhering to a tile of standard size, thereby gaining manufacturing and assembly advantages.

Circular Patterns

In this late twelfth-century encaustic tile pavement in the Abbey Church of St. Pierre-sur-Dives near Caen in Normandy, the two-color pattern is yellow on black/brown. The dark coloring has been obtained by covering the red clay of which the body of the tiles are made with a fine layer of black clay. The pavement is made in a circular pattern so that the tiles are of several different sizes. Although each tile bears a discrete design, so that the pavement was more straightforward to assemble than a mosaic pavement, circular patterns like these must, nevertheless, have been more complicated to produce than floors made of standard square tiles.

FURNISHING THE HOUSE OF GOD

Altars & Reredos

The spiritual heart of a cathedral was the sanctuary, or presbytery, which housed the high altar. The altar itself was simply a table, but inevitably it became the focal point of an elaborate, sometimes theatrical, setting. Some were housed beneath a freestanding canopy known as a ciborium or baldachin. A small screen, or retable, decorated with images and often made in wood, might be set up on the back of the altar. A more ambitious version of this was the reredos, a screen of an architectural nature, situated behind the altar and serving as a frame for sculpture, creating an imposing background for the celebration of Mass. Other features within the sanctuary, often built into the fabric of the church, were the piscina, or basin, in which the chalice was washed after Mass; the sedilia, the seats provided for the officiating priests; and, occasionally, an Easter sepulchre, used in the Easter ritual.

PARIS ALTAR
Based on a seventeenth-century drawing, this is Viollet le Duc's reconstruction drawing of the high altar of Notre-Dame de Paris, which dated from the late thirteenth or early fourteenth centuries. The simple altar was fitted with a retable and flanked by four copper columns surmounted by statues of angels bearing the instruments of the Passion. Behind the altar, and dominating the whole arrangement, was a lofty canopied structure housing the reliquary of St. Marcel, a former bishop of Paris.

ALTAR AT GERONA
The high altar of Gerona Cathedral is notable for its fourteenth-century retable and baldachin. Both are made of wood and covered with silver plate, and there is, in addition, a good deal of enamel work. The retable has three tiers of niches containing religious imagery, including saints and episodes from the lives of the Virgin and Jesus. Rising from the top of the retable are three figures, including a Madonna (center) standing under canopies. The baldachin is supported on four shafts with dark marble bases, and the canopy, which is in the form of a low quadripartite vault, is a representation of heaven, with the Coronation of the Virgin in the center.

WINCHESTER REREDOS

(Left) The late fifteenth-century reredos of Winchester Cathedral is an immense structure that towers over the high altar and sanctuary and that forms a dramatic setting for the liturgical proceedings; its great height is symptomatic of late medieval reredos design. This illustration, made before the nineteenth-century restoration, shows that the screen contains three tiers of canopied niches (which would have been filled with sculpture) and rises to a traceried stone cresting. In the center of the screen, directly above the high altar and forming the centerpiece of the design, is a large cross, and above it, at cresting level, an openwork traceried canopy from which the pyx (the receptacle containing the Host) would have been suspended. There are two doorways in the screen, leading to a space behind the altar known as the feretory, a repository for holy relics.

LINCOLN EASTER SEPULCHRE

(Above) The Easter sepulchre was a representation of Christ's tomb. It contained an opening into which the Host (the consecrated bread symbolizing Christ's body) was placed on Good Friday and from which it was removed on Easter Day amid great rejoicing. Most Easter sepulchres were temporary structures, and this example of ca. 1300, on the north side of the sanctuary in Lincoln Cathedral, has survived because the opportunity was taken to create a monumental feature as a permanent part of the cathedral fabric. Only the three niches to the right (east) comprise the Easter sepulchre; the western half of the monument symbolizes the tomb of Bishop Remigius, who built the Norman cathedral. Carved in relief below the three niches of the Easter sepulchre are the images of three sleeping soldiers, the watchers who became "as dead men" when the angel of the Lord rolled away the stone from the entrance to Christ's tomb at the Resurrection.

Screens

The medieval great church was divided into sections by a whole number of screens of both wood and stone. The choir was entirely enclosed from the rest of the church, and subsidiary chapels might be partitioned from the greater building. The main division in the length of a great church was between nave and choir, a separation that was effected by the construction of a double stone, or occasionally wooden, screen known as a pulpitum, which delineated the western end of the liturgical choir, and against which the returns of the choir stalls might be built. The pulpitum had a central entrance into the choir, flanked by a pair of altars toward the west. There was a gallery above, approached by a staircase, which accommodated the organ and from which readings were made.

The pulpitum was both a physical and symbolic barrier, forming the gateway to the religious hub of the cathedral, and it was often treated with elaborate designs of sculpture. These were sometimes in relief, but often the pulpitum was constructed with a series of niches in which to display figure sculpture, as at Lincoln and Salisbury cathedrals, although in both these cases the sculpture itself no longer exists. The sculptured decoration of a pulpitum might be religious in nature, although by the fifteenth century it was possible to house such overtly political imagery as that in the screen at York Minster, which proclaims the legitimacy of the House of Lancaster in its portrayal of England's kings from William I to Henry VI.

While York is a rarity in retaining its pulpitum complete with sculpture, the Lincoln screen, which dates from ca. 1330, is complete apart from having lost its freestanding sculptures. It has four niches on each side of the central gateway. There are no bare surfaces, the whole structure being sumptuously carved with a checkerboard pattern of fleurons (carved flowers). Such overall treatment is reflected in another fourteenth-century Lincoln screen—that which divides part of the southeast transept from the south choir aisle. This screen was made of a single thickness of ashlar blocks held together by iron clamps.

In monastic houses, where the area in front of the pulpitum was used by the monks, the length of the church was also interrupted by a rood screen, usually of wood, situated a bay to the west of the pulpitum. It supported a large wooden cross and had a nave altar placed in the center of its western face. In nonmonastic cathedrals, however, where there was no separate rood screen, the pulpitum sometimes carried a cross.

Paris Pulpitum

(Above) The pulpitum of Notre-Dame de Paris (no longer extant) was probably built ca. 1250–60 between the eastern piers of the crossing. It was a stone screen, approximately 16 feet 6 inches (5 m) high with scenes of the Passion carved in relief. The central entrance had a gabled canopy, above which rose a large crucifix. To the left and right of the entrance was an altar, and a pair of stair turrets at the two ends led to the gallery.

Zamora Screen

In this late fifteenth-century screen at the west end of the *coro* (choir) of Zamora Cathedral in western Spain, the central entrance is blocked, and the nave altar has been placed in front of it. On the other side of the screen, this central position is occupied by the bishop's throne—part of the integral seating arrangements in the *coro*—the canopy of which can be seen rising above the screen. Instead of the usual central entrance, the screen has two side entrances.

FURNISHING THE HOUSE OF GOD

Bishops' Thrones & Choir Stalls

The liturgical choir was furnished with wooden stalls for the accommodation of the clergy who sang the offices. It was in the construction of the choir stalls, which were often highly ornate works of art, that the medieval woodworker was able to rival the achievements of his masonic counterpart. Choir stalls were arranged hierarchically from east to west, and it was also customary to provide a more distinguished seat, or throne, for the bishop, also situated within the choir; in England, it was normally at the east end on the south side. Such features were the work of some of the finest craftsmen of their time.

EXETER BISHOP'S THRONE
(Left) Built for Bishop Stapledon in 1316–17, the bishop's throne of Exeter Cathedral is the earliest wooden bishop's throne to survive in England and the most impressive, its canopy rising to a height of nearly 60 feet (18 m). The principal craftsman was the master carpenter, Robert Galmeton, whose surname suggests a local origin (probably Galmpton near Torbay, approximately 20 miles/32 km south of Exeter). Galmeton was principal carpenter at the cathedral between 1313 and 1322 and would have been assisted by a team of workers in wood. The throne is unparalleled in the ambitiousness of its scale and is one of the most significant pieces of medieval church furniture to have survived. It was probably designed by the master mason Thomas of Witney, who gave advice in the selection of the wood for the throne in 1313, when he was master mason of Winchester Cathedral, taking up the position of principal mason at Exeter in 1316.

DURHAM BISHOP'S THRONE
(Right) The bishop's throne of Durham Cathedral is an elaborate construction of architectural character made for Bishop Thomas Hatfield between 1362, when the monks gave their consent to its erection in the cathedral, and 1381, when Hatfield died and was buried in the tomb that forms the base of the monument. Built within one of the arches of the choir arcade, Hatfield's tomb is set beneath a vault that carries the platform on which the throne is constructed. The throne itself forms the centerpiece of an openwork stone screen that fills the upper part of the arch. The name of the master craftsman responsible for the design is unknown, but it is probable that the Lady chapel of York Minster (1361–73) was his principal source, and that he had trained or worked in Yorkshire.

ELY STALLS

(Right) The choir stalls of Ely Cathedral were made between 1336 and 1348 and belong to the construction work that followed upon the collapse of the central tower in 1322 and the construction of the lantern (see page 112). The king's master carpenter, William Hurley, designed the timberwork of the lantern, and it is probable that the design of the stalls is also to be attributed to him. The stalls have tall canopies with cornice above and then canopied niches (containing nineteenth-century sculptures) surmounted by spirelets and interspersed by pinnacles. The woodwork is of a highly ornate character.

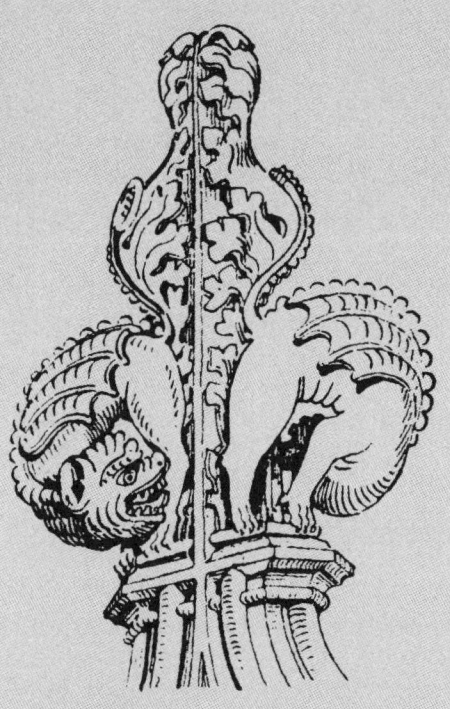

POPPY HEAD

Bench and desk ends were usually surmounted by an enriched finial in the shape of a fleur-de-lys, known as a poppy head. These prominent terminals gave the medieval sculptor an opportunity to show off his skill, and they are usually carved with foliage and other details. In this early fourteenth-century example from the Winchester stalls, a pair of dragons has been carved into the shapes of the two lower lobes of the finial.

WINCHESTER STALLS

(Above) Winchester Cathedral houses a set of choir stalls of European significance. Begun in 1308, they were made by the carpenter William Lyngwode of Blofield in Norfolk, a town some 5 miles (8 km) east of Norwich. Interestingly, letters written by the Bishop of Winchester to his counterpart in Norwich, in which he requested that Lyngwode be excused the duty of attending Blofield manorial court, indicate that the master carpenter was resident in Norfolk over the period that the stalls were being made. The Winchester stalls are arranged in pairs under traceried arches with richly carved spandrels surmounted by triangular crocketed canopies.

FURNISHING THE HOUSE OF GOD

Misericords

Seating in medieval cathedral choir stalls was not fixed but comprised individual hinged seats, somewhat in the fashion of wooden theater seating, that were tilted back against the stall when the choir stood to sing the offices. The clever part of the design was that the underside incorporated a bracket, or misericord, so that, when the seat was in the upright position it formed a ledge or small seat. The purpose of this humane facility was to allow the less robust members of the choir some relief from the long bouts of standing to which the long round of services might subject them, without the ignominy of sitting down. The misericord (meaning "act of mercy") became an object of the sculptor's attention, and the brackets were carved with scenes depicting religious, moralistic, mythological, humorous, and satirical themes. The standard arrangement was for the misericord to be carved with the principal scene, with smaller supporting scenes filling the spaces on each side.

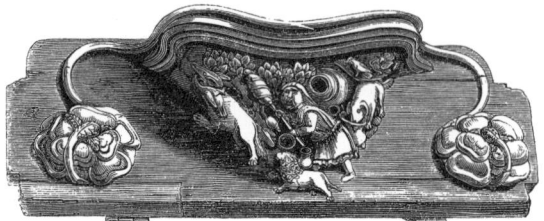

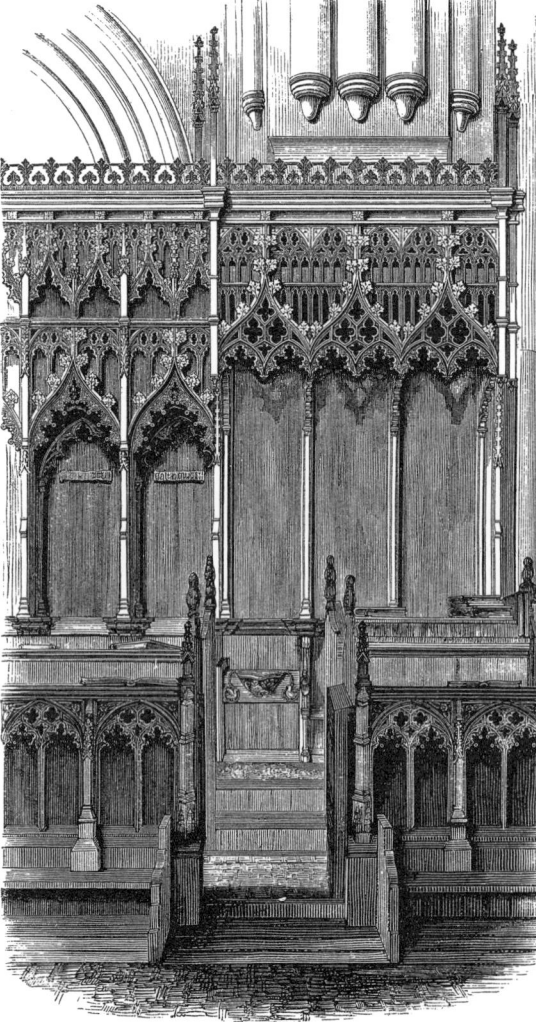

NORWICH CATHEDRAL
Norwich Cathedral choir was refitted with stalls ca. 1420, but a fire in 1463 destroyed a large number so that only thirty-two survive. Additional stalls were made ca. 1480, although another fire, in 1509, caused further destruction, prompting the introduction of several new ones ca. 1515. The existing stalls are, therefore, of these three different dates. The illustration shows the junction of the two earlier phases (those of 1420 to the left). Both are in an intricately carved perpendicular style with ogee-arched canopies containing lierne vaults. The stalls retain a collection of fifteenth- and sixteenth-century misericords, in addition to some later ones, which display a broad range of subjects.

Three misericords from Norwich are shown here (far left). The top one shows a wrestling bout in progress, in which the two bare-legged wrestlers try to gain a purchase on one another while their seconds hover in the background. The center drawing, which represents the vice of lechery, shows a man riding a hart. His left hand holds onto his mount's antler, while he holds a hare in the other. The supporters are a pair of Blemmyae, legendry beings without heads, whose faces appear on their breasts; they both carry swords. The third misericord, which depicts sloth, presents a very animated scene: a fox on the left, with a fowl in his mouth, is being chased by a dog and a woman brandishing a distaff. On the right, a pig takes advantage of the chaos by helping itself from an upset cauldron. The scene echoes an episode from "The Nonne Preestes Tale," one of Chaucer's Canterbury Tales *of the 1380s, in which a fox runs off with the cock, Chauntecleer, and is pursued by the whole household, including the dogs and the widow "Malkin, with a distaff in hir hand," and it may have been this story that the sculptor had in mind.*

BEVERLEY MINSTER

(Below and below right) The stalls of Beverley Minster choir date from ca. 1520, the desks displaying highly ornate ends, including blind tracery and poppy heads. The sculptor of this misericord in Beverley Cathedral has used the concluding episode from the romance of Reynard the Fox, in which the arch criminal, Reynard, is condemned to death. In this particular interpretation of the tale, he is being hanged by a gaggle of geese, who are, of course, some of his chief victims. In the left-hand scene, he is shown creeping up on two sleeping geese, and on right the noose is being released from his prostrate form by an ape, possibly hinting at one version of the story in which Reynard escapes punishment.

HENRY VII'S CHAPEL

(Above and right) The construction of Henry VII's Chapel at the east end of Westminster Abbey at the beginning of the sixteenth century was one of the last major medieval additions to an English great church. The stalls, which date from ca. 1520, are equipped with misericords as usual, and the example given here is the well-known biblical story of the Judgment of Solomon. King Solomon is called upon to preside in a dispute between two women who have given birth, one to a stillborn child and the other to a healthy child. Solomon must judge which is the mother of the healthy child. He sits on a throne beneath a baldachin. Before him is the dead child, to each side one of the mothers, and to the left-hand side a man-at-arms with a drawn sword holding the live child by the ankle.

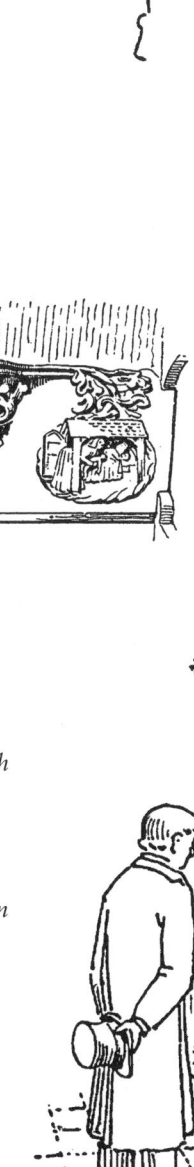

FURNISHING THE HOUSE OF GOD

Decorative Ironwork

Iron was much in use at a major building site, and the blacksmith was a constant presence. Not only did he manufacture construction materials—including armature, clamps, tie bars, nails, and door furniture—he also made tools and other iron building equipment and carried out maintenance on them. In addition to its practical use in construction, iron was also used as an artistic medium to create decorative features within a cathedral, including gates, grilles, railings, and door hinges.

Ornamental ironwork was being used to embellish cathedrals at least from the early twelfth century. One of the earliest examples of a decorative iron screen in northern Europe is the Pilgrim's Gate at the entrance to the south choir aisle of Winchester Cathedral. This wrought-iron screen, which probably dates from the early to mid-twelfth century, has a vertically orientated design filled with regularly disposed scrolls with leaf- or flowerlike terminations also composed of scrolls. Scrolls were standard elements of medieval ornamental wrought ironwork and would have been formed on a mandrel (a conical block of iron) or a scrolling iron, a spiraled iron pattern of the requisite shape, around which the scroll could be formed with comparative ease.

During the thirteenth century, stamped details were developed using steel or hardened iron dies. An early example, dating from the 1240s, is at Notre-Dame de Paris, where the large and wildly extravagant hinges of the western doors feature die-stamped work. In England, the earliest example, which also dates from the 1240s, is the metalwork of the original western door of St. George's Chapel at Windsor Castle, which was made for Henry III's chapel in ca. 1243–45. The hinge work is stamped with the name of the master craftsman who made it: "GILBERTVS," possibly Gilbert de Bonnington, who became the king's moneyer in Canterbury in 1248 and who is likely to have been a goldsmith by training.

The decorative iron grille of 1292–93 over the tomb of King Edward I's queen, Eleanor, in Westminster Abbey, was made by the master smith Thomas of Leighton for the sum of £12 plus carriage (now roughly the equivalent of £6,400, or $10,200). Thomas of Leighton probably came from Leighton Buzzard in Bedfordshire, some 35 miles (56 km) from London. Interestingly, the door of the church of All Saints in Leighton Buzzard bears elaborately scrolled thirteenth-century hinges, which are probably the work of Master Thomas. The scrolling decoration of the Eleanor grille is secured to the front of the main framework instead of being an integral part of the structure.

Ornamental Ironwork

(Below) A fragment of ornamental ironwork from the Abbey of St. Denis, which probably dates from the late twelfth century. This attractive but rather staid design comprises a regular pattern of scrolls embellished with grapes, flowers, and leaves and contrasts with the florid and more naturalistic designs of the thirteenth century.

Die-Stamped Ironwork

(Above) Part of a grille from the Abbey of St. Denis, recorded by Viollet le Duc in the nineteenth century, is an example of thirteenth-century, die-stamped ironwork, in which the scrolled decoration has been riveted to the plain frame. The most remarkable aspect of this artifact, however, is that the design is almost identical to that of the Eleanor grille in Westminster Abbey made by Thomas of Leighton (see opposite). The process by which this came about is unknown, but one must have influenced the other, either because the same master smith was responsible for both, which seems unlikely, or because the drawings of one were available to the maker of the other.

Stained Glass

The process of designing a stained-glass window began with the patron. Most designs, which, like those rendered in sculpture, were predominantly of a religious nature, would have been devised by clerics. The patron's requirements might be enshrined in a drawing, which would serve as the basis for the glazier's final design. This would, of course, depend upon the window-tracery pattern, and, although the essence of the design could have been settled as soon as the master mason produced his drawings for the window tracery, it would not have been prudent to have begun cutting the glass until the window had been built and final measurements could be taken. In fact, there was often a hiatus between a window's construction and its glazing, during which the openings were temporarily filled with some other material.

In creating his pattern, a glazier would prepare a drawing, or cartoon, at full size, divided into sections to represent the shapes of the individual glass sheets that would constitute the picture. This would be carried out on a wooden board, or table, that had been whitened with chalk or limewash, although, from the fourteenth century onward, it is clear that some drawings were being made on parchment. The cartoon prepared, the glass could then be laid over it and the shape marked on it with chalk, preparatory to cutting the sheets to size. The initial cutting was done using a hot iron rod scored around the outlined pattern, and the final trimming was done with a grozing iron. Once it had been cut to shape, the glass would be painted with the details of the drawing—facial features, drapery folds, ornamental patterns, and inscriptions, for example. This was done with a brush using a black pigment, and the sheets were then fired in a furnace.

The edges of the finished sheets were framed with H-section strips of lead known as calmes. These were cut to the shape of the glass and soldered together to form panels of convenient size containing several panes of glass; the lead-frame panels were then transported to the site for assembly within the window. The stone window frames incorporated ironwork expressly for the purpose of holding the glass panels in place. This included vertical (stanchions) and horizontal (saddle bars) members, and there was also shaped gridwork (armature) that filled geometrical traceried windows in the twelfth and thirteenth centuries. The lead-frame panels were attached to this ironwork by means of wire strips or clips.

Amiens Armature

(Right) The integrated ironwork to which the glass panels were attached can be seen in this drawing of one of the transept clerestory windows in Amiens Cathedral. The lower lights incorporate vertical and horizontal bars, while the tracery above contains individually designed patterns of armature.

Cartoon to Glass

(Above) These two figures show the glazier's cartoon (right) that formed the pattern from which the glass sheets were shaped and the finished glass figure (left), onto which the details have been painted. The cartoon has the divisions of the glass sheets marked clearly in thick lines.

FURNISHING THE HOUSE OF GOD

Stained-Glass Design

At their most didactic, the subjects of stained glass, like the great designs of figure sculpture, were intended primarily for the instruction of an illiterate congregation. Biblical scenes and narratives, the lives of significant individuals, including saints and martyrs, and, above all, the life and passion of Jesus, were woven into a tapestry of translucent color that gave glimpses of the heavenly kingdom and the everlasting life that might be conferred upon a Christian. Such designs, however, were not a universal requirement, nor were they always desirable, due both to costliness and the quality of the light they produced. In addition, the Cistercians, who were known for their puritanical attitude to ornamentation in their churches and who had a good deal of influence on Gothic architecture, actually banned the use of colored glass and the depiction of figures, so other types of window glass were also in use, notably grisaille (see below).

GRISAILLE
In 1134, the Cistercians banned the use of colored glass, so a different kind of decorated window glass known as grisaille (a name derived from the French gris, or "gray") was developed to coexist alongside the richly decorated stained glass from the thirteenth century. Made mostly from white glass, grisaille was thinly painted with foliage and interlaced geometrical patterns and crosshatching and achieved considerable popularity in the thirteenth century. One of the most impressive examples of grisaille glazing is the Five Sisters Window, of ca. 1250, in the north transept at York Minster. The panels shown here are from Troyes Cathedral and date from the late thirteenth century.

ARCHITECTURAL DETAIL
(Right) The main subjects of stained-glass windows were augmented with peripheral detail and infill so that the entire space was taken up with decorated glass. As well as being used to glaze entire windows, grisaille was also used in the borders of colored windows, but other motifs also occur. Architectural details are common, including canopied niches, which sometimes appear over images of individuals. This drawing shows an early fourteenth-century architectural detail that appears in one of the chapel windows of Beauvais Cathedral.

MEDALLION WINDOWS

A popular way of dividing a moderately large area of glass in the twelfth and thirteenth centuries was to break it up with a number of panels, or medallions, each containing a scene. This was the technique used by Suger's glaziers at St. Denis and in many subsequent cathedrals. The central lancet of one of the apsidal chapels that make up the chevet of Bourges Cathedral, for instance, contains a window depicting the life of St. Stephen, the first Christian martyr. This drawing, which is copied from one of the panels of which the window is composed, shows a scene from the martyrdom of Stephen by stoning. Like this one, each of the twenty scenes in the window is set within a vesica, or medallion, and forms one of a pair, arranged one to each side of the center.

BIBLICAL SCENES

(Top and above) A detail from one of the late thirteenth-century windows of the Church of St. Urban de Troyes, set in a frame constructed of four touching circles, the centers of which are connected by a square drawn at a 45-degree angle. The picture, which depicts Christ deliberating with the priests in the Temple of Jerusalem, is in the naturalistic style that was characteristic of late thirteenth-century art. The drapery folds, the bodily attitudes, and facial expressions are observations from life. In the background are trailing vines with scrolled buds and leaves.

THE TREE OF JESSE

A popular subject for medieval stained-glass windows was the Tree of Jesse, in which Christ's earthly pedigree is shown by means of a family tree stemming from Jesse, the father of King David, founder of the royal house of Israel. The tree ascends through the height of the window, and its branches bear a series of kings, ancestors of Christ, with Christ himself at the top. In the mid-twelfth-century Jesse window in the west front of Chartres Cathedral, of which a detail is shown here, the tree is rooted in the recumbent figure of Jesse, four tiers of kings peer through the branches, the whole surmounted first by the Virgin, then by Christ.

BUILDING SALISBURY CATHEDRAL

Furnishing the House

We have moved on to the year 1265. Not only has the cathedral been completed but the cloisters and chapter house have been finished as well. Now that the chapter house has been built, one of the final tasks is to fit the ceramic tile pavement (see page 138), which is now being laid down. Like other aspects of the chapter house, the floor emulates that of Westminster, but only in that it uses encaustic tiles because the design is highly individual. The tilers are working to the pattern drawn by the master tiler, laying it segment by segment, working from the east toward the vestibule, which links the chapter house with the east cloister walk. This is a skilled operation that must be carried out with precision if the pavement is to fit correctly within the prescribed space.

Following the completion of the eastern arm and crossing, the choir screen, or pulpitum, is being completed. This stone screen, which is being built between the east crossing piers, divides the choir from the crossing. The view here is from the west looking toward the choir. At the center of the structure is a double entrance giving access to the choir and a blind arcade to each side. The heavily molded arcade is supported on Purbeck marble colonettes, and the spandrels of the arches are decorated with carved angels. Although the stonework for the left-hand (north) side of the screen has been finished, the stone sculptures that will occupy the niches have yet to be placed in position. On the right-hand (south) side, the masons are placing the cornice stones in position. When the structural work has been done, the painters will get to work on decorating the sculptured arcade, and, once they are in position, the statues.

Layers placing the cornice stones in position

Niches for statues

Entrance to the choir

Purbeck marble colonettes

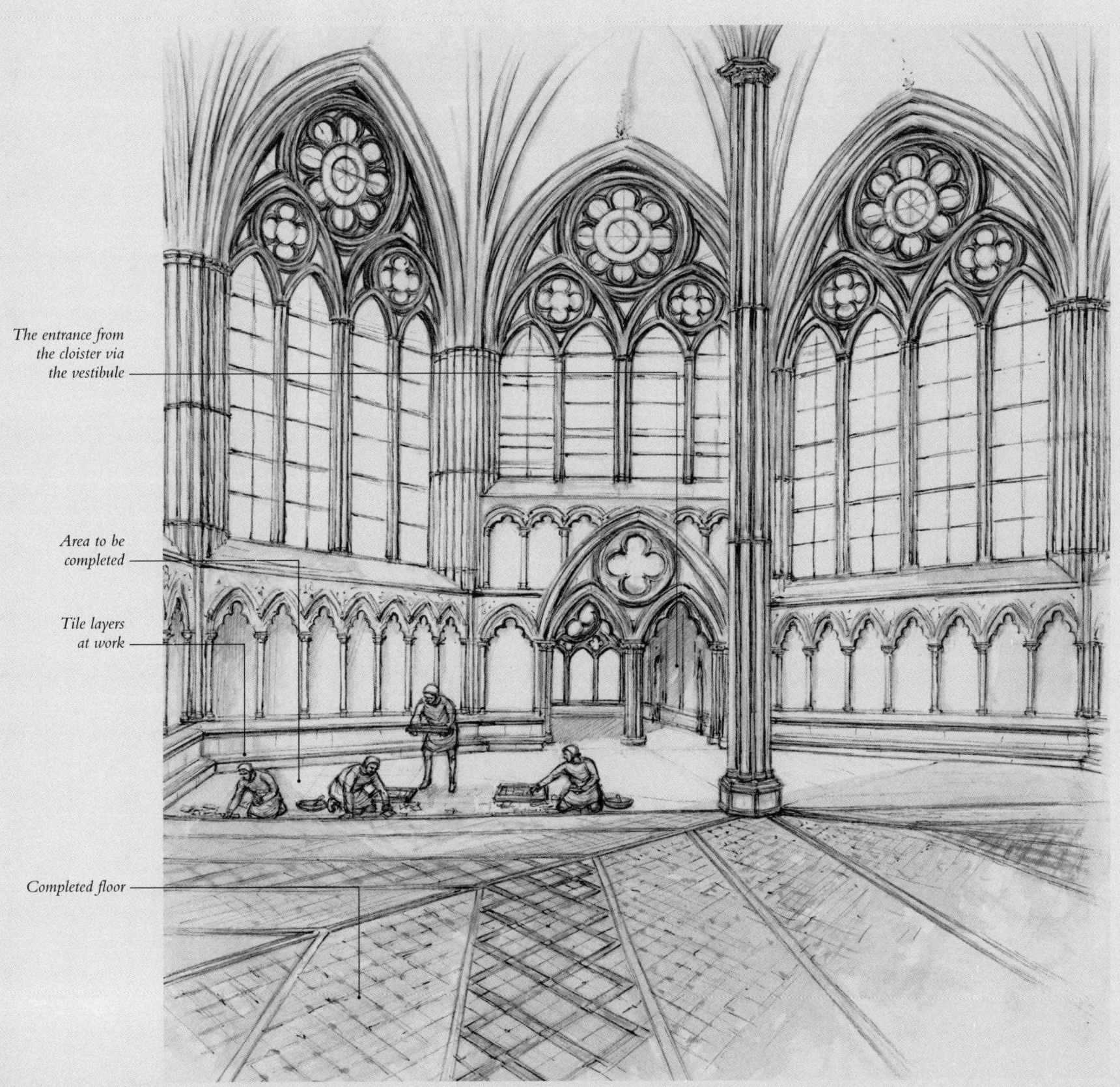

Timeline

Eleventh to Twelfth Centuries

1093
Durham's Saxon cathedral demolished. Work on the present cathedral begins, the first building in Western Europe to incorporate rib vaulting over the central vessel.

ca. 1125
Collapse of the nave vault over the abbey church in Cluny in Burgundy. Proto flying buttresses added in response.

ca. 1130
Pointed arch used in the construction of the rib vault over the nave of Durham Cathedral. This is the earliest surviving example of a rib-vaulted nave.

The nave at Durham Cathedral

1135–40
Abbot Suger begins the reconstruction of the abbey of St. Denis with the replacement of the west front of the church. Suger's work at St. Denis is the first major exercise in the Gothic style.

1140–50
Work continues at St. Denis with the replacement of the choir, incorporating one of the earliest systematic deployments of flying buttresses.

1175–84
Reconstruction of the entire eastern arm of Canterbury Cathedral in the Gothic style under the supervision of a French architect, William of Sens.

ca. 1180
Rebuilding of Wells Cathedral begins.

1192
Reconstruction of the Norman cathedral at Lincoln begun with St. Hugh's choir, under the control of a highly original architect. The vault has some of the earliest tierceron ribs.

ca. 1194
The newly rebuilt Chartres Cathedral destroyed by fire except for the west front. Work begins on a new church incorporating the crypt and west front of the former building. Prominent plate-traceried roses used with the clerestory windows.

Chartres Cathedral

1211
Destruction of Reims Cathedral by fire. The replacement church begun by the master mason Jean d'Orbais is the first to use bar tracery, and the first to weight its flying buttress piers with pinnacles to counteract the lateral thrust of the vault.

Window tracery at Reims Cathedral

1218
Fire destroys Amiens Cathedral (but not St. John the Baptist's Head).

1218–58
A new cathedral built at Salisbury on a virgin site as the focus of a new town.

---

ca. 1225–50
Rebuilding of York Minster transepts; the north transept includes the Five Sisters Window of ca. 1250, the last major composition of lancet windows.

1227
Laying of the foundation stone of Toledo Cathedral. The plan is based on that of Bourges.

ca. 1230–40
West front of Wells Cathedral built as a screen containing statuary.

Nave of Peterborough Cathedral

1230–50
The raising of the painted timber ceiling over the nave of Peterborough Cathedral. It is the only one of its type to survive in England.

1231–ca. 1250
Replacement of the nave and transepts of St. Denis in a style strongly influenced by Amiens, with very emphatic clerestory windows.

---

ca. 1250
The nave of Freiburg-im-Breisgau in Bavaria is begun, influenced by Strasbourg Cathedral.

1250–70
Extension of the transepts of Notre-Dame de Paris under the architect Jean de Chelles.

León Cathedral

1255
León Cathedral begun, probably by a French architect, in the rayonnant style prevailing in France.

1256–80
Construction of the Angel Choir, Lincoln Cathedral.

1259
Completion of first phase of Westminster Abbey (eastern arm, transepts, crossing, and chapter house).

1260
Chartres Cathedral dedicated in the presence of Louis IX.

ca. 1155–1230
Reconstruction of Laon Cathedral, one of the earliest cathedrals in the Gothic style.

1160
Maurice de Sully becomes Bishop of Paris and begins to rebuild a new cathedral (Notre-Dame) in the Gothic style.

1163
The foundation stone of Maurice de Sully's new Cathedral of Notre-Dame is laid by Pope Alexander III.

ca. 1170
Church of St. Remi, Reims, begun. Retains one of the earliest examples of an external flying-buttress system.

St. Remi

1174
The eastern arm of Canterbury Cathedral is severely damaged in a devastating fire. The decision is taken to demolish this part of the cathedral and rebuild.

Thirteenth Century

1195–1266
Bourges Cathedral under construction. Choir in use by 1232. The double-aisle plan is probably based on that of Notre-Dame.

ca. 1200–12
Soissons Cathedral rebuilt, strongly influenced by Chartres, including plate tracery in the clerestory windows.

Soissons plate tracery

1200–45
Construction of the west front of Notre-Dame de Paris.

Notre-Dame

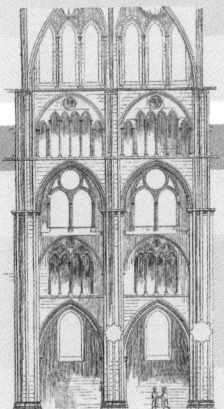
Bourges Cathedral

1220
Foundation stone for the new cathedral of Amiens laid. The architect is Robert de Luzarches. Unusually, work begins with the nave instead of the choir; the nave has been completed by 1236.

Foundations at Amiens

ca. 1220
Villard de Honnecourt prepares drawings of the new cathedral of Reims.

ca. 1220–45
West front of Notre-Dame de Paris built.

1221
Foundation stone of Burgos Cathedral is laid. Burgos has affinities with French cathedrals, notably Bourges in central France.

ca. 1225–60
Construction of the eastern arm of Beauvais Cathedral. This is the tallest cathedral in France.

ca. 1240–45
Nave of Strasbourg Cathedral begun.

1242–80
Chapel of the Nine Altars built across the east end of Durham Cathedral, based on the design of the early thirteenth-century Chapel of the Nine Altars at Fountains Abbey in Yorkshire.

1243–48
Building of the Ste.-Chapelle in Paris. One of the earliest uses of naturalistic foliage, a style that quickly spreads to other churches in France and England.

1245
Henry III of England begins the reconstruction of Westminster Abbey under the master mason Henry de Reyns (fl. 1243–50) who introduces some of the ideas used by French architects, especially Reims, Amiens, and the Ste.-Chapelle in Paris.

Westminster Abbey

1248
Work on Cologne Cathedral begins, the most ambitious cathedral-building project in Germany, strongly influenced by French precedents, notably Amiens and St. Denis.

St. Urbain de Troyes

1262
Church of St. Urbain begun in Troyes, Champagne, by Pope Urbain IV, who was a native of the town.

1268
The great opus sectile pavement is laid down in the presbytery of Westminster Abbey by Italian craftsmen recruited by Abbot Richard de Ware.

ca. 1270
The rebuilding of Exeter Cathedral begins.

1272
On the death of Henry III of England, the Westminster Abbey project comes to a halt.

1275–1301
Lower stages of the west tower of Freiburg Minster built.

Timeline

1277
West front of Strasbourg Cathedral begun.

ca. 1280–90
Building of the chapter house of York Minster.

1282–1390
Albi Cathedral, in the south of France, built at the instigation of Bishop Bernard de Castanet. It is unusual in being as much fortress as church.

Albi Cathedral

1284
Failure of the flying buttresses at Beauvais brings down part of the choir vault.

ca. 1290
Orvieto Cathedral begun.

Palma Cathedral

1306
Palma Cathedral on the island kingdom of Mallorca begun.

ca. 1310
Raising of the central tower and construction of the spire of Salisbury Cathedral, the tallest medieval structure in Europe.

ca. 1310–50
The openwork spire of Freiburg Minster built on top of the thirteenth-century west tower.

Freiburg Minster spire

ca. 1350
Building of the cloisters of Gloucester Abbey with the earliest fan vaulting in England.

1361–73
Construction of the Lady chapel of York Minster, marking the change from decorated style to perpendicular.

York Minster

1368
A revised design for Florence Cathedral agreed.

1375
Work recommenced on Westminster Abbey under the master mason Henry Yevele, who started the rebuilding of the Norman nave.

1379–1405
The nave and south transept of Canterbury Cathedral are finally rebuilt by Henry Yevele.

Burgos Cathedral

1442–58
Openwork spires of Burgos Cathedral built by the German master mason Juan de Colonia (Johann von Köln).

1446
The lantern of Florence Cathedral begun on top of the dome.

1465
A new crossing tower begun at Durham Cathedral, probably by the master mason Thomas Barton, who had formerly worked at York Minster.

ca. 1483–90
Upper stage of the crossing tower of Durham built, probably by the master mason John Bell.

1493–1503
Building of Bell Harry, the central tower of Canterbury by the architect John Wastell.

1492
The lantern topping the dome of Florence Cathedral is struck by lightning.

Seventeenth Century onward

1584
Gales bring down Lincoln's central timber spire.

Lincoln Cathedral

1643
Lichfield Cathedral is shelled during a Civil War siege and vandalized by Parliamentary troops. Reconstruction begins in 1660, inaugurating a long sequence of restorations.

1666
Destruction of St. Paul's Cathedral in the Great Fire of London. It is replaced by the present building designed by Sir Christopher Wren.

1793
French revolutionaries vandalize Notre-Dame; the thirteenth-century flèche is badly damaged.

1842–80
The towers and spires of Cologne Cathedral west front completed based on medieval drawings.

Lichfield Cathedral

Fourteenth Century

1291–1360
The nave of York Minster rebuilt.

1297
Construction of Florence Cathedral begun to the design of Arnalfo di Cambio.

ca. 1300–20
Completion of towers and spires of Lichfield Cathedral, the only English cathedral to retain all three of its spires.

1302–10
West font of Orvieto Cathedral begun under the Sienese architect and sculptor Lorenzo Maitani.

1304–1510
Rebuilding of Vienna Cathedral as a Hallenkirche.

1322
Dedication of Cologne Cathedral choir.

1322
The central tower of Ely Cathedral collapses into the choir.

1322–28
The replacement of the Ely tower begins with the construction of an octagonal stone base.

1328–32
Construction of timber lantern on top of the octagon at Ely carried out by the king's master carpenter, William Herland.

ca. 1331
Remodeling of the south transept of Gloucester Abbey. It is the earliest surviving building in the English perpendicular style.

1338
Glazing of the great west window of York Minster, one of the masterpieces of curvilinear tracery.

1344–85
Building of the choir of Prague Cathedral in a French style by the French master Matthew of Arras, and, after his death in 1352, the German master Peter Parler.

Fifteenth Century

1386
Milan Cathedral begun.

1402
Seville Cathedral begun. It is to become the largest of all medieval cathedrals.

1407
The thirteenth-century central tower of York Minster collapses. The master mason William Colchester is appointed by the king to take charge of the rebuilding.

1418–36
Dome of Florence Cathedral built by Filippo Brunelleschi, remarkably, without centering.

Florence Cathedral

Sixteenth Century

1500–50
Transepts of Beauvais Cathedral built.

ca. 1503–1509
Construction of Henry VII's Chapel at the east end of Westminster Abbey by the masons Robert and William Vertue. It is one the last important ecclesiastical works in England in the Gothic style.

1506
Completion of the nave of Westminster Abbey.

1527
A lightning strike destroys Amiens' central spire. A new spire is commissioned and completed in 1533.

1536–41
The Dissolution of the monasteries in England by Henry VIII results in the destruction of many great churches. Some abbey churches become cathedrals.

1561
A lightning strike brings down the central spire of Old St. Paul's Cathedral, London.

1573
Beauvais' central tower, completed in 1569, collapses.

The flèche of Notre-Dame

1858–60
Reconstruction of the timber flèche of Notre-Dame by the architect Viollet le Duc.

1885–90
The upper stage of the west tower and spire of Ulm Minster completed based on a fifteenth-century drawing by Matthäus Böblinger.

1917
The shelling of Reims Cathedral during World War I causes the destruction of the fifteenth-century roof after it catches fire.

1918
Soissons Cathedral bombarded during World War I and severely damaged.

1940
Coventry Cathedral gutted by fire during a World War II bombing raid.

1984
Fire destroys the medieval roof over the south transept of York Minster.

Cathedral Locations

The great Gothic cathedrals are concentrated in northwestern Europe, particularly France, which may be considered the birthplace of the Gothic style, and England, which also made important contributions and where a separate tradition grew up from early beginnings. The maps here show the more significant buildings mentioned in the text.

ENGLISH CATHEDRALS

Unlike some other European countries, the development of the Gothic cathedral in England was the product of an independent evolution, albeit sometimes with infusions of French inspiration. The greatest concentration is in the more prosperous south, although the largest (York) is the north.

1 *Carlisle Cathedral*
2 *Durham Cathedral*
3 *Whitby Abbey*
4 *York Minster*
5 *Beverley Minster*
6 *Lincoln Cathedral*
7 *Peterborough Cathedral*
8 *Ely Cathedral*
9 *Norwich Cathedral*
10 *St. Albans Cathedral*
11 *Westminster Abbey / Old St. Paul's Cathedral*
12 *Canterbury Cathedral*
13 *Winchester Cathedral*
14 *Salisbury Cathedral*
15 *Exeter Cathedral*
16 *Wells Cathedral*
17 *Gloucester Cathedral*
18 *Hereford Cathedral*
19 *Worcester Cathedral*
20 *Coventry Cathedral*
21 *Lichfield Cathedral*

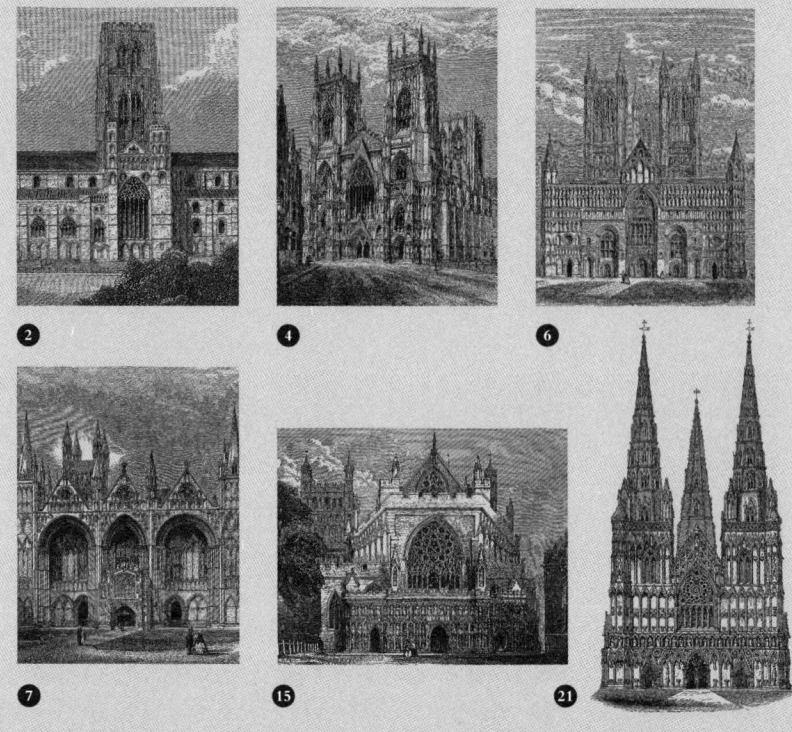

EUROPEAN CATHEDRALS

The distribution of sites in continental Europe reflects the fact that northern France was the epicenter of the Gothic style, most of the principal developments taking place here. The peripheral groups of central Europe and Spain were to a great extent influenced by French precedents. Italy, which had its own practices based on classical tradition, never fully embraced the Gothic ideal.

1 *Palma Cathedral*
2 *Valencia Cathedral*
3 *Tarragona Cathedral*
4 *Toledo Cathedral*
5 *Ávila Cathedral*
6 *Sigüenza Cathedral*
7 *Burgos Cathedral*
8 *León Cathedral*
9 *Narbonne Cathedral*
10 *Carcassonne Cathedral*
11 *Albi Cathedral*
12 *Séez Cathedral*
13 *Clermont-Ferrand Cathedral*
14 *Nevers Cathedral*
15 *Bourges Cathedral*
16 *Le Mans Cathedral*
17 *Chartres Cathedral*
18 *Sens Cathedral*
19 *Troyes Cathedral*
20 *Strasbourg Cathedral*
21 *Reims Cathedral*
22 *Laon Cathedral*
23 *Soissons Cathedral*
24 *Notre-Dame de Paris/ Basilica of St. Denis*
25 *Bayeux Cathedral*
26 *Rouen Cathedral*
27 *Beauvais Cathedral*
28 *Amiens Cathedral*
29 *Cologne Cathedral*
30 *Bamberg Cathedral*
31 *Speyer Cathedral*
32 *Freiburg Minster*
33 *Ulm Minster*
34 *Prague Cathedral*
35 *Vienna Cathedral*
36 *Milan Cathedral*
37 *Florence Cathedral*
38 *Orvieto Cathedral*

Glossary

AMBULATORY An aisle to the east of the sanctuary linking the side aisles of a church.

APSIDAL Semicircular in plan.

ARCADE A row of arches supported on piers or columns.

ARCHIVOLT The molded underside of an arch, which, in Gothic portals, is usually divided into several concentric tiers corresponding with the imposts lining the sides of the entrance.

BUTTRESS A localized thickening of, or projection from, the wall of a building to strengthen or shore, or to counter lateral thrust from a vault or roof.

CAPITAL The feature at the head of a column, shaft, or pilaster, usually molded or sculpted.

CENTERING Temporary wooden support used in building an arch.

CHAPTER HOUSE In a cathedral, the meeting place for the dean and canons to discuss business.

CHEVET French term for the east end of a church, including the ambulatory and radiating chapels.

CHOIR Strictly the part of a great church in which the choir stalls were situated and in which services are sung, but usually applied to the whole of the eastern arm.

CIBORIUM A canopy over an altar, usually vaulted- and supported on columns.

CLERESTORY The uppermost story of the central vessel of a church.

CORBEL A projecting block supporting something on its upper surface.

CROSS FRAME A transverse wood-frame construction including a roof truss.

DIAPER PATTERN A surface decorated with a repeated motif of lozenges or squares.

ENCAUSTIC TILE Floor tiles inlaid with a pattern in different colored clay to that of the main body.

ENTASIS A very slight convex curve to counter the optical illusion of concavity

FLAMBOYANT STYLE The final phase of French Gothic architecture characterized by flowing tracery and ranging in date from the fourteenth to the sixteenth centuries.

FLÈCHE A French term used to describe a spire.

FLYER The element of a flying buttress that transmits the thrust from the vault to the buttress pier.

GALLERY An upper story over an aisle with arcaded openings looking into the central vessel of a church; sometimes called a tribune, or (incorrectly) a triforium.

GOTHIC A style of architecture based on the pointed arch that was prevalent in western Europe between ca. 1130 and ca. 1530.

HURDLE Panels made from woven withies and used as scaffold platforms on medieval construction sites.

INTRADOS The underside of an arch.

KEYSTONE The stone at the apex of an arch.

KING POST The vertical element of a roof truss extending from the tie beam to the apex.

LADY CHAPEL A chapel dedicated to the Virgin Mary (Our Lady).

LANCET A narrow pointed window characteristic of the early Gothic period.

MISERICORD Bracket on the underside of the folding wooden seat of a choir stall, used by a chorister to rest on when the seat is in the upright position. It is often decorated with sculptured scenes.

MORTAR A mixture of sand, lime, and water used as a bonding agent in stone construction.

MULLION One of the principal vertical divisions of a traceried window.

NAVE The western arm of a church, often flanked by side aisles.

OGEE Double curved profile comprising a concave and convex part to form an S shape, and much used in flowing tracery.

OPENWORK Perforated stone or

PERPENDICULAR STYLE The final phase of English Gothic architecture dating from between ca. 1330 and ca. 1530, characterized by tracery of rectilinear form.

PIER Vertical masonry support usually for an arch.

PULPITUM A stone screen separating the choir from the nave.

RAYONNANT STYLE A phase of French Gothic architecture dating from ca. 1220 to ca. 1350.

REREDOS A decorative screen behind the high altar.

RETRO-CHOIR In a major church, the area between the high altar and eastern chapels.

ROMANESQUE A style of architecture based on the semicircular arch, prevalent in Western Europe during the eleventh and twelfth century.

ROOD SCREEN A screen extending across the eastern end of the nave and supporting a rood, or crucifix.

SOFFIT The underside of an arch, beam, or other architectural element.

SPANDREL The (roughly triangular) space between an arch and its rectangular frame.

SQUINCH ARCH A diagonally positioned arch spanning an internal corner to carry a polygonal or circular superstructure on a square substructure.

STRINGCOURSE A continuous horizontal projection with a molded profile, used to articulate the wall surface of a building.

TAS-DE-CHARGE The lower courses of an arch cut with horizontal upper and lower surfaces and bonded into a wall.

THRUST LINE The path taken by the vertical thrust exerted by a load.

TIE BEAM The principal transverse wooden member connecting two walls, on which a roof truss is built.

TIERCERON An intermediate vaulting rib extending from the corner of a vaulting compartment to the ridge rib.

TRACERY Pattern of open stonework or woodwork in a Gothic window. *Bar tracery*: A framework made from ribs or "bars" of molded section that superseded plate tracery in the early thirteenth century. *Flowing tracery*: A form, also known as curvilinear, based on the ogee, so that the pattern consists of uninterrupted curves. It dates from ca. 1300 to ca. 1340 in England, but was developed in France (as flamboyant tracery) from the late fourteenth century onward. *Geometric tracery*: An early form of bar tracery with patterns based on geometrical figures. It is largely associated with the thirteenth century. *Panel tracery*: Perpendicular tracery, comprising straight-sided upright panels, also known as rectilinear tracery. *Plate tracery*: Late twelfth- and early thirteenth-century form of tracery made from stone blocks or "plates" that form part of the wall structure to produce a pattern of perforations.

TRANSEPT The transverse element of a church, usually associated with the projections from the crossing of a cruciform church, but also occasionally found at the east or west end.

TRIFORIUM An arcaded wall passage at the level of the aisle roof.

TYMPANUM The space between a lintel and the arch above it.

VAULT An arched stone ceiling or roof. *Barrel vault*: a continuous vault made of homogenous structural character, also known as a tunnel vault. *Fan vault*: A highly decorated vault based on a series of inverted half cones made up of panels covered with blind tracery patterns. *Groin vault*: A vault created by the intersection of two barrel vaults. *Lierne vault*: A rib vault containing a pattern made from liernes, or intermediate decorative ribs. *Rib vault*: A vault formed from a framework of arches, with infill panels in the spaces between them.

VOUSSOIR One of a series of wedge-shape stones making up an arch.

WINDLASS A hoisting device based on an axle or drum.

Resources

Books

The Accounts of the Fabric of Exeter Cathedral
A. ERSKINE (ed.)
(Devon and Cornwall Record Society,
n. s. 24, 1981; 26, 1983)

The Archaeology of Cathedrals
TIM TATTON-BROWN and JULIAN MUNBY (eds)
(Oxford Committee for Archaeology, 1996)

Les Bâtisseurs des Cathédrales Gothiques
ROLAND RECHT (ed.)
(rev. ed., Musée de Strasbourg, 1989)

Brunelleschi's Dome: The Story of the Great Cathedral in Florence
ROSS KING
(Penguin, 2001)

Building in England Down to 1540
L. F. SALZMAN
(rev. ed., Oxford University Press, 1967)

Building Troyes Cathedral
STEPHEN MURRAY
(Indiana University Press, 1987)

The Cathedral Builders
JEAN GIMPEL
(Perennial, 1992)

The Cathedral Builders of the Middle Ages
ALAIN ERLANDE-BRANDENBURG
(Thames and Hudson, 1995)

Les Chantiers des Cathédrales: Ouvriers, Architectes, Sculpteurs
PIERRE DU COLOMBIER
(rev. ed., Picard, 1992)

Chartres: The Masons who Built a Legend
JOHN JAMES
(Routledge and Keegan Paul, 1982)

The Construction of Gothic Cathedrals
JOHN FITCHEN
(University of Chicago Press, 1961)

The Engineering of Medieval Cathedrals
LYNN T. COURTENAY (ed.)
(Variorum, 1997)

English Medieval Architects: A Biographical Dictionary down to 1540
JOHN HARVEY
(rev. ed., Alan Sutton, 1984)

The Gothic Cathedral
CHRISTOPHER WILSON
(Thames and Hudson, 1992)

Masons and Sculptors
NICOLA COLDSTREAM
(University of Toronto Press, 1991)

The Master Builders: Architecture in the Middle Ages
JOHN HARVEY
(Thames and Hudson, 1971)

The Medieval Architect
JOHN HARVEY
(Wayland, 1972)

Medieval Masons
MALCOLM HISLOP
(rev. ed., Shire, 2009)

Salisbury Cathedral: The Making of a Medieval Masterpiece
TIM TATTON-BROWN and JOHN CROOK
(Scala, 2009)

York Minster: An Architectural History c. 1200–1500
SARAH BROWN
(English Heritage, 2003)

Web sites

The Corpus of Medieval Narrative Art
www.medievalart.org.uk
Photographic images of medieval stained glass and sculpture.

Images of Medieval Art and Architecture
www.medart.pitt.edu/index.html
Web site of English and French medieval buildings including photographs and information.

Mapping Gothic France
www.mappinggothicfrance.org
Web site dedicated to the Gothic cathedrals and churches of France including high-quality photographs and information.

The Medieval Stained Glass Photographic Archive
www.therosewindow.com
Photographic archive of medieval stained-glass windows of England and France.

Index

A
ad quadratum designs 30–31
ad triangulum designs 30–31
Adam the Carver 172
Agnes, the lime burner 39
aisles 17
Alan of Walsingham 40, 112
Albi Cathedral 73
Alexander of Abingdon 174
allegorical sculpture 176–177
altars 198
Amiens Cathedral
  bays 55
  crossing tower 110
  flying buttresses 67, 69, 74
  foundations 41
  horizontal articulation 50
  labyrinth 18
  plan 21, 22
  sculpture 178, 179, 187
  sectional profile 26
  spire 115
  western portals 140–141
  windows 155, 164, 209
angels 182
arcading 52–53
arches
  construction 44–45
  ogee 162
  quadrant 62, 64, 65
  strainer 111
  transverse 65
  trefoil 53
architects 12, 13, 18, 121
architectural drawings 13, 28–29
Arnalfo di Cambio 124
Auxerre Cathedral 183
Ávila Cathedral 24, 99

B
Bamberg Cathedral 176
banker marks 47
bar tracery 154–155
Bayeux Cathedral 101
bays 48, 54–56
Beauvais Cathedral
  buttresses 72
  sectional profile 26
  stained glass 210
  tower 107
bell towers 108
Bernard, Abbot of Clairvaux 12, 171
Beverley Minster
  misericords 205
  nave arcade 45
  sculpture 174, 181
  tower 12
  windows 163
Binham Priory, Norfolk 154
Bishop's Eye windows 156
bishops' thrones 202
blind arcading 52
bosses 170, 175
Bourges Cathedral
  design 30, 54
  plan 20, 22, 23
  sectional profile 26
  windows 149, 152, 154, 211
broach spires 122
Brunelleschi, Filippo 124, 125
bubble foliage see undulating foliage
Burgos Cathedral 101, 121
Bury St. Edmunds, abbey church 101
buttresses 62, 63, 76–77
  case studies 72–73
  drainage systems 100–101
  embellishment and effect 74–75
  flying buttresses 63, 64–69, 72, 74, 75, 160–161
  pinnacles 70–71
Byland Abbey 194

C
Canterbury Cathedral
  buttresses 63, 70
  fire damage 80
  plan 12, 16, 22
  sculpture 180
  spire 107
  transport of stone to 38
  windows 150, 193
Carcassonne Cathedral 84
Carlisle Cathedral 107, 163, 180
carpenters 39, 80, 92, 95, 132, 192
Cartagena, Bishop Alonso de 121
Castanet, Bishop Bernard de 73
ceilings 96–97
chapels 24–25
  Lady chapels 14, 24
Chartres Cathedral
  bays 54
  facade 173
  flying buttresses 68
  horizontal articulation 50
  rebuilding 16
  roof 18, 99
  sectional profile 26
  spire 122
  tower 108
  windows 43, 142–145, 152, 153, 185, 211
chevets 22, 24–25
chisels 184
choir stalls 202–203
  see also misericords
choirs 14, 15, 22
cimborio 113
Clarendon Palace, Wiltshire 196
claw chisels 184
clerestories 26, 50, 51, 148, 149
Clermont-Ferrand, Cathedral of 183
Cluny Abbey 62, 64
clustered piers 49
Cole, John 119
College of the Vicars Choral, York 184
Cologne Cathedral 22, 25, 110
Colonia, Juan de 121
column construction 48–49
compasses 129
compound piers 49
consecration crosses 52
Corvey, Germany, abbey church 108
counter-relief tiles 196
Coventry Cathedral 118, 122, 123
cranes 42, 135, 136
crockets 180
crossing towers 107, 110–111
cruciform plans 20, 21
curvilinear tracery 162
cylindrical piers 49

D
Dean's Eye windows 156
demonic figures 182, 183
dome, Florence Cathedral 124–125
Durham Cathedral
  bishop's throne 202
  Chapel of the Nine Altars 24
  fire damage 80
  flying buttresses/quadrant arches 65
  rib vaulting 82–83
  spire 107
  tower 110
  windows 158

E
Easter sepulchres 199
Edward I, of England 174
Eleanor Cross, Geddinton 174
Ely Cathedral
  ceiling 96
  choir stalls 203
  foundations 40
  lantern 112
  lighting 148
  plan 20, 22
  sculpture 181
  spire 107
  web coursing 87
encaustic tiles 196
Ensingen, Ulrich von 28, 108
entasis 122
Exeter Cathedral
  bishop's throne 202
  plan 22
  rib vaulting 89
  sculpture 175, 180, 186, 188
  spire 107
  west front 173

F
facade design 57
false galleries 158
fan vaulting 90–91
figure sculpture 178–179
Finchale Priory 98
Fioravanti, Neri di 124
fire 80–81, 96
flamboyant style 162
fleches see spires
Florence Cathedral 107, 124–125
flowing tracery 162
flying buttresses 63, 64–69, 72, 74, 75, 160–161
foliage sculpture 175, 180–181
foundations 34–35, 40–41
Fountains Abbey 110, 194
freemasons 131, 136, 161
freestone 38
Freiburg-im-Breisgau Minster 23, 108, 120, 177

G
galleries 50, 51
  false galleries 158
Galmeton, Robert 202
gargoyles 170, 183
geometry 30–33
Gerhard, Master 25, 108
Gerona Cathedral 198
Ghiberti, Lorenzo 125
Gilbert de Bonnington 206
Glasgow Cathedral 96
glass production 193
Gloucester Cathedral
  fan vaulting 90
  groin vaulting 81
  tower 107
  windows 161, 162
Goldclif, Hugh de 12
Govair, John 98
green men 183
grisaille glass 210
groined vaulting 81
ground plans 20–23
guttering 100

H
Hagia Sophia, Constantinople 64
Hallenkirche (hall churches) 26, 27, 50
Hardingstone Cross, Northamptonshire 174
Hatfield Cathedral 202
Haughmond Abbey 186
Henry de Reyns 75
Henry III, of England 69, 96, 196
Hereford Cathedral 24, 107
Honnecourt, Villard de 28, 29, 32, 157
horizontal articulation 50–51
Hültz, Johan 121
hurdles 42, 131
Hurley, William 112, 203

I
ironwork 206–207
Ixeworth, William 172

J
Jaime II, King of Mallorca 75
Joy, William 111

K
keystones 84
Kirton, Abbot 90

L
labyrinths 18
ladders 42, 131
Lady chapels 14, 24
lancets 150–151
lanterns 112–113, 125
Laon Cathedral
  column construction 48, 49
  flying buttresses 64
  horizontal articulation 51
  lantern 112
  tiles 197
  tower 29
  tracery 152
Lausanne Cathedral 157
Le Mans Cathedral 25, 75
lead
  guttering 100
  roof covering 98, 99
Lechler, Lorenz 32
Lemyng, Lawrence 119
León Cathedral 108
lewis 42
Libergier, Hugues 19
Lichfield Cathedral
  facade 57
  plan 22
  sculpture 170
  vault 96
liernes 88, 89
lightning 107
lime putty 39

222

Lincoln Cathedral
  bays 54
  Easter sepulchre 199
  facade 57
  horizontal articulation 50
  plan 20, 22
  pulpitum 200
  ridge ribs 88
  roof 92
  rose windows 156
  screen 200
  sculpture 170, 174, 180, 182, 186
  spire 107
  tower 110
  vertical articulation 48
  wall arcading 53
  windows 151, 158, 162
Llobet, Marti 113
lucarnes 123
Luzarches, Robert de 21, 155
Lyngwode, William 203

M
masons 39, 43, 131
  see also freemasons;
    master masons;
    roughmasons
masons' marks 46–47
master masons 12–13, 18–19
Meaux Abbey 194
Melrose Abbey 22
Milan Cathedral 13, 26, 30, 31
misericords 204–205
mortar 39, 136

N
Narbonne Cathedral 85
naves 14, 17
Nepveu, Jehan 98
Nevers Cathedral 85
Norwich Cathedral 107, 172, 204
Notre-Dame, Semur-en-Auxois 187
Notre-Dame de Paris 20
  altar 198
  bays 54
  choir 15
  column construction 49
  crossing tower 110

flèche 116–117
flying buttresses 64
ironwork 206
plan 22
pulpitum 201
roof 94–95
rose window 156
sculpture 178, 181
sectional profile 26
wall construction 42
western tower 109
windows 148, 165

O
ogee arches 162
Old St. Paul's, London 107, 108
openwork spires 120–121
opus sectile work 138, 194
Orbais, Jean d' 25, 155
Ordoricus, Petrus 138
Oxford Cathedral 122

P
painted decoration 52, 96, 97, 140, 188, 192
Palma Cathedral 75
parapets 53
Parler family 108, 121
patrons 12, 13
pavements, tiled 138
perpendicular style 162
Peterborough Cathedral
  fan vaulting 90
  painted ceiling 96, 97
  spire 107
Pevsner, Nikolaus 174
piers 49
pinnacles 70–71
plate tracery 152–153
plumb lines 42
plumbers 98, 101
poppy head decoration 203
profiles 26–27
proportional measurement systems 33
pulpitums 200–201
punches (points) 184

Q
quadrant arches 62, 64, 65

quadripartite vaulting 82
quicklime 39

R
Ramsey Abbey 107
rayonnant style windows 156
Reims Cathedral
  bar tracery 154, 155
  five-chapel chevet 25
  flying buttresses 28, 70, 74
  labyrinth 18
  pinnacles 71
  planning and construction 49
  roof 93
  rose window 157
  sculpture 179, 182, 188, 189
  sectional profile 26, 27
  spires 106
relief tiles 196
reredos 198, 199
retables 198
reticulated tracery 162
rib vaulting 81, 82–85, 88–89
ridge ribs 88
ridge tiles 99
Rievaulx Abbey, Yorkshire 38, 194
Ripon Cathedral 107, 150
roof construction 80–81
  coverings 98–99
  drainage 100–101
  Notre-Dame de Paris choir 94–95
  Salisbury Cathedral 102–103
  timber 92–95, 102–103
Roriczer, Mathes 32
rose windows 144, 149, 152, 156–157, 165
rotated square technique 33
Rouen Cathedral 22, 74, 108
roughmasons 39, 161
rubble 38

S
St. Alban's Abbey, Hertfordshire 12, 19, 20
St. Alban's Cathedral 96, 107
St. Denis Abbey, near Paris and Abbot Suger 25
  flying buttresses 64

ironwork 207
mosaic tiling 195
roof 92
rose window 156
windows 150, 160, 211
St. Germain, Auxerre 122
St. James, Louth, Lincolnshire 114, 119
St. Martin, Tours 106
St. Nicoise, Reims 19
St. Ouen, Rouen 55, 113
St. Pierre Abbey Church, Chartres 85
St. Pierre-sur-Dives, Caen 197
St. Remi, Reims 64, 68
St. Riquier, France 110
St. Stephen, Vienna 26
St. Urbain de Troyes
  flying buttresses 69
  parapet decoration 53
  water conduits 100
  windows 159, 211
Ste.-Chapelle, Paris 180, 181, 182, 183
Salisbury Cathedral
  buttresses 76–77
  construction and planning 48
  foundations 34–35, 40
  furniture 212–213
  painted decoration 192
  plan 20, 22
  pulpitum 200
  raising the walls 58–59
  roof construction 102–103
  sculpture 170
  spires 106, 118, 126–127
  tile pavement 138
  tower 108, 110
  wall treatments 52
  windows 166–167
San Zeno Maggiore, Verona 152
sanctuaries 14
scaffolding 42, 118, 126, 135
Schmuttermayer, Hans 32
screens 200–201
sculpture 170–175
  allegorical 177
  figures 178–179
  foliage 175, 180–181

positioning marks 189
techniques 184–189
Scune, Christopher 119
sectional profiles 26–27
Séez Cathedral 56, 121, 123
Sens Cathedral
  roof tiles 98, 99
  sculpture 175, 177
setters 39, 164
Seville Cathedral 22
Sigüenza Cathedral 108
slates 98
slings 42
smiths 39, 192
Soissons Cathedral
  buttresses 70, 71
  plate tracery 153
Southwell Minster 180
Speyer Cathedral 81
spires 106–107
  broach spires 122
  managing the effect 122–123
  Notre-Dame de Paris 116–117
  openwork 120–121
  Salisbury Cathedral 126–127
  stone 118–120
  timber 114–117
stained glass 148, 208–211
  Chartres Cathedral 43, 142–145, 185, 211
  glass production 193
stiff leaf decoration 180, 181
stone
  roof covering 98, 99
  spires 118–120, 126–127
  transport of 38
strainer arches 111
Strasbourg Cathedral
  screen 52
  sculpture 182
  tower 106, 108
Street, George Edmund 99
stringcourses 51, 52
structural theory 62–63
  see also buttresses
Suger, Abbot of St. Denis 12, 25, 92, 156, 160

T
Tarragona Cathedral 112

tas-de-charge system 85
Thomas of Leighton 206
Thomas of Witney 202
thrust lines 62–63
tiercerons 88, 89
tiles
  counter-relief 196
  encaustic 196
  manufacture 193, 195
  pavements 138, 194–197, 212
  relief 196
  ridge 99
  roof covering 98, 99
timber
  roof construction 92–95, 102–103
  spires 114–117
  vaults and ceilings 96–97
Toledo Cathedral 22, 24, 108
towers 106–109
  bell towers 108
  crossing towers 107, 110–111
tracery 149
  bar tracery 154–155
  late medieval style 162–163
  plate tracery 152–153
  Salisbury Cathedral 166–167
tracing floors 164
transepts 20, 22, 24
transverse arches 65
Tree of Jesse 211
trefoil arches 53
tribune gallery 50
triforium 51
Troyes Cathedral 98, 210

U
Ulm Minster 28, 108, 121
undulating foliage 180, 181
Urban IV, Pope 159

V
Vale Royal Abbey 38
Valencia Cathedral 113
vault bosses 170, 175
vaulting 81
  groined vaults 81
  infill panels 86–87
  rib vaulting 81, 82–85, 88–89
  timber 96–97

vertical articulation 48–49
Vertue, Robert and William 91
Vézelay Abbey, Burgundy 81, 98
Viollet le Duc, Eugène 15, 18, 29, 41, 43, 54, 116, 117, 165, 198, 207
voussoirs 44
voûtains 86

W
wall bands 48
wall treatments 52–53
walls 38–39, 42–43, 58–59, 134
Walter the Imager 172
Waltham Cross statues 174
Ware, Abbot Richard de 138
Wastell, John 90
Wells Cathedral
  lancet windows 150
  plan 22
  roof 98
  sculpture 170, 171, 186
  towers 108, 110, 111
  tracing floor 164
Westminster Abbey
  ad quadratum design 31
  arch construction 44
  bar tracery 154
  blind arcading 52
  buttresses 74
  and Henry de Reyns 75
  and Henry III 69, 196

horizontal articulation 50
misericords 205
nave 16
plan 22
sculpture 172, 180, 182
sectional profile 26
tile pavement 138, 194, 196
vault construction 91
Whitby Abbey 45
William of Ireland 174
William of Sens 12–13, 38, 63, 92, 150, 180
William of Strand 98
Winchester Cathedral
  choir stalls 203
  ironwork 206
  plan 20, 22
  reredos 199
  vaulting 89, 96
windlasses 42
windows 148–149
  Bishop's Eye 156
  construction techniques 164–165
  Dean's Eye 156
  flying buttresses and 160–161
  lancets 150–151
  late medieval design 162–163
  Rayonnant 156
  rear frames 158–159
  rose windows 144, 149, 152, 156–157, 165

Salisbury Chapter House 166–167
see also stained glass; tracery
Windsor Castle: Chapel of St. Edward 96
Worcester, William 40
Worcester Cathedral 22, 80, 107, 108
workshops 39, 134

Y
Yevele, Henry 16
York Minster
  foundations 40
  nave 17
  pinnacles 70
  plan 21, 22
  roof 96
  sculpture 180, 200
  towers 107, 109
  wall treatments 52
  windows 149, 150, 161, 162, 164, 210

Z
Zamora Cathedral 201

Acknowledgments

AUTHOR'S ACKNOWLEDGMENTS

In acknowledging the help given to me during the creation of this book, I would first of all like to thank my principal contacts at the Ivy Press: Caroline Earle, Jamie Pumfrey, and Michael Whitehead, together with all the members of staff who contributed to the project. The publication is enormously improved by the reconstruction drawings of Adam Hook, to whom I am greatly beholden. Thanks are also due to Simon Smith, who acted as copy-editor. In addition, a debt of gratitude is owed to the pioneers of the study of medieval cathedrals, as well as subsequent researchers, without whose recording and interpretation this volume, in its existing form, would not have been possible. My greatest thanks, however, are reserved for my wife, Anne, who, as on other occasions, has acted as research assistant, proofreader, critic, and translator.

IMAGE CREDITS

The publisher would like to thank the following individuals and organizations for their kind permission to reproduce the images in this book. Every effort has been made to acknowledge the pictures, however we apologize if there are any unintentional omissions.

Alamy/Photos12: 129.

AKG Images: 132, 136; Massimiliano Pezzolini: 140; British Library: 19L, 131, 133; Erich Lessing: 135, 144; Gilles Mermet: 29R, 28C.

Getty Images/William Johnstone White: 139.

Adam Hook: 19R, 34, 41, 45, 58, 75TR, 76, 102, 126, 166, 189L.

Photos.com: 2, 134, 137.

Society of Antiquaries of London: 138.

Topfoto/The Granger Collection: 130.

V&A Images, Victoria and Albert Museum: 28L.